Ancient Shock

Monsters, Philosophers, & Saviors

How Neanderthals Became Sapiens

~!~

The Untold Story of Humanity

Real Sagas of DNA, Body, Mind & Spirit

Steven A. Key

The NEW MUSE Book Series

The books of the New Muse Series, by Steven A. Key, are a collection of writings focusing on the genres of Body, Mind & Spirit; neuroscience; psychology; consciousness; and ancient histories.

Ancient Shock ~ Monsters, Philosophers, & Saviors ~ How Neanderthals became Sapiens

(2020)

How to Be Immortal ~ The Adventures of King Gilgamesh and the Wildman

(2020)

The Vikings Secret Yoga ~ The Supreme Adventure

(2019)

Future Books in the NEW MUSE Series

The Colors of Mind in the Garden of Knowledge

Psyche in the Theatre of the World

The Deeper Mysteries

The Colors of Mind in Ancient Times: Egypt, India, Greece, China

The Death of Atheism and the Rise of the Spiritual Maverick

LIZ: Messages from Mother; The Connections beyond the Veil

Yeshua Esoterica: The Untold Story of Jesus

The Jungian Supernova: A Secret History of Psychiatry

Gotama's Take: The Rise and Fall of Mystical Buddhism

Dedication

This book is dedicated to the kindness, patience,

and heart-love of my Mother and to the strength,

discipline, and spirit-seed of my Father.

Hence, my Being.

~!~

This book is also dedicated to Stan Gooch (1932–2010), the world's first paleo-psychologist, for his brilliant insight into the neuropsychology of the Neanderthals and their descendants, and to the untold legions of Neanderthal-Sapiens souls that were our distant ancestors. Without them, we wouldn't be here.

Acknowledgements

First, I want to thank Baa'l Animingus as the one who assisted in the overall idea generation of this book and the *New Muse Book Series*. Turning an author's manuscript into modern book formats is somewhat of a miracle in itself. The creation of this book, in both print and eBook form, was facilitated by the many helpful, creative, & professional folks at BooksGoSocial, under the strong leadership of owner Laurence O'Bryan.

Literature is the faint remembrance of Experience.

Steven A. Key

Contents

Introduction

ONCE Upon a Time. ..

is not just the usual introduction to a fairy tale, but rather, in its first use, the phrase has its roots in the earliest Pali language; the language spoken by Siddhartha Gotama, the Buddha, in 450 BCE. Thus, his biography, in Pali, begins with those very famous words.

As the author of this surprising, surreal book, I feel the choice words of 'Once upon a time' has a certain romantic appeal, and certainly does apply to the hoary content, about the little-known, sometimes dark, sometimes bright, passages of our evolutionary past, involving several well-known figures, hence the title: *Ancient Shock ~ Monsters, Philosophers, & Saviors ~ How Neanderthals became Sapiens.*

Many ideas in this book were originally written as Part Two of another New Muse Series book: *How to Be Immortal ~ The Adventures of King Gilgamesh and the Wildman*, which is a full, alternative historical review of the great saga of an ancient Sumerian King, known as the great 4,000-year-old Story of King Gilgamesh, the world's oldest known poem. After writing that book, I couldn't resist investigating several suspicions I had concerning Enkidu, the King's great, mysterious wild friend. And so, as my research progressed and expanded, it became necessary for *Ancient Shock ~ Monsters, Philosophers, & Saviors* to stand on its own, and even expand into a second book titled *The Deeper Mysteries*. Both books are focused upon a mysterious expression of hybrid humanity; those creatures of mixed Neanderthal-Sapiens heritage and ancestry, and how they greatly influenced Sapiens, in both their humanity and their history.

The New Neon

In Part I of this book, aptly titled, *Neanderthal as The New Neon*, we cover many of the latest, remarkable scientific findings of pure-blooded Neanderthals, who disappeared around 25,000–40,000 years ago. In this book, to set the record straight, we kindly rename Neanderthals to *Neons*, meaning, the *bright* ones. We also note that these creatures 'gifted' many marvelous things to Sapiens, as they co-existed millennia ago.

The basic, scientifically supported premise presented here, is that the reader, the author, and nearly everyone on the planet has 2–4% (or more) Neanderthal DNA in their body. Where and when did this Neon DNA come from, in our distant past? Who were these other ancestors of ours? The theme of this book, our premise, must also strongly suggest, even mandate, that our ancient ancestors surely must have contained much larger amounts of hybrid DNA than we do today.

The Mixed Breeds

In Part II, *The Mixed Breeds of The Story of King Gilgamesh,* we approach prehistoric history with a keen eye focused on detecting ancient figures with the tell-tale characteristics of a Neanderthal-Sapiens DNA admixture, whom we will also refer to as hybrid-hominids. We evaluate, for our hypothesis, 4,000-year-old historical figures, such as The Story of King Gilgamesh's Enkidu the Wild Man, and Huwawa the Monster.

The Strange Players

In Part III, *The Strange Players*, we depict many more historical figures as being hybrid Neanderthal-Sapiens creatures—Beowulf and the monster Grendel, and, shockingly, even the great leader of Western Philosophy— Socrates himself. Information will be provided that relates how Socrates had more Neanderthal DNA than modern people. He was not seen as the usual Grecian model of a man. Why?

The Hidden History of Saviors, Monsters, and Kings

Part IV, *The Hidden History of Saviors, Monsters, and Kings,* casts a new, dramatically shocking light on several important historical personages. Here we portray extraordinary new information, seen for the first time, and must ask sensitive hybrid-hominid questions. What of Jesus the

Christ . . . and the Buddha himself—Siddhartha Gotama? Just who were their parents, really? The answers will startle you.

In *Ancient Shock ~ Monsters, Philosophers, & Saviors*, the 'standard model' of academic history gets broken into pieces. In this book, it will be convincingly shown that our current 'Sapiens only' history, is really just a convenient, somewhat ignorant arrangement, for uninformed historians, religionists, and those powerful political forces in the past. To move towards a better understanding of our histories, we *must* fully accept the full DNA spectrum of our ancestors, to gain a better view of the past. Not doing so will merely propagate a rather long lie.

"History is the Lie commonly agreed upon."
Voltaire (1694–1778 AD)

The Author must warn the Reader: prepare for a considerable shock; this is the first and only book to **examine** the hidden history, and the lives of our hybrid humanity. In history, much has been obscured because we, and the academic scholars, simply thought of ourselves as Sapiens creatures . . . and wrote our entire history according to that thinking. The whole time a hidden, alternative, hybrid-hominid history . . . has been hiding in plain sight.

"The Unexamined Life is not worth Living."
Plato

If the reader will be courageous and keep an open mind, the obviousness of this approach regarding the existence of a hybrid-hominid hidden history, will become readily apparent, as you read along the many examples that are given in each chapter. Hopefully, you will find the entirely new presentation of information contained in *Ancient Shock* strange but fascinating, intriguing, and able to grab your attention.

Simply put, without being too adamant, it is a **logical *necessity*** that our ancestors had more mixed hominid DNA, mainly Neanderthal-Sapiens admixtures, than humans living today. Who were these people?

In *Ancient Shock ~ Monsters, Philosophers, & Saviors* there are given numerous, startling examples of a hidden, relict Neanderthal presence in our supposed 'all Homo sapiens' society, in ancient literature, legends, and monumental artwork, as in the Great Sphinx of Giza. Using recent scientific discoveries of Neanderthals and their cultures, we are simply looking for, and finding, remnant traces of Neanderthal descendants, who match certain traits and attributes, which are explained as we proceed. It is vitally important to release the old notion of a dumb, knuckle-dragging brute, and to replace that image with an intensely spiritual, visually acute, powerful creature. The information contained within, concerning our hybrid ancestry, will be very startling for some, yet arouse an "*Aha!*" from others. Good reading to you, my brothers and sisters, the modern hybrid-hominids, who are also part Monster, Philosopher, & Savior.

4

PART I ~ Neanderthal as the New Neon

The New Man

In 1856, a large limestone quarry excavation was in full production in a large German valley. The excavation stopped for a brief moment when workers discovered the bones of a skeleton which was removed and stored. Later, anthropologists would examine this unusual skeleton, and declare that it was not human in origin. It's a marvelous coincidence that the skeleton was named after the valley which was called Neander, after a beloved 17th-century German theologian and composer, Joachim Neander. The meaning of Neander's name was very telling: Neander meant 'New Man,' and thus the naming of the Neanderthal species came to be.

In this book, we will often refer to Neanderthal as 'Neon,' to offset the incorrect notion of the dumb brute—an image fostered by early anthropologists. And replace that idea with a new image of an intelligent humanlike creature in our distant past, as well as to exemplify their rather amazing traits, including that of having dramatically superior eyesight and a greater capacity for imagination and dreams, due to their much larger eyes and a rear-brain vision center that was 400% larger than modern humans.

Science has studied the evolution of man for quite some time now. Until the early 1950s, most anthropologists thought that Neanderthals were not related to humans. Since then, Neanderthal DNA has been found and widely acknowledged in humans—most likely you are approximately 2–4% Neanderthal in your genome and only 96–98% human, or Homo sapiens. Although many missing links still exist in the scientific explanation, scientists now generally accept that our species, Sapiens, was preceded by other, older hominid species by several million years. Neanderthals, like Sapiens, were relative newcomers, springing up as a hominid sub-species perhaps 450,000 years ago, before dying out only 25,000 years ago, in the Gorman caves near the Rock of Gibraltar. This dating places a time range of only 21,000 years between the last-known Neanderthal by the Gibraltar Strait, and the 4,000-year-old Story of King Gilgamesh in ancient Sumer, which we discuss in Part II.

Enkidu, the ancient Wild Man, who befriends King Gilgamesh

The two breeds of humankind overlapped perhaps 50,000 years ago or more, and produced a hybrid species, that at one point, must have been approximately 50% human, or Sapiens, and fully 50% Neanderthal, after the first mating between the two species. This ancient mating produced the first Neon-Human hybrid children, many thousands of years ago. Research indicates that the range of Neanderthals was well extended into the Eurasian geography, including most of Europe, the Far East, the Middle East and Mesopotamia, which includes the land of ancient Sumer, where King Gilgamesh and Enkidu the Wildman may have possibly lived, once upon a time. This sexual interbreeding between male and then females of different hominid species, of course, could only be accomplished by either rape or mutual desire. Perhaps the Roman Lucretius (99–55 BCE) said it best, writing in 100 BCE, *On the Nature of Things*, concerning the hoary past:

"But the race of men at that time was much hardier on the land, as was

fitting inasmuch as the hard earth had made it, built up within it was with

bones, larger and more solid, fitted with strong sinews throughout the

flesh, not such as easily to be mastered by heat or cold.

7

And Venus joined the bodies of lovers in the woods; for either the

woman was attracted by some mutual desire or caught by the man's

violent force and vehement lust, or by a bribe.... acorns and arbute-

berries or choice pears."

When Lucretius writes of the larger bones and 'strong sinews' of the earlier 'race of men,' we may suspect that this race was a hybrid-hominid reference. Lucretius' words also describe, as we shall see in Part II, the greater strength of such creatures, such as that of Enkidu the Wildman, in The Story of King Gilgamesh, a full 2,000 years before Lucretius.

Science has since found that the bones of Neanderthals, and thus most likely their hybrid ancestors, were indeed much larger than their Sapiens counterparts.

In most animal species, mutual sexual desire appears to be the purpose as both male and female often go into a type of sexual swoon, torpor or trance, which, in our case, might be called intense hominid lust today. A timid anthropology is stumped on this one, as scientists largely avoid the sexual issues involved with hybrid-hominid creation. Their entire toolkit of evidence revolves around a small number of Neanderthal fossils, from perhaps fifty cavernous sites in Eurasia. Normally, an analytical science simply glosses over, and only depicts the physiological changes in mankind's evolution as seen below, and largely ignores the living being:

A Brief History of Man

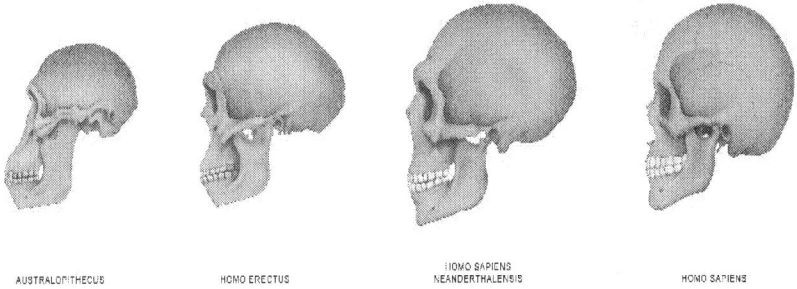

A Sapiens-to-Neanderthal skull comparison beginning with AUSTRALOPITHECUS, moving to HOMO ERECTUS, then HOMO SAPIENS NEADERTHALENSIS and ending with HOMO SAPIENS. The Neanderthal skull contained a brain with a smaller frontal hemispheric set than ours, but their rear brain had a visual cortex four times larger than Homo sapiens. As we shall see, this large visual cortex was an important key in the early spiritual and cultural development of humanity.

~!~

The systematic genus, Homo, is designed to include both anatomically modern humans and extinct varieties of archaic humans. While Homo sapiens is considered the intelligent (sapient) creature, we can consider Homo Neanderthals, our Neons, to have greater 'visual' intelligence,

9

obtained through enhanced eyesight, visions, dreams, and imagination. They were unlike Sapiens, and more advanced in this way.

For several decades, the science of anthropology has debated over the fact that ancient Neanderthals buried their dead, usually in magnetic red ocher; what could this mean? Some scholars have speculated that a 'Cult of Immortality' may have existed in the mind of primitive man, as Neanderthals and Cro-Magnons, the earliest Sapiens, co-existed.

A New Neon

Meet
Homo neanderthalensis

"The conclusion has to be that Neanderthals were cognitively indistinguishable from Homo sapiens, and the Neanderthal versus sapiens dichotomy is therefore invalid, Neanderthals were Homo sapiens, too."

Archaeologist Joao Zilhao, University of Barcelona

Y es, our new conclusion must drop the notion of our Neanderthal ancestors as dim-witted brutes. As Neanderthal evidence continues to accumulate, and as we hear of Joao Zilhao's interesting research and findings, his remarks suggesting equal 'humanism' between species remind us of a professional woman in an unrelated field—Dr. Elizabeth Kubler-Ross. Kubler-Ross, as the world's first death-and-dying psychologist, performed her humanitarian work in a post-World War II setting, and developed a keen insight into the nature of Homo sapiens and their ancestors. A famous author, she once wrote that the origins of humans reaches back into the dim past, for perhaps millions of years. Unlike the cold view of an anthropologist, an insightful Elizabeth considered that *all* of our distant ancestors, whether Homo erectus, Homo sapiens, Homo neanderthalensis, or the newly discovered Denisovans, were our kin. Yet, like all kinfolk, we have our differences, especially in the neural sense. In this book, after focusing upon the more ancient Neanderthals, we then shift to observe those potential hybrid descendants of the Neons and early humans, as our ancestral past, for the past 10,000 years.

~!~

A rather strange coincidence, or synchronicity, occurred to me recently, while I was researching for this book. I live in Colorado, and was relaxing in the Pueblo Athletic Club sauna, listening to esoteric author Manley P. Hall (1901–1990) on my headphones. Hall, a 33rd-degree initiate of the clandestine Free Masonry Society, who wrote the staggering tome *The Secret Teachings of All Ages*, was discussing the subject of ancient man and his use of magical talismans. Hall stated these were shamanistic and prehistoric in nature. Prehistoric Shamanism is considered a precursor to today's organized religions. Hall's description was overwhelmingly simple. One day, while out in the wilderness, a prehistoric human, either man or woman, spied a real beauty of a small rock or stone; perhaps its unusual colors or sparkly nature appealed to that particular person, and the pebble or stone was picked up and carried back to the home cave and placed in a special, perhaps secret corner of the cave where no one would find it. The special stone would work its way into the mind of its new owner, and a type of psychological bond would soon be established in the mind of the cave-dweller. A talisman is often further personalized by its owner creating marks or additional signs upon it. It becomes precious. The word talisman derives from the Greek, meaning 'consecrated.' Whoever picked up the beautiful stone eventually placed a lot of mental energy upon it; neurons fired. The stone became valuable. Today, talismans are always associated with luck, good fortune, and protection; this notion may stem from really hoary days in the unknown past. Talismans have existed for perhaps 100,000s of years, as ancient people, including the Neons and their descendants, developed their own personal sacred collections, and used them alongside their tools, weapons, jewelry, and musical instruments. The symbolic art of the Neons may date back 250,000 years or more.

A few days later, after my sauna experience concerning Manley P. Hall and his story of an ancient talisman, I noticed an article on Neanderthals on Arttrak.com, a website that tracks art development in early tribal cultures. The article cited several new scientific observations, one of which was about their possible use of talismans. The article, dated 12/22/2017, cited recent findings, and a surprisingly developing anthropological view, that advanced our dim knowledge of the so-called brute; excerpt follows:

"Once upon a time, about 130,000 years ago, a Neanderthal fancied a

peculiar pebble. He or she picked it up and took it home. "Home" was a

cave in modern Croatia, at the Krapina archaeological site. The cave

was sandstone, while the rock was a brown piece of limestone with black

patterns. Among the 1,000 stone pieces extracted from Krapina, nothing

matched the pebble. The striking rock probably piqued the curiosity of

the Neanderthal who found it. In 2015, a collection of eagle talons was

found at the same site. The talons had been carved and made into a piece

of jewelry. In other locations, Neanderthals gathered shells and even adorned them with pigments. The limestone rock was originally found

during excavations that lasted from 1899 to 1905 and was forgotten until

the same team who found the talons researched the site's past finds.

That's when they found the rock, which appeared to have no purpose

other than to look pretty. It had no modifications as a tool or piece of

jewelry."

So, in the 1920s, while the esoteric author Manley P. Hall was referring to prehistoric man's use of a special talisman stone, perhaps 10,000 years ago, we can flash forward to the recent Arttrek Neanderthal article and find a direct match for the mind-to-talisman relation. However, the date of the 2017 discovery has shifted far back . . . to 130,000 years ago. To clinically minded anthropologists, such a special stone reflects a potential *cognitive symbolism*, which is considered a progressive evolutionary mental trait. Although the Arttrek article doesn't specifically mention a 'consecrated' object or the word 'talisman,' as we shall see later, the Neons, and many of their hybrid descendants, exhibited a remarkable tendency towards a deep psychological spirituality. Can we also say, in the philosophical sense, that such a talisman could be appreciated, simply because of its beauty, and beauty alone, a trait highly valued by those of a philosophical bent? John Hawks, a paleoanthropologist at the University of Wisconsin-Madison who wasn't involved with the study, commented upon its findings:

"Neanderthals appear to have had a cultural competence that was

shared by modern humans. They were not dumb brutes; they were

recognizably human."

The previous, long-held scientific notion of Neanderthals as 'knuckle-dragging brutes,' should be entirely discarded as an immature, assumptive, scientific conclusion.

Another cave in southeastern Spain, Cueva de los Aviones, also yielded 115,000-year-old seashells that had been delicately perforated and could be strung together as a 'Neon necklace.' Neanderthals are now thought to have used strings, and perhaps even ropes. Neon artwork and clever handywork were obvious aspects of their lifestyle. As research continued into the nature of the illusive Neons, another 60,000-year-old cave near Barcelona, Spain, already known for its many ancient wall paintings, yielded yet one more startling insight into our distant past.

The Ancient Hearth

As our knowledge of the Neons has recently expanded, and is constantly being revamped, scientists finally concluded that the ancient Neons utilized their caves in much the same way we do our own homes today.

A sleeping area was your bedroom, a bathroom area was set aside, as was a kitchen area for meat carving, meal preparation, and trash disposal, and then there was the living room with the lit fire, roaring and warming the cave. Impressive skulls, as memories from previous hunts and battles, were lined up as trophies and hung upon the hearth wall. Yes, the Neanderthals are now thought to have used, and perhaps created fire and the earliest hearths. By their roaring fire, Neons would likely crouch, not sit, and create their weapons, tools, and artwork using wood, sharp rocks, and even pigments, and powerful glues to finish their creations. These ideas and processes they would later reveal to Sapiens, their hominid cousins, as they came onto the scene, arriving after the Neanderthals, by several hundred-thousands of years. If you have ever gazed into a surreal fire, try to imagine the Neons' experience, with much larger eyes and a huge visual cortex. Color appreciation is something that Neons would have had in a much greater degree than we, with their remarkable eyesight and rear vision center braincase. Bright colors were best.

Let us imagine ancient Neon folks, reeking strongly of an animal smell, perhaps painted and bejeweled, looking strangely akin to the American Indians of the 1700–1800s, entering into and living in this ancient cave, in a day-to-day life setting.

One of the more startling archeological findings in the Barcelona cave is the 2015 discovery of a large hole, dug directly in front of the ancient Neon fire hearth. Archeologists studying Neanderthals consider the most likely use for such a well-placed hole in the ground, was for containing water, which would be conveniently heated, and possibly brought to boiling temperature for cooking, cleaning, or bathing, or all three typical behaviors. This was an early form of having hot water in the abode, similar to our uses today, say, as in a hot bath, or jacuzzi. When dry, the hole could be used for sleeping by the fire. The bright Neons were seemingly much more organized, and more intelligent than previously imagined.

Neanderthal fossilized teeth have been found to contain cooked starches, further confirming their ability to cook foods. Were there ancient clay or stone pots for cooking these vegetables? No one knows; however, this finding of cooked vegetables raises another important question. When did hominids, or a portion of them, decide to become vegetarians? In The Story of King Gilgamesh, in a scene where Enkidu destroys the traps of the hunter, the poet-scribe is portraying the Wildman as abhorring the killing of animals; as someone who certainly doesn't desire or eat living meat. Perhaps, somewhere in the distant past, Enkidu survived not as a hunter but as a gatherer of eggs, nuts, roots, and berries for his daily fodder, until that fateful day, when he arrived at the city of Uruk, in ancient Sumer. It is likely that meat-eaters and vegetarians co-existed far back into the past. One man, a paleo-psychologist named Stan Gooch, actually predicted that some of the Neanderthals would be vegetarian; we discuss his remarkable ideas in upcoming pages. Further, we can ask: did Neons also develop plants and herbs into their culture, possibly to be used for healing purposes? Some anthropologists have suggested that the Neon culture had its own type of medical-healing culture based upon the healed wounds observed in their craniums and the dental tartar in the teeth. Neons appear to have used yarrow, chamomile, and poplar as natural antibiotics. By comparing the fossilized teeth found in different caves in Spain and Belgium, researchers found that the Belgium cave's fossils revealed that both plants and meats were in the diet of the northern Neon. However, in El Sidron, the Spanish cave, only the remnants of a vegetarian-based diet were found, namely forest moss, pine, and mushrooms.

~!~

Thus, moving forward in time, it is entirely reasonable to believe the poet-scribe of The Story of King Gilgamesh was depicting a real hominid creature. Yes, Enkidu the Wildman, as we shall see, was a relict Neon who chose to be vegetarian, or something very close to it.

Is it reasonable to believe that early Greek, Hindu, Chinese, and Egyptian

17

medical notions had a far distant prehistoric precedent, possibly stemming thousands of years into the past, to a time when Neons or their remnant ancestors had already generated this knowledge, slowly developed over hundreds of thousands of years?

"Let food be thy medicine and medicine be thy food."

Hippocrates (460-360 BCE)

~!~

Some Neanderthal researchers have also suggested that, based upon newer, expanded findings, the Neons would have developed skilled midwives to help in the birthing practice, perhaps complete with sterile, boiled water and a prepared soft landing spot replete with warm furs for the newborn babe and its mother. On the other hand, in our particular case, at some later point, we must consider that Enkidu himself, must have been born in the wild, in a rather raw setting, devoid of culture and civilization, and was abandoned early in life, and yet still survived to become a Mesopotamian Wild Man, only 4,000 years ago.

Another remarkable, clever Neanderthal finding was observed in France in 2016 at the dig site known as Pech-De-l'Aze, where several groups of archaic Neons apparently collected manganese dioxide to help them start their fires. This particular mineral, at first glance, doesn't appear to be combustible material, yet 50,000-year-old blocks of the stuff kept turning up during the ongoing dig. Archeologists at first assumed the Neons were using the substance for black pigment for painting, but the Neons already had copious amounts of charcoal from their hearths for cave and body painting. Fire experts were called in, and subsequent tests proved that the dark mineral, when completely ground down to a powder, creates a much more stable and long-lasting fire. Somehow, Neon figured out that by pulverizing it with stones, a non-burning piece of earth could dramatically improve their fire-making; they then harvested the substance for their homes and hearth in the dim past, for untold millennia.

Rollover Prometheus

The astute reader may have realized, as did I when I read the latest Neon research, that it is highly likely that Homo sapiens and Neanderthals shared much more than just DNA via sex. Neanderthals are now known to predate humans by many thousands of years, yet . . . they still used fire, charcoal, etc. It may be reasonable to consider that it was the other, older species, the Neons, that actually gave fire to mankind. Science has also considered that the first use of fire occurred well over 100,000 years ago, with Homo erectus, an even earlier hominid species. Yet, with the many comparisons to be made here on the New Neon, transferring the knowledge of fire use to our earliest human cultures seems likely. Sex in the cave between a male and female of different species, if not too violent, was likely followed by a warming by the fire hearth, or even, as a few archeologists suggested, by getting into an ancient, soothing hot bath, which likely also served as the only water 'vessel' in the cave, during a freezing winter.

The Sights, Sounds, and Scratches of Olden Days

T he line separating Homo sapiens and Neanderthals has been rapidly thinning, or even evaporating in the minds of some anthropologists. Perhaps we can even allow consideration for a link between King Gilgamesh and the Wild Enkidu, as they considered each other as brothers.

As we have seen, Neons and their hybrid descendants created many beautiful visual delights. Their exquisite cave paintings are often compared to modern artists, such as Picasso, for their in-depth, symbolic portrayals . . . but there is more. The Neons, like us, also practiced art in the vocal sense.

Author Steven Mithen, an anthropologist who focuses on Neanderthal development, wrote a most intriguing book, entitled; *The Singing Neanderthals*. Based upon the freshest archeological evidence, Mithen informs his readers of many details concerning the prehistoric mind and the cognitive origins of music, singing, art, religion, and science, all of which congeal in the developing psyche—the anima of the creature we call Neanderthal. As we shall see in a few pages, at least one scientist thought them capable of chanting, which, like the ancient talisman, is another step towards seeing the earliest vestiges of our world religions . . . pushed back over 100,000 years. Today historians generally agree that organized religion is only 5,000 years old, yet this seems an academically necessary, politically contrived date and was created while scientific research still portrayed ancient cavemen as grunting, apelike creatures not capable of speech or forming words, let alone singing. We can recall Voltaire's words here:

"History is the Lie commonly agreed upon."

In 1989, several things changed in the course of Neanderthal study. A 60,000-year-old Neanderthal hyoid bone was discovered in Israel. This small bone connects to the tongue and helps with speech. In other hominids, the hyoid bone is placed in such a way that they cannot vocalize like modern people, however, the Neon hyoid bone was basically identical to that of modern humans, thus speech such as ours would have been physically available to them.

Further, new Neanderthal DNA evidence also reveals that our critical FOXP2 gene, which is essential for 'proper speaking and language' in Homo sapiens, was originally handed down to us from the Neon species. This, along with other cranial-mouth observations, suggests that Neon could do far more than merely utter cave-grunts while dragging her knuckles.

A cross-disciplinary scientific team, headed by Dr. Daniel Dediu, from the Max Planck Institute for Psycholinguistics, Netherlands, studied the vocal bone structures of the Neanderthals and wrote:

"Speech and language is an old feature of our lineage going back at least

to the last common ancestor that we shared with the Neanderthals."

Additional linguistic animal research with monkeys and baboons now shows that language, with the ability to create clear vowel sounds, is likely millions of years old, and so is not really a new development to just humans. In the upcoming New Muse Series book, *The Colors of Mind, in Ancient Times,* it is revealed, for the first time, how animal and human languages interacted, in a precedent-setting example of linguist Noam Chomsky's theory of Universal Grammar. Chomsky claimed that Universal Grammar arose from animal vocalizations, and it appears that it does!

Vocal communication containing key vowel sounds may be a primary tool in the development of an animal's primitive language. With lungs, mouth, and jaws up to one-third larger than our own, the Neon's vocalizations were likely far more powerful than ours and had a greater range of audible sounds; anything from soft and wispy vocalizations to extremely loud calls might be expected. As for singing sounds, or even the singing of Neon songs, we might expect the usual ranges of baritones, tenors, and sopranos, only delivered with more vocal force than a Sapiens. Aside from peaceful times and music, truly formidable, harrowing roars might be heard from the strong Neon males when hunting or in battle in defense of the caves. The terrifying roar of a modern gorilla comes to mind. Stronger and louder than other early humans and equipped with vastly enhanced vision, we can speculate that they were mighty creatures, and quite possibly superior in many ways to Cro-Magnon, our other, smaller ancestors.

As Cro-Magnons, our frontal brain hemispheres were large, as they are today, and a more polished language may have developed as a strong aspect of the left-brain hemisphere, which controls speech. The Cro-Magnon's right hemi-field was silent, without direct speech capabilities; same as ours at the present day.

Recent computer modeling of the skull indicates that Neanderthals could not only talk, but were likely capable of moderately complex language, perhaps even conversation. But the anthropological trail goes cold here.

The shorter, muscular Neon had strength estimated at twice that of the ordinary, leaner Sapiens-human, who was usually 4–6 inches taller. If you, as an early human, encountered one, and quickly realized the superior strength of their muscular bodies, plus their massive cranial-facial size, was so much larger than our own, it would be hard not to have been intimidated. Their overwhelming physical strength was much greater than that of early mankind. Perhaps, at times, the only way for Cro-Magnons to survive a lethal Neanderthal attack was to band together in greater numbers. Many anthropologists consider that the population ratio of Cro-Magnon man and Neanderthals may have been lopsided—even 10–1 odds. So the stronger, perhaps greater Neanderthal creatures may have been taken down, and gone extinct, against sheer, overwhelming numbers. Science is unclear on this point. It's certainly interesting that Stanly Gooch, perhaps the world's first paleo-psychologist, was the first person to advance the likelihood of Neanderthal and Cro-Magnon mating, before modern anthropological science could swallow the idea. Even as today, one might expect the usual admixture of desires; lust, rape and/or compassionate affections may have existed between the different hominid species. There should have been codes of ethics, however primordial, that developed and existed between the two. We can no longer rely on the older, outdated anthropology notion that we are dealing with base animals, hardly removed from the great apes themselves.

After the discovery of Neon's bones in 1856, in Germany, it wasn't until the year 2000 that geneticists began extensive DNA analysis upon their ancient fossils. Then, suddenly, anthropology was again upended, this time in 2008, by the discovery of ancient fossils in the Denisova cave in the Altai mountains of Siberia, by a group of Russian anthropologists. Yet another new humanlike species had been discovered, and named the Denisovans, after the location of the ancient cave. The Denisovan skull case was even larger than the Neanderthal's! The age of the fossils of the new species was placed at 160,000 years by Swedish geneticist Svante Paabo, director of the Max Planck Institute for Evolutionary Anthropology in Leipzig, Germany.

~!~

In the Mesopotamian area, where The Story of King Gilgamesh was first written down around 4,000 years ago, it is more likely that Enkidu, the red-haired Wildman, would have been an admixture of Sapiens and Neanderthal DNA. The main thrust of the Epic's poet, concerning hairy Enkidu, is simply to introduce a moralistic wild creature who instructs King Gilgamesh in how to properly live life, and with the Wildman's untimely death, how to begin a spiritual search, and move beyond the egotism of a young King.

~!~

Our scientific expectations of Neanderthals as being our 'kissing cousins' may have to change. Even the mouth and nasal passages of the Neons were 30% larger than Cro-Magnon man. The larger jaws imply a much greater biting strength than we have today; many indigenous cultures make great use of their mouths to bite or hold the essential objects in their environment. Because of the huge size of the nose and mouth, larger quantities of oxygen could be breathed in and quickly sent into the body . . . perhaps into larger hearts and lungs as well, which are needed to support the exceptionally strong muscles. In the past, larger percentages of oxygen, 50% or more in the primordial air may have been a factor in their strength; oxygen is greatly reduced in our atmosphere today, down to roughly 20%. Their capacity for smell could possibly surpass that of today's modern canines. An intricate olfactory sense dominates the reality of a dog's brain, getting equal priority with vision itself. The worldview of the Neons must have been extremely rich in sensory perceptions. Theirs was an exceptional world of sheer, raw beauty contrasted with the stark, physical reality of the wild Megafauna environment in which they lived, with its saber-toothed tigers and wooly mammoths. Their perceptive ears, also likely 30% larger than ours, may have heard sounds we will never hear, in a way similar to our inability to hear the full range of sounds that our dogs can hear.

On the Origin of Writing

From Scratch to Cuneiform to Alphabet

"Writing—a system of graphic marks representing the units of a specific language—has been invented independently in the Near East, China and Mesoamerica. The cuneiform script, created in Mesopotamia, present-day Iraq, ca. 3200 BC, was first. It is also the only writing system which can be traced to its earliest prehistoric origin. This antecedent of the cuneiform script was a system of counting and recording goods with clay tokens."

Denise Schmandt-Besserrat; University of Texas at Austin

Our singing, far-sighted Neon may be implicated in yet another way—that of prehistoric writing. Recent Neanderthal archeological findings reveal that patterns of ancient cut marks upon stone, bone, and other materials, indicate that Neon had cognition skills that included symbols.

The scratched floor of Gorham's Cave: Neanderthal engraving in Gibraltar, By Stewart Finlayson(Gibraltar Museum): CC: SA 4.0

These 35,000-year-old cutting marks appear to show that a type of *single-line cuneiform* style was used. These simple cut marks, arranged in a single row, if multiplied and placed side by side, might construe an earlier *proto-cuneiform* style, which humans might have once mimicked, and/or altered, as needed, for simple accounting and perhaps astronomical purposes, such as noting the phases of the sun and moon.

Is it a coincidence that the Levant, especially early Phoenicia, where caves have produced significant Neon fossils, also produced the world's first alphabet in prehistoric times? This alphabet is still in use today, having been adopted by the early Greeks. Could sexual mating and cohabitation between these two hominid species have eventually contributed to a cross-culture learning system? Chants and songs were exchanged or developed, and perhaps the curious scratches evolved to proto-writing styles, which eventually became either a cuneiform or alphabetic method of describing one's thoughts. One can picture two ancient Neon-Sapiens hybrid-hominids sitting quietly by a good fire in

25

their cave, one making tools and weapons, the other making art, and calculating her cut marks. Perhaps they could occasionally laugh, and make a singsong, if the day and night had been good, safe and warm for them. These early Neon and Neon-Sapiens minds were imaginative marvels and had the massive visual neurons to prove it.

"If you can talk then you can sing."
Old Swahili Proverb

The Dream Culture of the Neanderthal

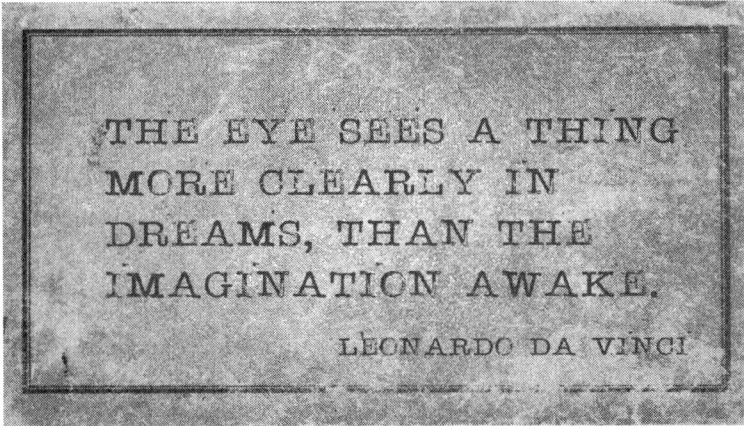

THE EYE SEES A THING MORE CLEARLY IN DREAMS, THAN THE IMAGINATION AWAKE.

LEONARDO DA VINCI

"Stan Gooch is one of the most underrated writers of our time."

Colin Wilson; author; The Outsider

Where did our religions originally come from, as we peer further back into our prehistoric past? Today's organized theologies would be shocked to learn their own relatively recent beliefs actually stem from much deeper times in our ancestral past.

British psychologist Dr. Stan Gooch (1932–2010) was the proverbial man before his time. Perhaps he is one of those people who will achieve much greater notoriety after his passing, having single handedly created a fledgling science of paleo-psychology, while studying Neanderthals and their hybrid descendants. His first book, *The Total Man,* was a psychological attempt to describe the many 'theories of personality' of mankind from a wide variety of sources such as Marx, Christianity, Freud, Pavlov, Nietzsche, and many others. Relatively successful as a result of his career and authorship, Gooch's curious genius soon led him to the outskirts and exit door of academia. He became an Outsider. As Gooch the psychologist followed his own keen interests in human evolution, he was criticized and ostracized by the anthropologists of his day, for theorizing that human evolution contained a hybrid-origin, indicating that a mixture of hominid species had mated and produced hybrid, crossbreed offspring. As the moralistic roar of pedantic skepticism abated, as often happens, he was later found correct by scientific research in the next several decades; nowadays anthropologists parrot Gooch's idea as if it were their own. In addition to the Human-Neanderthal connection we have discussed, as we have seen, there is also good anthropological evidence of a Denisovan connection in Russia and southern Asia, where humans have DNA relations (1–4%) with yet another ancient hominid species. This human-Denisovan relation, however, does not appear to extend westward geographically, to ancient Sumer in Mesopotamia.

Stan Gooch was the first to write of the hitherto, dumb apelike Neanderthal in a dazzling, new insightful light. But Gooch's precocious view of our ancient hominid ancestor was dimly received by knuckle-dragging anthropologists. His view is that much of the Neanderthal culture was swept underground and lost to the modern historical view.

"Many writers, some with good reason but others with none, speak of an

'Ancient Wisdom', of some great body of knowledge and of great

civilizations that produced and enshrined it...is now lost to us. Fragments

of this knowledge, it is said, are found all over the world and they are

proof that the complete body of knowledge once existed. When

Neanderthal and Cro-Magnon met and mingled to produce ourselves,

modern man, I believe each side made a unique contribution. This was at

one level a cultural cross-fertilization; but at a deeper level it was a

genetic one. Neanderthal contributed our religious/intuitive genes and

Cro-Magnon our scientific/logical endowment."

Stan Gooch

Alternative-history authors, such as Robert Bauval and Graham Hancock, write that human civilization likely existed far into the past, well beyond the 5,000-year limit taught in schools and academia. Hancock, with his famous book, *Fingerprints of the Gods*, and his research showing a 12,000-year-old catastrophe, where comets from space likely rained God's fire upon mankind, nearly wiping out civilization, broaches the difficult idea to his readers, of extending the academic notion of civilization. Stan Gooch takes the notion of previous civilizations even further and turns them on their head with his interpretation of a lost and forgotten *Neanderthal civilization*, which was largely internalized, thus endearing paleo-psychologists but leaving the shovel-digging archeologists . . . without a clue. Colin Wilson, in his book *Atlantis and the Kingdom of the Neanderthals,* also suggested that academia had 'forgotten' over 100,000 years of prehistoric civilization. Gooch wrote of an ancient prehistoric religion, which is largely forgotten today, extending back perhaps several hundred-thousands of years, when Neanderthal was in her prime. In Britain, his book, *The Guardians of the Ancient Wisdom,* was given a revealing new title when it was published in the United States: *The Dream Culture of the Neanderthal*.

With this provocative new title, Gooch was making a rather shocking statement to the scientific community, who is constantly searching for ancient artifacts as proof of the lifestyle and technology of the cultures that produced them. Gooch, as a psychologist, went beyond the need for physical proofs and entered into an entirely new arena: he postulated that, aside from the outer rigors and dangers of their daily lives, that the Neon folks also lived deeply inside of their minds:

"What my book precisely offers is very strong evidence of a hidden, lost

civilization. But this was more a civilization of the mind than of buildings.

*For the lost ancients built not cities of stone, but **cities of dreams**."*

At first glance, Gooch's notion of a Neanderthal dream civilization makes no sense at all in the context of the usual scientific logic applied towards the benefits of a highly technological, outwardly focused human civilization. That's the modern, utopian life that everyone wants, right? Well, truly, not at all, if we listen to our deepest psychological sense. In the ancient, often violent times of our brilliantly painted Neon, we might expect that they, like us, experienced extreme terror, due to the hostile elements in their environment. After all, anthropologists know that the remains of Neanderthals were routinely found in the stomachs of ancient saber-toothed tigers, hyenas, bears, large predatory birds, and a long list of other predators. The terror of seeing your clan members killed, or yourself being close to death or severely wounded by a large predator, even while you are on the hunt for prey, would produce a deep, lasting impact on the mind of the Neanderthal. This psychological impact is similar to what is known in modern humans as PTSD, or Post-Traumatic Stress Disorder.

"All of Life is Suffering."

Siddhartha Gotama, 450 BCE.

The pain of the external conflict often drives one inside, away from the physicality and pain of an often cruel world, and into the mental dream worlds of which Gooch spoke. Although our brains might be structured differently from the Neon's, it would appear that our pleasure and pain responses were remarkably similar.

Today, this psychological method of mental retreating, on a much lesser scale of intensity, can be observed in a person opening a good book and losing themselves in it, after a really stressful, bad day.

Following a close encounter with death, and with PTSD setting in, a wounded Neon would retreat deeply into his cave complex; sometimes he would be with the clan, and at other times, he would seek to retreat deeply away from others and settle into his own interior world, as Gooch suggested. As Neons were blessed with remarkably superior vision (with their large eyes, their rear brains, and a visual cortex four times larger than ours), they might actually have had a greater opportunity to experience extraordinary dream realities. This would be a dream capacity far beyond that of modern humans, where dreams are either diminished in intensity and are not common, and/or they take the form of 'bad' dreams, nightmares, etc. Indeed, modern analytical scientists, such as Carl Sagan or Richard Dawkins, stated in their own words, that they themselves rarely dream poignant dreams, if ever, and thus the importance of their dreams fades away, becoming nonsensical and therefore unnecessary. A large portion of the scientific community now finds dreams and their analysis to be meaningless and random. One could say they seem clueless, or that this finding may be due to left-brain dominance, a condition which can shut down, ignore, or occlude, the marvelous dreaming capabilities of the hominid species. This was not the case in the hoary past of the Neon folks, where natural dreams were extremely important. To Neon, his dreams, whether light, or deep, or during the daytime, may have seemed extremely trancelike. Flash forward hundreds of thousands of years and we find shamans, Yogins, and even modern science informing us that physical reality is either an illusion or a holographic generation, depending upon your belief system. Is it possible that the Neons intuited their harsh yet beautiful, natural surroundings as a type of daily dream itself? Just how long has our species, Neon and Cro-Magnon, thought of daily reality as being a vivid, surreal, dreamlike setting? The Australian Aboriginal culture, now estimated to be over 50,000 years old, has always believed in the world as a Dreamtime, as have others.

"Life is a Dream."
Leonard Tolstoy

"Reality is an Illusion, although a very persistent one."
Albert Einstein

In modern times, another remarkable development of a dreamlike retreat into another reality, is seen in American filmmaker Steven Spielberg's 2011 movie, ReadyPlayerOne, based upon a book by Ernest Cline. The plot is set in the year 2027, when exterior civilization has dramatically collapsed, and humans utilize a techno-mask computer system to create their own dreamlike reality, in a computer matrix called 'The Oasis,' to escape from the dreary pressures of external life. The principle is similar, but to a far lesser degree of intensity, than that of the 250,000-year-old escape of the Neon, hiding in a cave from wild beasts, and then slowly relaxing into her or his own dream reality. We and the Neons can be similar in our approach to dreams and reality, if we choose an open mind.

"I'm a Dreamer, I build Worlds.

Get Yourself a Clue."

Ready Player One

"Create your own mental world and environments."

Sri Sivananda, Yogin.

"All is True."

Hamlet, **Shakespeare**

In *The Dream Culture of the Neanderthal,* Stanley Gooch writes of the Neanderthal's love, or worship for the moon; he considers Neons may have been semi-nocturnal and avoided the full, hot sun. His suggestion of a moon-worshipping, dream-cultivating Neanderthal civilization is also seen, much later, in Sumer's culture of 4,500 years ago. Both King Gilgamesh and Enkidu have intense dreams, all of which foretell of a foreboding future in the Epic, written by an unknown author who called themselves, 'Moon God, Hear My Plea.'

Another dream culture example is St. Augustine's notion, made in AD 400, of an inner 'City of God' which rivaled and conflicted with the outside 'Earthly City,' where man's precious attention was caught in the desires of his senses. After his terrifying, external experience with a saber-toothed cat, or a pack of hyenas, an injured Neon, or his hybrid descendants, might be expected to stay deep in a hidden recess of his cave for days or weeks, surviving near a well-kept, roaring fire, on a small cache of food and slowly wandering into a dreamy state which we call trance today.

Today we know that in primitive societies, from which our own civilization has developed, hunters would withdraw from society before a hunt, and undergo a type of sensory deprivation via several methods. An ancient Neon man may have experienced something similar way back in his cave, whether injured or not. Sensory deprivation, and the revealing dreams that then occur, can happen quite naturally, under certain conditions.

In our modern state, we often speak of spiritual and/or artistic retreats to a safe, secluded place, where we enter into our innermost thoughts and experiences.

In numerous cultures, some type of sensory deprivation experience, such as retreats, fasts, total silence, darkened rooms, etc., have been utilized to train shamans, witchdoctors, priests, monks, gurus, mediums, hermits, amongst others. Few people know that Plato, at age 47, underwent Egyptian Initiation rites; he was underground, beneath the pyramids for several months. Sworn to secrecy, he later wrote his mysterious *Allegory of the Cave* as an encrypted device, where the implications of caves, illusions of reality, and dreams are fairly obvious, of his own cave-like experience.

But where, in our distant Cro-Magnon and Neanderthal ancestry, did such practices, such as sensory deprivation causing extended dreaming, truly begin?

Is it possible to consider that, due to our somewhat related neural connections, that Gooch is right, that the Neon folks were the 'Guardians of the Ancient Wisdom' and that this Ancient Wisdom has survived and morphed, in clandestine forms throughout the ages? He considered that faint traces of a Neanderthal occult influence can be seen in the esoteric histories of Witchcraft, Kabbala, The Knights Templar, the Rosicrucian's, and even in Christianity, and Judaism. The quintessential, inward retreat of our long-lived species, including that of the distant Neons, can be seen in a simple poetic phrase of Jesus, taken from Matthew 6:6, King James version, a mere 2,000 years ago:

"But thou, when thou prayest, enter into thy

closet, and when thou hast shut thy door, pray

to thy Father which is in secret; and thy Father

which seeth in secret shall reward thee openly."

Gooch also considered that the Neons were our forebearers in the areas of spiritual and psychic experience. If so, did they have great spiritual leaders or shamans, the names of which we shall never know, akin to our Buddha, Jesus, and Osiris?

Manley P. Hall's classic book, *The Secret Teachings of All Ages*, will have to be reconsidered in favor of the truly ancient ages, and sages, of the Neanderthals.

Other interesting, modern analogies might be made, concerning our scenario of an ancient Neon, injured or not, who retreated far back into his cave and entered into his own dream world. These may have been our first shamans.

The recent case of a severely ill neuroscientist named Eben Alexander is pertinent here. Alexander, while seemingly unconscious and in a full coma due to the presence of an advanced bacterial brain infection, awoke several days later . . . and reported a highly visual out-of-body experience that had lasted for days. His entire life changed as a result of his dreamlike experience.

In Plato's *Myth of Er*, a scene is described where a fallen soldier lies for days upon the battleground, taken for dead, and then awakes and describes an incredible series of intense experiences, which some analytical philosophers have called 'merely dreams.'

In today's Buddhist meditative practices, monks are routinely instructed to focus their vision inwardly and purposely produce 'mental creations.' These mental worlds are called 'Tulpas.' Similar to Gooch's notions about the Neanderthal dream culture, the Tibetan Monks create their own unique, inner life, whatever it may be. Purposeful practices, such as Tulpa mental creation, is likely an ancient, neural birthright of our cognitively aware species, and is likely a gift from our unknown prehistoric past. The Western metaphysical notion of 'thought-forms' stems from this Tibetan practice. In the 19th century, Theosophist Annie Besant, in her book, *Thought-Forms*, divided these Tulpas or Thought-Forms, into three classes: forms in the shape of the person who creates them, forms that resemble objects or people and may become "ensouled" by "nature spirits" or by the dead, and forms that represent "inherent qualities" from the astral or mental planes, such as emotions.

You say it's a crazy scheme

I already bought the dream

Steely Dan

Imagine what visual Tulpa worlds could be created by an ancient Neon ancestor, whose rear-brain visual cortex was 400% larger than ours? Gooch may be right, in that the Neons, with such a potential neuropsychological visual approach, may have strongly preferred to create nearly endless dream worlds, and then went to live in them for long periods of time, recessed safely into their deep caves. Today, cognitive man, rapidly advancing through the desires and limited merits of his left-brained Ego, finds science, logic, analytics, and mechanical-thinking simply irresistible, thus we are developing a runaway technological system that is out of control and definitely destructive to nature. While pedantic skeptics raise their usual negative dust, our premise here is that these and other types of spiritual experience have occurred for hundreds of thousands, if not millions of years, in our ancestral background. Our modern religions are dim reflections of a spiritual culture in the distant past. History is politically timid and inaccurate.

There are strong similarities in Gooch's notion of a Dream Culture of the Neons, and modern, spiritual experience. As an intriguing coincidence, anthropologist Werner Herzog recently completed a 3-D documentary on the Chauvet caves in Southern France, and entitled his film, "The Cave of Forgotten Dreams." We can agree; for a long-dreaming Neanderthal,

Gooch's prescient knowledge of the large-brained Neon favoring dream worlds is similar to the simple concept of a modern artist.

Excuse me if I have some place in my mind, where I go time to time

It's Good to be King; **Tom Petty**

In our modern world, people develop their own worldview and inner view. To recall Joseph Campbell's notion, these views may collectively be referred to as one's personal myth. Personal myths are not a new development. We can consider, as we slowly evolved through the life-forms of apes and early humans, such as the Neanderthal, that they must have possessed their own evolving brand of inner psyche and personal myth. Early Western thoughts on personal myths were given by Joseph Le Conte, writing in 1897 on *Evolution, Its Nature, Its Evidences and Its Relation to Religious Thought*;

"I believe that the spirit of man was developed out of the anima or conscious principle of animals, and that this, again, was developed out of the lower forms of life-force and this, in its turn, out of the chemical and physical forces of Nature; and that at a certain stage in this gradual development, viz., with Man, it acquired the property of immortality precisely as it now, in the individual history of each man at a certain stage acquires the capacity of abstract thought. Material evolution finds its goal in man, psychic evolution in the divine man"

Le Conte considered that the anima of animals was a 'spirit-in-embryo' and that evolution, with the 'birth of man' created an organic-based Immortality of the Psyche, as a result of the evolved neural matter of

36

humans. This neural matter may be thought of as the Wisdom Body of humans, with the heart center driving the three cranial brains. Le Conte advocated the idea that an omnipresent divine energy individuates into a separate, personal entity in the human. We can now consider Enkidu, as a Neon-Cro-Magnon mix, as mankind slowly evolves, or is this process a devolution, in a spiritual sense? Svante Paabo, that Swedish purveyor of ancient Neanderthal and modern man, once commented that the Neanderthals seemed intelligent and 'reasonable' in their approach to themselves and their environment, and that rather, it was an overly modern mankind, with his destructive ways, that seems mad, and out of control.

And if your head explodes with dark forebodings too

I'll see you on the dark side of the moon

Pink Floyd

The Neanderthal Marco Polo

It's noteworthy that the left hemisphere of our Sapiens brain is endlessly interpreting the outside world, as presented to it by the right hemisphere and rear brain, a few milliseconds after the images arrive optically, via the eyes. This neural necessity implies that all ancient and modern myths created by human beings . . . are actually attempts by the left brain to process the huge amounts of incoming information, which then creates a fanciful story, or concept to try to understand, or limit, what has been seen and heard in its life. Our challenge is to understand our neural position, to be whole-brained, and to realize that human left-brain myth-creation results in what we have to sometimes call history and legend. This interpretive human 'history' happens side by side with a deeper and ancient, hybrid-hominid reality, with its own unknown history, throughout the whole existence of ancient humanity. Author Colin Wilson once remarked that over 100,000 years of hominid history has been totally forgotten and overlooked, yet there are a few tantalizing traces. This forgotten history includes Sapiens, and the hybrid descendants of a mixed Sapiens, Neanderthal and/or Denisovan sub-species. These hybrids, with

37

their sloping front skulls, had a left-brain hemisphere that is not as pronounced as in modern man, however, their rear-brain case and vision center, would have greatly exceeded our own.

Yet another startling new anthropological finding was recently reported by Chinese media and was picked up by international news outlets. Readers are familiar with the romantic story of the Italian Marco Polo, and how he traveled to China in the 13th century AD, roughly following the ancient, prehistoric Silk Road of antiquity. Now, paleoanthropologists from Spain and China have found extremely ancient evidence of Neanderthals traveling west to east, perhaps as long as 130,000 years ago. In 1958, Chinese farmers digging in the Maba township in the southern province of Guangdong unearthed an object that they thought was a human skull; the unremarkable skull sat on a dusty shelf until recently, when it was re-evaluated by scientists. Referred to as the 'Maba Man,' the skull specimen was neither the oldest nor the best-preserved early human remains found in China, but it had a strangeness that set it apart—it had a "European" face, yet with distinct features that resembled those of a Neanderthal. Researchers described the Pleistocene-era skulls as having "a morphological mosaic with differences from and similarities to their Western contemporaries." Specifically, the brow ridges and front skull shape closely resembled the early peoples of prehistoric Europe, while the skulls had a flat brainpan like other eastern Eurasian humans of the time. Maba Man's ear canals and large rear skull were similar to those of a Neanderthal's. This combination poses two possibilities. Researchers conclude that Maba Man was either an early Neanderthal, meaning the Neanderthal's eastern range must have included China, or it shared a common ancestor with the Neons. This finding, of course, makes this fossil a perfect fit for our own hybrid-crossbreed hypothesis, specifically in the case of our Chinese Shennong, who descended eons later, upon the same general area as did the Maba Man, perhaps 100,000 years earlier. The likelihood of myriad crisscrossing migratory waves of crossbreeding hominids of Sapiens, Neons, and Denisovans, has only been hinted at thus far in a fledgling paleoanthropology, which is now constantly breaking new ground, with new tools and expanding their concepts of the Neanderthal, and the Denisovans.

"There is room to think about

an unknown Euro-Asian evolutionary process."

Professor Emiliano Bruner: University of Colorado

PART II ~ Mixed Breeds in The Story of King Gilgamesh

And What of Enkidu?

In the ancient Sumerian poem, The Story of King Gilgamesh, which is over four thousand years old, scholars have long puzzled over the strange attributes of Enkidu, the great Wildman who became a close friend of King Gilgamesh. In this chapter we discuss a possible alternative to the traditional, academic view, namely, we present the red-haired, speechless Enkidu as a Wildman, with possibly 10–20% Neanderthal DNA. The first question we should ask is: why the ancient scribe, using a sharp stick to press poetic marks into twelve clay cuneiform tablets that became The Story of King Gilgamesh, would seek to install such an anomalous character as a key player, as a companion to a great King? Was the scribe trying to communicate, four thousand years ago, that a hybrid humanity existed, in the form of strong Enkidu, and that they sometimes made contact with Sapiens humanity, as was done in ancient Sumer?

Could there possibly be an inkling, say, a remnant, or a shred of truth to this noble animal-man creature, Enkidu, as actually having existed, many thousands of years ago? Truth is Stranger than Fiction!

As we mentioned earlier, Enkidu is described as a strange wild man whose body is entirely covered, from shaggy head to hairy toe, in massive amounts of matted red hair, or fur. At first, before he meets Gilgamesh and ancient Sumer civilization, he is an outsider. Enkidu lives in the wild, grazes amongst the animals, cannot speak and knows nothing of human life.

And my dear mother left me, when I was quite young.

On the Road Again; **Canned Heat**

He has no recollection of neither mother nor father: Enkidu has simply lived on the plains and mountains of ancient Mesopotamia for as long as he recalls, being an orphaned Wildman, before being spotted and lured into human society.

"Sprouted luxuriant growth of his hair-like, the awns of the barley,

Nor knew he people nor land; he was clad in a garb like Sumuqan.

E'en with gazelles did he pasture on herbage, along with the cattle

Drank he his fill, with the beasts did his heart delight at the water."

The Story of King Gilgamesh
(Sumuqan; the Sumerian God of cattle and the river plains)

In the Epic, the ancient poet begins the story, by having a wild Enkidu slowly drift with the migrating gazelles, towards human civilization in the ancient Mesopotamian city of Uruk, ruled by King Gilgamesh. This is seen as a metaphysical response to the prayers of the oppressed people, who pray to the moon above, seemingly to represent those who are desperately seeking relief from the young, evil King.

The Gilgamesh Epic also has a strange sounding author; Sin-Leqi-Unninni, whose name translates to "Moon god, Hear my plea." Thus, we don't know the anonymous poet's true name, as if he or she were deliberately hiding their identity, while acknowledging a deep, nighttime prayer of remorse. The author's name, given in the form of a prayer, would have been in direct response to the evil youthful days of King Gilgamesh, when he greatly oppressed his people by slavery and rape. We can consider that Sin-Leqi-Unninni may have been a woman, anguished for her children, and venting her tears to the moon above.
Thus, Fate looms in ancient Sumer. Enkidu is eventually is spied by a hunter:

"Then did a hunter, a trapper, come face to face with this fellow, came

on him one, two, three days, at the place where the beasts drank their

water. Sooth, when the hunter espied him, his face o'er mantled with

42

terror."

The Story of King Gilgamesh

It's important to note that the wild Enkidu inspires absolute terror when a human first sees him; his appearance may not seem human at all, not taking into account the red hair, or fur. He is extremely intimidating, like a wild animal, and has overwhelming, powerful strength in his limbs. This overwhelming strength marks Enkidu as a remnant Neanderthal-Sapiens creature. Millenia before, pure-bred Neanderthals are considered by anthropologists to have had nearly twice the strength of their Sapiens counterparts and could have easily overcome the weaker species.

The hunter from Uruk knows he is no match for the strange, hairy wild man and quietly retreats. The wild Enkidu sees animals as his kin and disables all of the hunter's traps. Traumatized, the hunter goes to Gilgamesh, the strong King of Uruk, the city Father, and informs him of the wild man:

"Open'd his mouth (then) the hunter, and spake, addressing his father:

"Father, there is a great fellow come forth from out of the mountains.

O, but his strength is the greatest (the length and breadth) of the country,

Like to a double of Anu's own self his strength is enormous,

Ever he rangeth at large o'er the mountains, and ever with cattle

Grazeth on herbage and ever he setteth his foot to the water,

So that I fear to approach him."

After listening, Gilgamesh responds to the hunter, by saying no, that it was he, as the King of Uruk, who was the strongest, mightiest fellow in the land. Then, as a ploy, the King tells the hunter to take a beautiful courtesan-girl, a hetaera from the sacred temple, into the wild with him, for the purposes of having her seduce the wild monster-man.

"Forth went the hunter, took with him a courtesan-girl, a hetaera,

So, did they start on their travels, went forth on their journey together,

Aye, at the term of three days arrived at the pleasance appointed.

Sate they down in their ambush, the hunter and the hetaera,

One day, two days they sat by the place where the beasts drank

their water. Then at last came the cattle to take their fill in their drinking.

Thither the animals came that their hearts might delight in the water,

Aye, there was Enkidu also, he whom the mountains had gender'd,

E'en with gazelles did he pasture on herbage, along with the cattle

Drank he his fill, with the beasts did his heart delight at the water,

So, beheld him the courtesan-girl, the lusty great fellow,

O but a monster all savage from out of the depths of the desert!"

The young King begins to have strange, foreboding dreams of the strange wild man.

The beautiful temple seductress lies with Enkidu for a full week and slowly coaxes him into entering into human habitation. They are near the city of Uruk. The Epic's poet informs us that during this time she teaches the Wildman to speak. Perhaps Enkidu develops a rather slow, stilted, grasp of the monosyllabic Sumer spoken language, accompanied by a strong use of sign-gesturing visual language. He also begins to wear clothing during this time, after which his gazelle companions will have

44

nothing to do with him. The courtesan informs Enkidu of King Gilgamesh. The Wildman hears of the distasteful actions of the young ruler and sets out to challenge him. The King and Wildman have a great fight which results in a stalemate, as well as form a new friendship, born out of respect for each other. The Wildman strongly persuades the young King to forgo his slavery and rape of his people, and instead, they set out on kingly adventures together. The King and the Wildman represent two small evolutionary paths. King Gilgamesh, like us, may have 2–4% Neanderthal DNA, while Enkidu the Wildman likely has 10–20%, which is reflected in his shorter height, total body hair, and his great strength. In the Epic, the story of a great monster, Huwawa, is the first of these adventures and his name will be linked to the Wildman, Enkidu, in a subsequent chapter.

In The Story of King Gilgamesh, let's recall the scene where Shamhat, the sexy courtesan, meets Enkidu, seduces him and then educates him rather quickly, before she takes him to the city of Uruk. Enkidu is naked when he first comes in from the wild, thus he likely dons clothes for the first time in his life. As a Wildman, he initially cannot speak, but we might surmise that the Wild Fellow learns a smattering of simple monosyllabic Sumerian words, along with a good dosage of sign language from his new courtesan friend. Today, we find hominids, such as gorillas, learning several hundred words of human languages, like English, via a signing and gesturing language, so the idea of a wild animal-man such as Enkidu learning to 'speak' amongst the Sumer peoples is entirely plausible, albeit in simple, direct, spoken statements, along with copious amounts of signing-signals. After Enkidu's training and taming by Shamhat, he found that his former friends and companions, the gazelles and wild beasts, would no longer tolerate him. He had changed rapidly, and perhaps, he had gained a strange, new smell from his contact with civilization, and so, his old migrating friends departed for new pastures.

The earliest Sumer cuneiform scripts are mainly monosyllabic; thus, the spoken language was as well. Perhaps the Sumer language was simpler and more direct, as compared to the many convolutions in today's extensive languages, with hundreds of thousands of words. It is noteworthy that the earliest prehistoric Egyptians in the Nile Delta, who had colonies in the ancient Phoenician-Israeli region where many Neon fossils have been found, also appear to have had an early terse form of monosyllabic language, which preceded the development of pictorial hieroglyphics, possibly by thousands of years. These simple words expressed important key concepts, as follows:

AB: heart

ANKH: eternal life

HA: body

TA: earth, ground

RA: Sun, light

KA: psyche, mind

BA: indwelling spirit

SA: to see, or saw

Putting these and several other monosyllables together yielded larger words and names in the earliest Egyptian language. Joining the KA, BA, and ANKH word-sounds together, for instance, constitutes a yoga-like spiritual path, joining mind and spirit, which early Judaism adopted as their mystical system of the KABBALA (KA+BA+ANKH). Each of these few words was highly charged with great meaning; when combined, they constituted a spiritual path, which remains true today. Perhaps the cognitively advanced Neon was capable of making similar or identical grouping of sounds.

Academia currently states that the earliest Egyptian culture is only 5,000 years old, although alternative-minded Egyptologists, such as John Anthony West(1932–2018), posit that the Egyptian culture existed thousands of years before that questionable date. The Great Sphinx is one example of greater age, with geological testing on the sculpture's water-eroded walls suggesting it may have existed 25,000 years ago or more.

Thus, the creation and existence of the Great Sphinx may have coincided with the last vestiges of the pure Neanderthal, along the considerable rim of the Mediterranean Sea. The last known Neanderthal fossil in that area is dated at 25,000 years old, at the Gorman caves near Gibraltar.

Neon's massive skull casing shows that their brain mass was over 20% larger than their early human counterparts—our other ancestors, the Cro-Magnons. Somewhat amazingly, their rear visual cortex was 400% larger than ours. The Neon's eyesight must have been stunning, precocious, and a big part of their life, since they may have had hawk-like perceptual acuity, with enhanced night vision. What would it be like to have such superior eyesight? How would the yellow moon appear, and the brilliance of the stars, and the Milky Way? It takes imagination to approach what they must have been like personally—as forerunners to the early humans. Beyond eyesight, dreaming, and imagination, capabilities would be greatly enhanced, as these aspects are also related to their larger rear vision center.

Deep in the cave, as a young Neon silently gazed into her precious talisman stone, the intensity of her visionary focus, may have at times taken her into mystical realms as a form of ancient scrying, of which visionaries in our own recent times often speak:

"To see a World in a Grain of Sand And a Heaven in a Wildflower,

Hold Infinity in the palm of your hand, and Eternity in an hour"

Auguries of Innocence (1803) **William Blake**

Johann Wolfgang von Goethe, Germany's great poet and author of the nineteenth century, was also known for his long, visually intense 'staring' trances, where all thought was stopped, and the deeper door of a vision was opened. Having such an intensive visual focus is akin to mystical scrying, which was an ancient priestly practice in Egypt, Phoenicia, and Sumer.

The Wild Men and Women of our Past

In The Story of King Gilgamesh, there is ample evidence that the ancient author was writing about a Wildman, matted in red hair, who is said to have 'come-in-from-the-wild,' and met humans for the first time, in the Sumerian city of Uruk, over 4,000 years ago. Let us ask, quite bluntly: were there truly wild people, both men and women, mixed in somewhere, in the ancient history of mankind, over the past eons of human civilization, as a result of Neanderthal and Sapiens mating? Yes, it appears so, is this author's researched answer, but, as it turns out, the likelihood of a hybrid, hominid species in our historical past is a subject scientists and historians apparently abhor and would rather forget, as there is no available research or study upon the subject of hybrid-hominid evolution, say for the past 10,000 years. Yet, the answer should now be obvious to the reader, that such an evolution must surely have occurred, since we ourselves are 2–4% Neanderthal. Of a necessity, we must pursue the dim path of available ancient leads and see where they will follow. When science chooses to ignore the possibility of a mixed species in our recent past of the past several millennia, they are choosing a dead-end path, for as we shall see, ample information is available to construct at least a hypothesis for the existence of the 'Wild People,' who were our very own ancestors as well, or perhaps the in-laws.

Huwawa: Monster or Friend to the Forest?

Mask of Huwawa (Humbaba): Monster-protector of the Cedar Forest. CC: SA 3.0 2nd millennia BCE.

I n the ancient Epic of Sumer, there is another storyline that occupies several of the twelve cuneiform tablets. As we saw earlier, after the initial struggle between King Gilgamesh and the Wild Enkidu, the two become fast friends with great respect for each other. Under Enkidu's moralistic direction, Gilgamesh ceases the rape and slavery of his people. Yet, the young Gilgamesh, still having a sizable Ego, decides to travel to far-off Lebanon for two reasons. First, he would meet and defeat a strange creature—Huwawa—said to be a monstrous ogre who guards the precious aromatic Cedar Forest, where the gods live. Secondly, the young ruler would bring fifty men to cut down as many sacred trees as they could, taking them back to Sumer for the glory of the King and the city of Uruk. These feats would assure King Gilgamesh of lasting fame, but they were totally unnecessary, in the eyes of the Sumer gods such as Enlil who lived in the Cedar Forest. As we have seen, Enkidu appears to be a strong candidate for a hybrid creature with perhaps 10–20% Neon DNA in him, and the wild character of Huwawa may appear to be even more of a monster than the terrifying Enkidu—perhaps his Neon DNA percentage is 20–25% or more. The size of a hybrid creature's face and skull, up to one-third larger than modern humans, as well as being extremely hairy, are two leading clues that large amounts of Neon DNA are present. Huwawa's fierce face, with its long shaggy head and long, wild facial hair, is described as being the face of a lion. Below, Gilgamesh tells Enkidu of his desire for travel. Enkidu responds that to meet and fight the Ogre of the Cedar Forest is unwise and dangerous. Gilgamesh feels a tinge of guilt at Enkidu's words, yet firmly states he will go to the Levant and defeat the roaring monster, regardless, because of his insatiable desire for fame.

"I, O my friend, am determined to go to the Forest of Cedars,

Aye and Huwawa the Fierce will o'ercome and destroy what is evil.

Then will I cut down the Cedar."

Enkidu open'd his mouth, and to Gilgamesh spake he in this wise,

"Know, then, my friend, what time I was roaming with kine in the

mountains, I for a distance of two hours' march from the skirts of the

Forest Into its depths would go down. Huwawa—his roar was a

whirlwind...,

Flame in his jaws, and his very breath Death! O, why hast desired

This to accomplish? To meet with Huwawa were conflict unequall'd."

Gilgamesh open'd his mouth and to Enkidu spake he, in this wise:

"Tis that I need the rich yield of its mountains I go to the Forest"

Enkidu open'd his mouth and to Gilgamesh spake he in this wise:

"But when we go to the Forest of Cedars, its guard is a Fighter,

strong, never sleeping, O Gilgamesh.

Enkidu then describes how Enlil, the Mesopotamian 'Lord of the Wind' appointed Huwawa, whom we describe as a relict Neanderthal, to be the guardian of the forest. Enkidu tries to persuade Gilgamesh that if one should go into the Forest of No Return, meeting the terrible Huwawa is like meeting instant death:

So that he safeguards the Forest of Cedars, a terror to mortals

Him hath Enlil appointed—Huwawa, his roar is a whirlwind,

Flame in his jaws, and his very breath Death! Aye, if he in the Forest.

Hear but a tread on the road—'Who is this come down to his Forest?'

So that he safeguards the Forest of Cedars, a terror to mortals,

Him hath Enlil appointed, and fell hap will seize him who cometh

Down to his Forest."

The very name of Huwawa is strangely akin to the roar attributed to large hominids, which we may depict as here as *Huuuwaawaa*! An expected violent roar, of say, a modern gorilla, defending his territory. King Gilgamesh responds that he is not afraid of death (at this early point) and that all mortals shall meet their own fate. He tries to cheer courage into the Wildman, and is disappointed at Enkidu's words, but he must press on, for fame and cedar:

"Gilgamesh open'd his mouth and to Enkidu spake he (in this wise):

"Who, O my friend, is unconquer'd by death? A divinity, certes,

Liveth for aye in the daylight, but mortals—their days are all number'd,

All that they do is but wind—But to thee, now death thou art dreading,

Proffereth nothing of substance thy courage I, I'll be thy ward!

'Tis thine own mouth shall tell thou didst fear the onslaught of battle,

I, forsooth, if I should fall, my name will have stablish'd (forever).

Gilgamesh 'twas, who fought with Huwawa, the Fierce!

Yea, when thou speakest in this wise, thou grievest my heart for the

Cedar I am determined to fell, that I may gain fame everlasting.""

While The Story of King Gilgamesh excerpts above are taken from the 1928 translation by R. Campbell Thompson (1899–1968), a recently recovered Story of King Gilgamesh clay tablet from the Museum of Sulaymaniyah portrays Huwawa in an entirely different light. In this alternative version of the story, Huwawa is not a monster at all, but rather a creature beloved by the creatures of the forest and the gods:

"Where Huwawa came and went there was a track, the paths were in

good order and the way was well trodden... Through all the forest a bird

began to sing: A wood pigeon was moaning, a turtle dove calling in

answer. Monkey mothers sing aloud, a youngster monkey shrieks: like a

band of musicians and drummers daily they bash out a rhythm in the

52

presence of Huwawa."

Wikipedia

In the Sulaymaniyah tablet, Huwawa, the partial Neon, is depicted as a kind Ruler of the Forest, like a man-beast King. The wild animals are very accustomed to his presence and do not fear him. He is likely a vegetarian, like Enkidu, which is why the animals loved them. Huwawa's dusky green palace reeks of the strong aroma of cedar resin. It's noteworthy that both Enkidu and Huwawa are seen in peaceful natural settings, before they encounter the violence and disease of civilization. The tablet goes on to portray King Gilgamesh in a negative light, as an egotistical aggressor, who unnecessarily destroys the largest trees in the Cedar Forest, so he can build a large gated entrance for his city of Uruk and gain fame for himself by fighting a well-known, supposedly hideous monster—Huwawa.

In returning to the earlier interpretations in 1928 by R. Campbell Thompson, we find that Gilgamesh acts deviously when he and Enkidu first encounter Huwawa in the forest. There is no initial violence or fighting. Instead, a deceitful Gilgamesh distracts Huwawa by innocently saying that he comes offering gifts—seven in total. While the ogre's guard is down perusing the new gifts, perhaps surrounded by dozens of the King's men, Gilgamesh suddenly deals Huwawa a near-fatal blow; a sucker punch. The ogre then pleads for his life, but the remorseless King then cuts off the head of the man-beast, with its bulging, staring eyes, while Enkidu looks on and laments Huwawa's death. Are they distant relatives, in terms of being relict-Neons?

Having accomplished his two Ego-driven goals, the Sumer King and his Wildman return to the city of Uruk (Erech) with their load of precious cedar logs:

"And now in the River Euphrates, washing their hands, they start on their

progress and come to the city; Now are they striding the highway of

53

Erech, the heroes of Erech. thronging about them to see them. Then

Gilgamesh utter'd a riddle unto the notables;

Who, pr'ythee, is most splendid of heroes,

Who, pr'ythee, is most famous of giants?

Gilgamesh—he is most splendid of heroes,

Enkidu—he is most famous of giants."

By referring to Enkidu as a red-haired giant, although shorter than himself, King Gilgamesh is describing a relict Neanderthal exactly as did Stan Gooch. According to Gooch, ancient folk often referred to hybrid creatures as giants, not because of their tall stature, but rather because of the greater size of their fierce faces and their greater strength. They could be an overwhelming force. The muscular Neanderthals are now considered to once have had nearly twice (2X) the physical strength of their human counterparts, so reports of 'extra' strength in literature may indicate a hybrid-hominid presence. In the Bible's Book of Numbers, there is a curious report from the spies of Moses, after they returned from their investigation of the land of Canaan. They exclaimed:

> *"We can't attack those people; they are stronger than we are.*
>
> *All the people we saw there are of great size.*

In AD 93, Josephus the historian described the nomadic, uncivilized Amorites as 'giants' in his *Antiquities of the Jews*. In 2100 BCE, the wandering Amorites had occupied a large area of land extending from Southern Mesopotamia to Canaan on the eastern shore of the Mediterranean Sea. He indicated that some sort of anomalous fossils may have been observed at that time:

"There were till then left the race of giants, who had bodies so large,

and countenances so entirely different from other men, that they were

surprising to the sight, and terrible to the hearing. The bones of these

men are still shown to this very day, unlike to any credible relations of

other men."

When Josephus says that the giants are terrible to be heard, the roaring of Huwawa comes to mind, as the sound of roaring, became his very name.

HUUUWAAWAA!

With these samples of note, we can appreciate that Gooch was correct in his early analysis that legends and myths of giants were likely originated from humans observing dramatically different ancient peoples, likely Neanderthals, and their hybrid descendants. Thus, Enkidu was a giant.

As Gilgamesh and Enkidu returned to the King's residence at Uruk, a mighty party was held in honor of a successful sojourn and a safe return.

"So, in his palace did Gilgamesh hold revel thereafter,

while all the heroes asleep, on their nightly couches were lying

Enkidu, too, was asleep, and a vision beheld, and so coming

Enkidu now his dream to reveal, thus, spake he unto his comrade.

"Why, O my friend, do the great gods now take counsel together?

The fever hath laid me on my back."

Enkidu has dreamt that the Gods have joined together to determine his fate. Enkidu is to die, but Gilgamesh to remain alive. It would appear from the succeeding material that Enkidu, stricken presumably by fever, attributes all his misfortunes to the hetaera Shamhat, whom he loads with curses.

In Enkidu's dream, the Gods of the Cedar Forest are enraged at the murder; the God Enlil decrees that the other man-beast, Enkidu, must also die, to balance the scales of justice. In the seventh tablet of the Epic, Enkidu curses Shamhat, the courtesan, the sacred temple prostitute, with whom he had lain, and wishes for her to become starving and homeless.

The Neon-Sapiens creature grows weak and contracts a fever; could these symptoms actually be a fatal case of syphilis? Then he has a vision of Shamash, the Sumer Sun God, who admonishes Enkidu for cursing the hetaera, the sacred prostitute:

"Heard him the Sun-god, and open'd his mouth, and from out of the heavens Straightway he call'd him: "
O Enkidu, why dost thou curse the hetaera? She 'twas who made thee eat bread, for divinity proper: aye, wine too. She made thee drink, 'twas for royalty proper: a generous mantle. Put on thee, aye, and for comrade did give to thee Gilgamesh splendid. Now on a couch of great size will he, thy friend and thy brother Gilgamesh, grant thee to lie, on a handsome couch will he grant thee Rest, and to sit on a throne of great ease, a throne at his left hand, so that the princes of Hades may kiss thy feet in their homage;He, too, will make all the people of Erech (Uruk) lament in thy honour, Making them mourn thee, and damsels and heroes constrain to thy service, while he himself for thy sake will cause his body to carry Stains, and will put on the skin of a lion, and range o'er the desert."

This portion of the Epic clearly shows the influences of hybrid-hominids upon the early literature of humankind, in both the dreaming and religious sense, as Gooch had predicted.

Shamash the Sun God finishes by stating the details of honor in Enkidu's impending funeral. In the Epic, Gilgamesh becomes 'stained' in a psychological way; he is both depressed and terrified at the sting of death upon his best friend, the wild giant, Enkidu. Thus, the grieving King dons a lion's skin and ranges over the desert later, in search of Utnapishtim, the Immortal Human. The Wildman relents to his vision of the Sun God and apologizes for his damning curse upon the temple courtesan. He continues to dream of his impending death; possibly delirious from his sickness. Enkidu experiences the Underworld in his mind's eye, as a premonition; he is a hybrid-hominid, who is having a near-death-experience (NDE),as he sees the gods of Sumer. The Wildman relates his vision to the King, his best friend in the world—this is the first time in recorded history, that a hybrid-hominid is describing . . . the Underworld:

Enkidu . . . woe in his belly . . . sleeping alone, came in the night to discover his heaviness unto his comrade: "Friend, O a dream I have seen in my night-time: the firmament roaring, Echo'd the earth, and I by myself was standing, when perceived I a man, all dark was his face, and his nails like claws of a lion. Me did he overcome, climbing up, press'd me down, Upon me, my body. Me did he lead to the Dwelling of Darkness, the home of Irkalla. Unto the Dwelling from which he who entereth cometh forth never! Aye, by the road on the passage whereof there can be no returning, unto the Dwelling whose tenants are ever bereft of the daylight; where for their food is the dust, and the mud is their sustenance. Bird-like, wear they a garment of feathers and, sitting there in the darkness, never the light will they see."

This is the End, Beautiful Friend

The End, **The Doors**

Enkidu's next vision reminds us of Plato's Myth of Er scenario, where the famous hero Odysseus, now in his afterlife, wisely chooses a lot for his next life, as a quiet, private man away from the glare of royalty, with its struggle of fame. We are about to hear a Neon-Sapiens, for the first time in recorded history, relate his prophetic dream of impending death. The dying Wildman continues to relate his vision to his human friend; where the once-powerful rulers are now humble servants in their afterlife:

"On the Gate, when I enter'd, on the house was humbled the crown,

For those who wore crowns, who of old ruled over the country, of Anu

and Enlil, 'twas they set the bakemeats, cool was the water they served

from the skins. When I enter'd into this House of the Dust, were High

Priest and acolyte sitting, Seer and magician, the priest who the Sea of

the great gods anointed. Here sat Etana, Sumuqan; the Queen of the

Underworld (also),Ereshkigal, in whose presence doth bow the Recorder

of Hades, Belit-ser, and readeth before her; she lifted her head and

beheld me"

After his strange revelation, now a weakened shell of his former strong self, the hybrid, red-furred Enkidu finally dies. Gilgamesh laments and roars loudly at the funeral for his Neon-Sapiens friend and brother. While staring at his dead comrade, the King has a sudden chill come over him as he realizes fear and death, perhaps for the first time, in his own mortal self. Thus, the young King begins his spiritual quest, as described earlier:

"Gilgamesh bitterly wept for his comrade, for Enkidu, ranging Over the

desert: "I, too—shall I not die like Enkidu also? Sorrow hath enter'd my

heart; I fear death as I range o'er the desert, I will get hence on the road

to the presence of Uta-Napishtim.""

Thus, the ancient King is suddenly awakened, alerted by the death of his hybrid-hominid, giant of a friend. And so, with the death of both Huwawa and Enkidu, our hybrid-Neons from 4,000 years ago in The Story of King

Gilgamesh, we turn our attention to more recent discussions of hybrid people, those people lost in time.

The Hybrids; People Lost in Time

Paleontologists have examined the 24,500-year-old skeleton of a young boy, discovered recently in a shallow grave in Portugal. Bred in the boy's bones seemed to be a genetic heritage, which is part Neanderthal, part early modern Homo sapiens. He was a hybrid, they observed, and represented the first strong physical evidence of interbreeding between the groups in Europe.

"This skeleton demonstrates that early modern humans and Neanderthals are not all that different. They intermixed, interbred, and produced offspring."

Dr. Erik Trinkaus, paleoanthropologist

Washington University in St. Louis

Some conservative-minded scientists disputed the interpretation, while other scientists who study human origins said the findings were intriguing, probably correct and certain to provoke debate and challenges to conventional thinking about the place of Neanderthals in human evolution.
Presumably, Neanderthals and modern humans were more alike than different, not a separate species or even sub-species, but two groups who viewed each other as appropriate mates.

The skeleton of the boy, buried with strings of marine shells and painted with red ocher, was uncovered in December by Portuguese archeologists led by Dr. Joo Zilhao, director of the Institute of Archeology in Lisbon. The discovery was made in the Lapedo Valley near Leiria, ninety miles north of Lisbon.

Realizing the potential significance, Dr. Zilhao called in Dr. Trinkaus, an authority on Neanderthal paleontology, who went to Lisbon and examined the bones in January.

The boy, who was about four years old at death, had the prominent chin and other facial characteristics of a fully modern human. But his stocky body and short legs were those of a Neanderthal. Dr. Trinkaus compared the limb proportions with Neanderthal skeletons, including some children. He said he was then sure of the skeleton's implications.

"It's a complex mosaic, which is what you get when you have a hybrid," Dr. Trinkaus said. "This is the first definite evidence of admixture between Neanderthals and European early modern humans."

The age of the skeleton, determined by radiocarbon dating, showed that full Neanderthals had apparently been extinct for at least 4,000 years before the boy was born. "This is no love child," Dr. Trinkaus said, meaning that this was not evidence of a rare mating but a descendant of generations of Neanderthal-Cro-Magnon hybrids.

~!~

Before we continue our discussion of a possible hybrid-hominid species that eventually led to a creature such as Enkidu, we must ensure that we dispel an older, pedantic, science-driven myth that Neanderthals were simply dumb brutes, not far removed from monkeys and the great apes. This was a huge scientific mistake, fostered by an insistence that signs of technology must be found amongst the Neon fossils, in order for them to be considered intelligent by using tools, etc. This unbalanced scientific view has become deeply imbedded in the public mindset and is difficult to dislodge. Thus, that is our task here: to reshape the public view, if possible, to accept the greater, expanded idea that our distant, ancient kinfolk were far more spiritual and in touch with themselves and with nature than people living today, who operate, psychologically, under the fraud of a technological cloud. As Gooch inferred, these Neons and their descendants were truly the guardians of an ancient wisdom which is nearly lost today.

Recent, provocative research now clearly shows that these people were far more advanced than previously thought, yet, still, the only anthropological interest to the analytic scientific mind, is in finding 'tools' that indicate technological development, while totally ignoring the mind and neuropsychology of those they study. Perhaps, these ancient ones, with their bright eyes, were far more spiritual than those who found their bones many thousands of years later.

As a scientific precedent, Gooch had correctly predicted that Cro-Magnon and Neon had mated in the dim past, and he was equally interested in how those first crossbreed matings had proceeded over the subsequent eons of time to the present, where modern humans now contain 2–4% Neon DNA. Since the first Cro-Magnon/Neon-hybrids contained an approximately 50/50% DNA mix, we can logically construct a rough timeline of how those original crossbreed matings occurred and then proceeded throughout time. This timeline is a not a scientific measurement tool, but rather a logical one.

We can choose a starting date of approximately 40,000 years ago, when most of the Neons had died out, or gone extinct, except for those in the Gorman caves along the Straits of Gibraltar, where fossils have been dated back to only 25,000 years ago. Over these eons of time, the Neanderthal DNA percentages would have dropped due to expanded crossbreeding, perhaps, as a speculation, 5–10% for every 10,000 years or so, to bring us to the present. A simple chronological ordering follows below:

The first crossbreed mating between pure Neanderthals and pure Sapiens occurs, producing the first hybrid children of Neon-Sapiens.

40,000 years ago:	Hybrid creatures:	50–50%	Neon DNA
30,000 years ago:	Hybrid creatures:	40–50%	Neon DNA
20,000 years ago:	Hybrid creatures:	30–40%	Neon DNA
10,000 years ago:	Hybrid creatures:	20–30%	Neon DNA
5,000 years ago:	Hybrid creatures:	10–20%	Neon DNA
Today:	Hybrid creatures:	2–4%	Neon DNA

Although these are obviously arbitrary numbers as simple postulates, our main point here is to try to associate the ancient names and faces over these eons, as likely Neon/Cro-Magnon hybrid candidates, because they must have assuredly existed, given our own mixed DNA today. Plus, we should consider that King Gilgamesh, of course, was likely 2–4% Neon DNA, like ourselves today, or perhaps a bit more. We can now examine several entities and groups, as listed below, for their crossbreed attributes, which may reveal them to be relict, remnant representatives of our Neon forebears that descended, unseen, throughout the ages. These are the 'lost people' who were hybrid humans, but were depicted as wild men and women, monsters, and even Gods. Stan Gooch wrote that ancient tribal folks may have seen these hybrid creatures as terrifying and giant-like, because of their extremely large faces, hairy bodies and great strength.

"History is the recital of facts represented as true. Fable,

on the other hand, is the recital of facts represented as fiction."

Voltaire

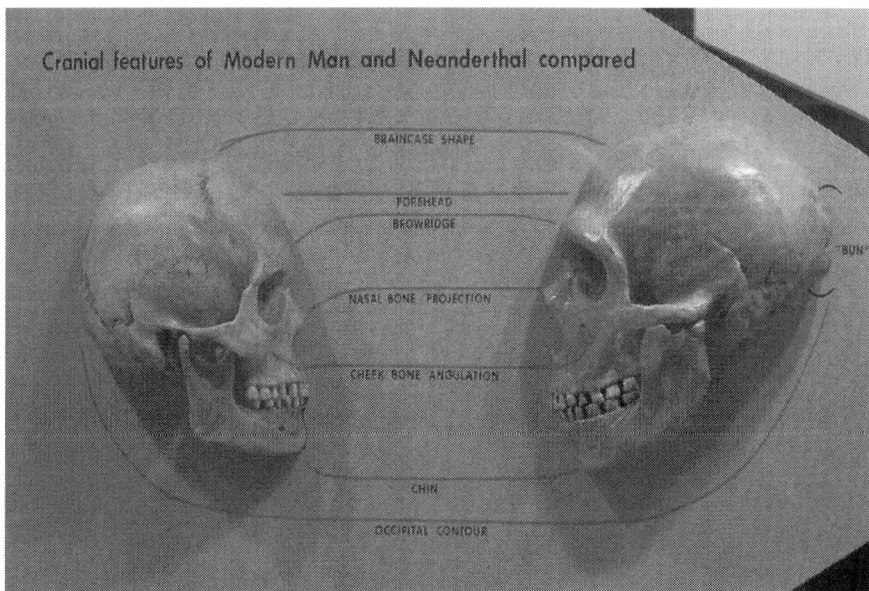

Cranial features of Modern Man and Neanderthal compared

BRAINCASE SHAPE
FORSHEAD
BROWRIDGE
"BUN"
NASAL BONE PROJECTION
CHEEK BONE ANGULATION
CHIN
OCCIPITAL CONTOUR

A 'giant' Neanderthal skull, as compared to a smaller Cro-Magnon

According to Gooch, these hybrid creatures later became known as those rare ogres, giants, trolls, and monsters in the ancient mists of legend and myth. Let's recall that, aside from these hybrid creatures, Gilgamesh, the King of Uruk is also being depicted by the Epic's poet-scribe, as being one-third human, and two-thirds God, so the scene is rich. Perhaps new understandings will grow here. The New Muse Series book, *How to Be Immortal: The Adventures of King Gilgamesh and the Wildman* further explores the neuropsychology of both King Gilgamesh and the Wild Enkidu, in much greater detail, while discussing the keys to understanding life, death, and the thereafter.

So, just where are these hidden crossbreed folks in the annals of history? In looking for certain Neanderthal physiological clues, we find that there is indeed a faint trace of their existence, although historians don't realize this, yet! In the future, academia will be compelled to realize that hybrid-hominid creatures have been poking their heads in and out of history for many millennia.

In Part III ~ *The Strange Players*, we will be studying and providing many more intriguing examples of Neon-Sapiens admixtures that likely existed in the past. A few samples follow below:

Zana: A crossbreed wild woman in 19th century Eurasia.

Getae-Dacian: A group of early tribal peoples in the East European area.

Bes: An ancient Egyptian God, similar to Huwawa in form.

Socrates: The Wild Man Philosopher of Greece.

Tibet-Sherpa: The Tibetan and Sherpa peoples and cultures.

Yeti~Shennong: A hybrid Yeti evolves into a Chinese Chan.

64

Additional notable hybrid-hominids in Part III include Beowulf and Grendel, Merlin the Ugly, Quasimodo the humpback, and Spartacus the gladiator.

PART III ~ The Strange Players

~!~

Who were our hybrid-hominid ancestors from the past?

Zana the Red-Haired Wild Woman and Other Modern Wild Folk

I n modern times, we have grown accustomed to numerous wild, bogus reports, and spectacular hoaxes concerning all types of strange creatures; the infamous Bigfoot and the shaggy mountain Yeti are primary examples of such ruses. In most cases, little or no helpful information can be gleaned. Usually, the glammed-up reports are mere distractions, without sufficient evidence.

But what if a real, hidden hybrid-hominid mystery exists behind the scenes?

As we shall see, in our chapter on the Yeti and the Shennong Clan, it is certainly possible, or even probable, that a hybrid creature may have existed, and was called a Yeti, but this name, however, is a slurred slang of the real name. Research indicates this is a likelihood, occurring over the past centuries, despite the ongoing, publicized hoaxes.

Our hypothesis of a Cro-Magnon/Neanderthal hybrid species emerging, perhaps thriving, and then slowly moving towards DNA extinction over the past 40,000 years must hold true, regardless of regularly occurring fake reports, hoaxes, and misunderstandings. Somehow, in a reverse calculation, we must account for our 2–4% DNA and also our distant, mixed-breed ancestors.

Zana the Wild Woman is a good place to start, as she most likely lived within the past 100 years. Stan Gooch, who postulated the original hypothesis of Cro-Magnon and Neon sexual relations, at a time when science abhorred the idea, later found evidence of recent Neanderthal-Sapiens crossbreeding, as described in his book, *Guardians of the Ancient Wisdom*:

"The Abkhazians (who live to the east of the Black Sea in the

neighborhood of Azerbaijan) tell of the wild men they call 'Abnauayu.' (It

is itself interesting that so many peoples from the Black Sea through to

the China coast each have a special name for the wild men.) The

Abkhazians reported the capture and domestication of one of

these creatures, whom they named Zana. She was covered with reddish

hair, with a flat nose and powerful jaws. Physically she was very robust.

She left several children by human fathers."

When Gooch states 'from the Black Sea to the China coast,' he is referring to several types of wild people, whom he distinguishes as relict Neanderthal types A, B, etc. Years later, research revealed that the newly discovered Denisovans were what Gooch was calling Neanderthal type B, generally found further to the east. Caves with fossils of crossbreed Denisovan-Neanderthal DNA mixtures have been found—as high as 17%. One of Zana's children was also examined after its death. Professor Boris Porshnev, Director of the Modern History Department of Moscow Academy, reported that the body and skull did indeed have 'Neanderthaloid' features, but DNA analysis was inconclusive (one can only wonder if Zana the Wild Woman ever spoke words or used sign language, as we suggested Enkidu did, in The Story of King Gilgamesh). Gooch goes on to describe several more recent human encounters with hybrid people:

"Several thousand miles further east the Kazakhs (Cossacks) also once

captured a male, wild man. He too had a body covered with thick reddish

hair. He had a sloping forehead, massive jaws, a small nose and pointed ears, and prominent eyebrows. A Mongolian scientist named Rinchen

collected many eyewitness accounts from the Gobi Desert region...of wild

men (Almas), who had sloping forehead, prominent eyebrows, large jaws,

and were covered with reddish -brown hair. A group of these were seen

as late as 1927."

Now, it is interesting, that while Gooch and others considered Neon-Human hybrid mating to be a distinct, shocking reality, that the old legends and myths of ogres, trolls, and satyrs were actually just folk names for Neon-Sapiens hybrid people. Other sources, such as the standard one below, still consider that Wild People are simply a cultural myth, while not understanding the real implications of hominid DNA crossbreeding:

"The wild man (also Wildman, or "Wildman of the woods") is a mythical

figure that appears in the artwork and literature of medieval Europe,

comparable to the satyr or faun type in classical mythology and to

Silvanus, the Roman god of the woodlands. The defining characteristic of

the figure is its "wildness"; from the 12th century they were consistently

depicted as being covered with hair. Images of wild men appear in the

carved and painted roof bosses where intersecting ogee vaults meet in the

Canterbury Cathedral. The image of the wild man survived to appear as supporter for heraldic coats-of-arms, especially in Germany, well into

the 16th century. Renaissance engravers in Germany and Italy were

particularly fond of wild men, wild women, and wild families."

Wild Man; **Wikipedia**

As we shall see, as Voltaire stated, it's unwise to consider all legends as pure myths, although humans are well known for their fabrications. Still, a faint light of truth can be perceived underneath the usual falsehoods of our often mythical history. Hybrid peoples, must, of a necessity, have actually existed, albeit away from the usual gaze of human civilization. They are a part of our ancestry, the 2–4% part. So, anthropologists still wonder, how and why did the Neanderthal species go extinct? Who were, and what happened to Zana the red-haired Wild Woman's great line of ancestors? It's still anyone's guess, but perhaps a few simple psychological points can be made. In the ancient caves bearing hominid fossils of different species, the social co-existence of either pure Neanderthals and pure Sapiens, or a hybrid Neon-Sapiens admixture must have been sorted out, in a rather rough fashion. Below, we see a simple explanation of this precarious hominid co-existence, as explained by H.G. Wells (1866–1946), in his book, *The Outline of History* (1920):

"Away from the fire other members of the family group prowl in search

of food, but at night they all gather closely round the fire and build it up,

for it is their protection against the wandering bear and such-like beasts

of prey. The Old Man is the only fully adult male in the little group. There

are women, boys and girls, but so soon as the boys are big enough to

rouse the Old Man's jealousy, he will fall foul of them and either drive them off or kill them. Some girls may perhaps go off with these exiles, or two or three of these youths may keep together for a time, wandering until they come upon some other group, from which they may try to steal a mate. Then they would probably fall out among themselves. Someday, when he is forty years old perhaps or even older, and his teeth are worn down and his energy abating, some younger male will stand up to the Old Man and kill him and reign in his stead. There is probably short shrift for the old at the squatting- place. So soon as they grow weak and bad-tempered, trouble and death come upon them."

Keeping on your Toes: In those early cave days, neither human nor Neanderthal had the luxury of sitting; everyone squatted, perhaps as a natural reflex to quietly approaching tigers or bears that broke in and suddenly attacked. Theirs was a different life; chairs were only invented a few thousand years ago. Sitting down would have meant instant death, while squatting would save a few precious seconds—enough to survive, while running away or grabbing a weapon, as done in the fight-or-flight psychological complex that psychologists today call 'acute stress syndrome.' A term that would certainly apply if a bear is going to eat you. Neanderthal, with his or her superior leg strength, would have an advantage against such predators, as compared to the weaker, slower Cro-Magnon. Anthropologists now consider that the Neons, with their powerful legs, would actually have been extremely fast sprinters, and could easily outrun the Cro-Magnons.

The Beauty and the Beast: Another possible avenue for Neanderthal extinction, in this author's simple speculation, is that a type of Beauty and the Beast situation existed between the different hominid species. That is to say, that the Cro-Magnon women were fancied as beautiful, petite, submissive females by the Old Man of the Cave; say a pure or relict Neon man. For their part, the human females may have found the beast (Neon) very attractive, because of his greater sense of lust and his greater strength, which could certainly be expressed, like a sexual jack-hammer, during robust crossbreed mating sessions, some of which must have been mutually pleasurable, while others were simply rape. As a modern example, in the world today, there is a small sub-culture of black men who prefer blonde white women over their own race, and vice versa. This cross-racial sexual exchange affects the DNA distribution in both groups. Even Aristotle is on record saying that blonde women are the best for romance and sex, yet his voice is alone, so his may be a particular bias, as we have mentioned sometimes occurs. So, interbreeding between races of Sapiens routinely takes place; we can extend this simple premise of racial sexual favoritism to the ancient crossbreed species of the past. Over the eons, a slight sexual favoritism would result in the slow eradication of pure Neons, and result in their eventual extinction, leaving only their hybrid children, which we still are, to a small DNA degree. Another point of conjecture might be related to the male Neon's great vision and appreciation of beauty. In Sapiens males and females today, it is stated that a man's sexual drive is strongly associated with his lustful vision, whereas women may *feel* their way into the bedroom. What of the male Neon's visual lust and appreciation of beauty, with his rear braincase and vision center being four times larger than ours?

I could picture every move than a man could make,

getting lost in her lovin' is your first mistake.

Sundown; **Gordon Lightfoot**

Did the male Neons favor the petite, easier to overcome female Sapiens, over the stouter females of his own species? Perhaps the Neon was attracted by his tremendous vision and lust, and the early Homo sapiens female was attracted by the strength of her Neon man, who was much stronger than the Sapiens males? It may have been a simple case of 'the

Beauty and the Beast,' eons ago. Was a flute-playing, fine-dancing Neon ever a heartbreaker, even with his rough looks? We can imagine how it must have started, in a cave entrance, long, long ago. Neon's enhanced vision would have also increased, and perhaps fine-tuned, the ability to track movements, and thereby increase the appreciation for sexual subtleties in body language and dancing.

Watching Girls passing by, it's not the latest thing.

The Rolling Stones

The male love of beautiful women has caused many a human conflict in our own known histories; this simple, yet intense attraction possibly spawned many Neon tribal conflicts and battles as well.
Could it be that human males observed lustful gazes between their own women and Neon males, and took action? Aside from the Beauty and the Beast extinction hypothesis, we can also imagine Sapiens males often eliminated their competition, when possible. The Tasmanian Aborigines, as an example, were hunted to extinction by early British settlers, the last dying in 1876. These creatures were likely Neon-Sapiens hybrids, suggested Gooch, because they, unlike their Australian counterparts, had thick, heavy, full-body hair, and eyes with projecting, exaggerated brow ridges, akin to the Wild Folk we have been observing. The British settlers, when they weren't shooting the Wild Folk, had copious sex with their females, and so thousands of mixed blood Tasmanian Aborigine-Anglo-Saxon children survive to this very day.

~!~

For untold thousands of years, hybrid-hominid creatures such as Zana the Wild Woman have been hiding on the outskirts of civilization, usually as Wild Folk. However, some of the Neon-Sapiens mixed breeds have been more casually accepted into human society.

"One can observe even the Neanderthal Type at any Public Gathering."

German Historian **Oswald Spengler** (1880-1936)

Loren Eiseley (1907–1977), that marvelous combination of anthropologist and philosopher, readily recognized that unusual Neon-Sapiens crossbreed folk were living among humans, as a small evolutionary portion of the Great Chain of Being. While on one of his anthropology journeys, he once wrote of an amazing hybrid-hominid female that he met:

"A stocky barefoot girl of twenty sometimes came hesitantly down the path to our camp to deliver eggs. Short, thickset, and massive, her body was still not the body of a typical peasant woman. Her head, thrust a little forward against the light, was massive boned. Along the eye-orbits at the edge of the frontal line I could see outlined an armored protuberance that, particularly in women, had vanished before the close of the Wurman Ice. She swung her head almost like a great muzzle beneath its curls, and I was struck by the low bun-shaped breadth at the back"

(Authors note: Since the Wurm Ice age was in the Alps mountains, 70,000–100,000 years ago, Eiseley is inferring that, somehow, Neanderthal-Sapiens hybrid-hominids still existed, in remote locations.)

In central Russia, around 1925, there was a noteworthy conflict between humans and a relict Neanderthal. For whatever reason, this creature was shot by Major General M.S. Topilsky and his men in the Pamir mountains. Topilsky wrote this in his official report, which was published years later in the Moscow Times in 1964:

"We recovered the body all right. It had three bullet wounds. At first glance I thought the body was that of an ape; it was covered with hair all over. The chest was covered with brownish hair and the belly with greyish hair. In general, the body hair was very thick; there was most hair on the hips. The color of the face was dark, and the creature had neither beard nor mustache. The eyes were dark, and the teeth were large and even and shaped like human teeth. The forehead was slanting, and the eyebrows were very powerful. The protruding jawbones made the face resemble the Mongol type of face. The nose was flat with a deeply-sunk bridge. The ears were hairless and looked a little more pointed than a human being's, with a longer lobe. The lower jaw was massive. The creature had a very powerful chest and well-developed muscles. The hands were slightly wider, and the feet much wider and shorter than man's."

What a superb, eyewitness account! One can see from such a description how the folklore and legends of ogres and trolls came about, as Gooch has indicated.

Going back a few hundred years to 1784, we find another early anthropologist, Michael Wagner, describing yet another Neon-Sapiens creature:

"Here you have information about the wild boy who was found a few years ago, in Romania and was brought to Kronstadt, where in 1784, he is still alive. This unfortunate youth was of the male sex and was of medium size. His eyes lay deep in his head. His forehead was strongly bent inwards. He had heavy brown eyebrows which projected out far over his eyes and a small flat pressed nose. His mouth stood out somewhat, and he had a dirty yellowish skin. The back and the chest were very hairy; the muscles on his legs were stronger and more visible than ordinary people. He walked erect but a little heavily. It seemed as if he would throw himself from one foot to the other. He carried his head and his chest forward..."

As I read Wagner's centuries-old account, I had to chuckle with a little amazement, when I read how the young boy walked, for the description is identical to Plato's, of how Socrates swaggered, to and fro, as he walked, in 500 BCE. As unusual as it sounds, we describe Socrates in an upcoming chapter, as also having a hybrid-hominid nature; his friends didn't think he looked Greek . . . nor did he! Socrates himself thought he looked rather unusual . . . and with good reason.

Spartacus; Enter the Getae

A s we recall, Neanderthal fossils have been found in numerous cave sites ranging from the Straits of Gibraltar near Spain, and eastward to the Levant, the Black Sea, and even China.

Euro-Levant map

In the map above, if we give our attention to the land directly above the Mediterranean area, we will find ancient tribes called the Thracians; this is the land where Spartacus, the famous slave rebel, was born and raised. Most readers will recognize the name 'Spartacus' as representing a pure-blooded white man, a view fostered by Hollywood's movies. However, it's more likely that this Caucasian portrayal is untrue.

Further to the north, the fierce tribes called the **Getae**, were nestled against the Black Sea. Also known as the Getae-Dacians, or Getae-Thracians, as similar-sounding titles, there are tell-tale clues that this tribe, in particular, may have had relict Neanderthals in their ranks. In the 500 BCE to 50 BCE time period, this large population of self-sufficient, red-haired tribal peoples could outfight, man-for-man, any armies sent against it by the Persians, Greeks, and Romans.

~!~

Authors Note: The Getae were also known as the Gets. It's very important for the reader to remember the key sound of 'GET' in the name of the Getae, for this sound, GET, has an extremely hoary beginning, and is thousands of years older than the Getae themselves. Its highly likely that this core sound of 'Get' was mispronounced, for their other two names are actually rhyming sounds for Get, which was likely the earliest name.

Core Sound	Resultant Tribal Names
GET	GET-AE
DAC (deck)	DAC-ian
THRAC (threck)	THRAC-ian

In later chapters, the amazing ancestors of the powerful Getae are discussed in an entirely new light.

~!~

Trajan, the Roman soldier-emperor, declared that the Getae warriors possessed the *greatest physical strength* of any enemy that they had encountered. We should ask an important question: Just how does one particular tribe's warriors develop such superior physical strength, so much greater than the other tribes, and the Roman Empire itself? Could this strength be obtained through training, diet, or perhaps a genetic predisposition? If it were simply training and diet, the Romans themselves would have become much stronger, and have been the more superior warriors. So, genetics, meaning a Neon-Sapiens admixture, may be the real cause of the greater strength of the Getae folk. Further, we can note that Trajan did not refer to the Getae as being larger or taller than normal. This omission may be important, for the typical Neon-Sapiens warrior would not be exceptionally tall; they were simply stronger by virtue of their Neon-Sapiens muscular structure. After several Getae victories over the Romans, Trajan finally succeeded in besting them, but only by bringing in additional legions of troops, finally achieving victory with far greater numbers of fighting men. This land area, which is now modern-day Romania, had many successive waves of humans and possibly Neanderthals roaming over it for several hundred-thousands of years. Is it possible that these ancient Getae folk, and the red-haired Spartacus himself, the best of the gladiators, were actually a slightly hybrid species, with perhaps, say, 7–12% Neon DNA, compared to our own 2–5% two thousand years later? Centuries after, on the other side of the Black Sea, we still find the reports of Zana the red-haired Wild Woman and numerous other Wild Folks. The fierce, wolf-like Getae were an example of how Neanderthals successfully formed large tribes with Sapiens folks, as compared to Zana, and the other hybrid people living near the Black Sea. These few mysterious hybrid-hominids usually lived in the wild, alone, or in exceedingly small groups.

In battle, the stronger Getae warriors did not use the traditional sword and shield but rather preferred an extremely heavy weapon called the 'Falx,' which required great strength to wield. A strong, red-haired Getae warrior with a six-foot long wooden rod with an attached curved steel blade intimidated even the toughest enemy soldiers, who would be quickly hacked to death. In 72 BCE, an attacking Roman army actually withdrew because of a great fear of accidentally encountering these fierce warriors in the forest, for whom they were no match. The Roman short sword and shield were ineffective weapons, as compared to the brutal, long-swinging Falx. Appropriately, theses tribal folk were also called 'MassaGetae,' meaning 'strong-Getae.'

The Getae warriors were intensely focused on animal-like behavior during battle; thus, they were called the Wolf Warriors, possessing a battlefield mindset not unlike that of the Berserkers of the 10th century

Vikings. Like the Berserkers, the early Getae warriors may also have imbibed a powerful potion of drugs and alcohol before going to war. Sooner or later, we must allow that some cultural expression of a Human-Neon mix did indeed occur throughout our history, but anthropology and historians apparently have no interest in this unclaimed, scientific area of hybrid peoples living in the historical past. Thus, there is parsimonious academic evidence, but fortunately, simply detecting the remnant physical traces of Neons and their hybrid descendants, may be enough to give a good start in unraveling this hidden history of hybrid peoples. *Ancient Shock ~ Monsters, Philosophers & Saviors*, as a New Muse book, relentlessly pursues this hidden history and breaks new ground in many cases.

Spartacus, the most famous Getae-Thracian of all, was captured by the Romans, and forced into gladiatorial combat, where, as a mixed-breed Neon-Sapiens, he would have had the advantage of greater physical strength, thus he went undefeated in the Roman Colosseum. This great warrior-leader escaped his bondage, along with a handful of other slaves, and later led a massive slave rebellion that, at one time, challenged the entire Roman Empire.

The Getae developed a system of worship based upon the teachings of Zalmoxis, who, according to Herodotus, was not a God, as was later believed, but rather a human who converted the Getae to his beliefs. As we shall see, this may be an example of a hybrid-hominid spiritual development.

"We have conquered even these Getai (Dacians), the most warlike of all

people that have ever existed, not only because of the strength in their

bodies, but, also due to the teachings of Zalmoxis who is among their

most hailed. He has told them that in their hearts they do not die, but

change their location and, due to this, they go to their deaths happier than on any other journey."

Trajan, Roman Emperor (98–117 AD)

Ancient images of Zalmoxis portray him as a thick-bodied, hairy man, not unlike our portrayal of many hybrid-hominids—the Wild Peoples. As Zalmoxis is Getae-Thracian, thus, Spartacus too would likely appear as a similar, hairy, muscular, thick-bodied man—not your typical modern white fellow, as seen in the Spartacus movies. As a genetic speculation, perhaps Zalmoxis and Spartacus had possibly 8–10% Neanderthal DNA, while the less-strong 100 AD-era Romans may have had, say, only 2–6% Neon DNA—more closely aligned to our own modern genetic disposition. So, in equal numbers, the Romans, Persians, and Greeks were always routed when fighting the MassaGetae, the strong ones.

There are several old Greek myths concerning these Getae. An old story once held that Agrius, a man-eating, Getae-Thracian giant, was half-man and half-bear. In another tale, Enceladus was a Getae-Thracian 'giant' who was reputed to have fought against the Gods. Alcyoneus was the eldest of the Thracian giants, who was killed by Heracles. Porphyrion was the King of these ancient Getae-Thracian 'giants' who may actually have been ferocious Human-Neon relics, perhaps similar to Sumer's Enkidu or Huwawa, as Enkidu is also repeatedly referred to as a giant. Stan Gooch pointed out several times that ancient folk tended to refer to strong, overwhelming, large-faced hairy people as ogres, giants, trolls, and satyrs. Pursuant to such early stories, and also according to legend, Zalmoxis, the Getae man-God, was born wrapped in a bear skin. This subtle hint may be significant. It is believed that Neanderthals had a special relationship with cave bears—possibly worshipping them, while also having to kill and eat them, all the while raising the surviving bear cubs to be pets and then cave guards (being semi-tamed). This worship-while-killing practice also existed for thousands of years, by way of example, amongst the American Indians and many other early hunter-gatherer cultures. In his legend, Zalmoxis later disappeared from the Getae people and lived for three years in a cave. Living in natural caves is a preferred Neanderthal habitat. When he emerged, he began instructing the Getae tribal folk in a heart-centered religion, where he taught that it is impossible to die, thus

81

rendering great courage in the Getae warriors, where dying in battle while you were protecting your tribe was considered a sacred privilege. The Getae never fought offensive battles. It's noteworthy that today's Yogins in India say practically the same thing—retreat to the awareness of your heart and consciousness is forever eternal. This eternal consciousness is seen as creatively manifesting in the outer universe, in various differing forms and bodies. Plato wrote that, aside from war, Zalmoxis was also skilled in the arts of incantation, or chanting, and that he created a unique type of song and dance called 'Hesych,' about which little is known.
As a quick speculation, based upon its sound, taken as He-sych, it's possible that the 'He' prefix would be chanted as an *inhalation sound*, and be followed by 'Sych' as the *sound of exhalation*.

In: HEEEEEEE; Out: SYYYYYCHHHH

In many older cultures, chanting was not just an exhaled sound, but rather the sound of both inhaling and exhaling. This chanting process is much older than simple exhaled chant-sounds, for the ancients knew the in/out sounds made by the breathing process, in both Sumer and Egypt, where chants were referred to as 'utterances.'
Taken together, Spartacus, Zalmoxis, and the Getae folk can be considered as a good candidate group for our Human-Neon hybrid theory. Being stronger than everyone else, and also being red-haired, are the primary clues here. Perhaps these Getae tribe's people had DNA that was 10–15% Neon. We will never know, unless DNA of their fossils can be located, exhumed, and checked for confirmation.
King Decebalus (r. 87–106 AD) was the last King of the Getae-Dacians and also fought several wars against the Roman Empire before finally succumbing to the Roman's superior forces, after being greatly outnumbered. The country of Romania recently portrayed their ancient red-haired hero with a remarkable rock-face sculpture, which shows a trace of Neanderthal features, with its large face and broad nose, as seen below.

King Decebalus, immortalized at the Iron Gates in Romania

The Wild Satyr: Looking again at Socrates

A thick-faced bust of Socrates in the Vatican

T hose who study Greek myths and philosophy are well acquainted with the ancient Grecian ideal form of a man. Exquisite, perfectly formed statues of Apollo and other gods and heroes were the ever-present illustration of what a Grecian youth could aspire to, as he cultivated and accordingly sculpted his own body. But how does the famous Socrates compare to these ideals? And who was he, really? As we shall see, Socrates is actually the atypical Greek, in that his physical body was peculiar and odd, in contrast to the regular Greek folk who favored the tall, slender, athletic body. Consider the excerpt below, taken from Standard University's website; Plato.Stanford.Edu;Socrates:

Socrates's Strangeness

"Standards of beauty are different in different eras, and in Socrates's

time beauty could easily be measured by the standard of the gods, stately, proportionate sculptures of whom had been adorning the Athenian acropolis since about the time Socrates reached the age of thirty. Good looks and proper bearing were important to a man's political prospects, for beauty and goodness were linked in the popular imagination.

*The extant sources agree that Socrates was **profoundly ugly**, resembling a satyr more than a man—and resembling not at all the statues that turned up later in ancient times and now grace Internet sites and the covers of books. He had wide-set, **bulging eyes** that darted sideways and enabled him, like a crab, to see not only what was straight ahead, but what was beside him as well; a **flat, upturned nose** with flaring nostrils; and **large fleshy lips** like an ass. Socrates let his hair grow long, Spartan-style (even while Athens and Sparta were at war), and went about barefoot and unwashed, carrying a stick and looking arrogant. He didn't change his clothes but efficiently wore in the daytime what he covered himself with at night. Something was peculiar about his gait as well, sometimes described as a **swagger** so intimidating that enemy soldiers kept their distance. He was impervious to the effects of alcohol* *and **cold weather**, but this made him an object of suspicion to his fellow*

soldiers on campaign."

Let's compare this information with the notes on our relict Human-Neon hypothesis.

We reported earlier how some of the Wild People had unusual gaits and swaggered as they walked. Socrates had bulging eyes, as did Neons and their hybrid ancestors—perhaps one-third larger than modern humans. Perhaps for this and other reasons, Socrates is said to have had a perpetual stare, and was capable of going into lengthy, day-long trances.

Socrates, like the Neons, had great tolerance to cold. Some anthropologists have postulated that the lips of Neanderthals may have been large and fleshy, as Socrates' were. As we stated earlier, the Greeks were bordered on the north by the red-haired Getae-Thracians, yet we have no information as to the color of Socrates' hair, although he was said to wear his hair differently to the normal Athenian fashion of his time— his locks were long and uncut, more like a Spartan warrior. With a strong, swaggering body, and unkempt beard and piercing eyes, he likely produced a very wild look indeed.

He was physically unattractive, and his peers sometimes referred to his physique as looking like a satyr, rather than a man. In an era when the ideal Greek man was tall and graceful with chiseled facial features, Socrates was short and stocky, with a broad, stubby nose. Many thought his appearance strange. Nevertheless, he eventually married, and sired three children, whom Aristotle later called unremarkable 'fools and dullards.' Later, when Socrates was accused, tried, and executed by his Greek foes, for 'corrupting' the youth of Athens, he accepted his fate, and drank the proffered hemlock. He died peacefully . . . in a modified cave, that had been converted to a prison cell.

Neanderthals and their descendants are often stated to have extreme cold-hardiness and remain unaffected by weather that would incapacitate a normal human being. We recall the Roman Lucretius, writing in 100 BCE, "On the Nature of Things," concerning the hoary past:

"But the race of men at that time was much hardier on the land, as was

fitting inasmuch as the hard earth had made it, built up within it was with

bones, larger and more solid, fitted with strong sinews throughout the

flesh, not such as easily to be mastered by heat or cold."

Is it possible that the *cold-enduring* Socrates was partially descended from such people, who may have been Neon-hybrids? The idea that Socrates could outdrink any Greek soldier and all of his friends is a very curious notion and suggests an adapted DNA pool that was not entirely Greek, but perhaps something more ancient.

While we don't yet know the drinking habits of Neanderthals, it follows that natural fermentation of grains has likely existed for hundreds of thousands of years. Thus, long ago, Neon and Neonette probably sipped a few beverages in their cave, by the roaring fire, before, say, wild sex.

Xenophon, Socrates' student, wrote of his teacher's strange appearance in his Symposia dialogue, where the philosopher defines his own facial features. In one of his last dialogues before his death, Socrates and Critobulus hilariously compete to win the Prize of Beauty—who provides the best Greek image? He, Socrates, or Critobulus, a newly arrived colonist? Socrates states that his nose bridge isn't high and straight as Critobulus' but, rather, his was "spread out wide and flat." Both Critobulus and Socrates also speak of the philosopher's "snub nose." Socrates also mentions that he has large, and thicker lips than those of his opponent and finally finishes by saying that he looks a lot like Silenus, a rough-looking, yet macho-handsome Greek God, who was also a wild Satyr—half man/half animal.

In Plato's Symposium, where a group of Greek men are having philosophical discussions, there are direct references to Socrates' non-human appearance, as seen in this excerpt, where Alcibiades, Socrates' friend, is speaking to the group, about Socrates:

*"Said Alcibiades, and if I say anything which is not true, you may interrupt me if you will, and say "that is a lie," though my intention is to speak the truth. And now, my boys, I shall praise Socrates in a figure which will appear to him to be a caricature, and yet I speak, not to make fun of him, but only for the truth's sake. I say that he is exactly like the busts of Silenus, which are set up in the statuaries, shops, holding pipes and flutes in their mouths; and they are made to open in the middle and have images of gods inside them. I say also that he is like Marsyas the satyr. **You yourself will not deny, Socrates, that your face is like that of a satyr**. Aye, and there is a resemblance in other points too. For example, you are a bully, as I can prove by witnesses, if you will not confess. And are you not a flute-player? That you are, and a performer far more wonderful than Marsyas. He indeed with instruments used to charm the souls of men by the powers of his breath, and the players of his music do so still: for the melodies of Olympus are derived from Marsyas who taught them, and these, whether they are played by a great master or by a miserable flute-girl, have a power which no others*

have; they alone possess the soul and reveal the wants of those who have need of gods and mysteries, because they are divine. But you produce the same effect with your words only, and do not require the flute; that is the difference between you and him. When we hear any other speaker, even a very good one, he produces absolutely no effect upon us, or not much, whereas the mere fragments of you and your words, even at second-hand, and however imperfectly repeated, amaze and possess the souls of every man, woman, and child who comes within hearing of them."

An early Artist's depiction of a Satyr's face

The above text strongly infers, as did paleo-psychologist Stan Gooch, that musical abilities were transferred from hybrid-hominids (satyrs) to humans, somewhere in the distant past. Further, some archeologists have associated Neanderthal fossils with flute-like carvings in the far distant past. Perhaps their descendants learned to play as well.

While Socrates is referred to as a bully, it is in the sense of verbal and visual intensity where he might sometimes force his glaring stare, and scintillating dialectic approach upon others who did not wish to be accosted. Alcibiades, while referring to Socrates as a flute-playing, ugly satyr, is not kidding at all. His main point to those in the Symposium is that Socrates is considered honey-lipped (like Plato himself) and that the satyr-philosopher produces a trancelike effect on his audience when he speaks.

"The etymology of the name Satyr (Greek: σάτυρος, sátyros) is unclear,

and several different etymologies have been proposed for it, including a

possible Pre-Greek origin. Some scholars have linked the second part of

name to the root of the Greek word θηρίον (thērion), meaning ""wild

animal."

Satyr: **Wikipedia**

There are also many earlier reports of satyrs in the Egyptian and Phoenician areas. In India, there are myths of Kings who assembled large 'armies of satyrs' to fight in their successful wars. Could these legends really refer to an ancient army of fierce, fighting hybrid-hominids? In the standard versions of the Greek myths, the elusive satyrs were usually considered aligned with Dionysus, the God of the wine, and thus were often considered extremely lustful with regard to wine, women, and song. Stan Gooch, who fostered the first hypothesis that Neons and Cro-Magnons mated long ago, also wrote that the Neon folk were extremely lustful and sexual in their nature. Greek artists often depicted satyrs with horse's tails and goat's feet, perhaps as an allegorical implication of their tremendous sex drives. Some scholars have speculated that satyrs, or Sileni, as they were also called, were actually red-haired savages living on certain islands of the Mediterranean Sea. Others favor the idea of the Sileni coming originally from the ancient land of Ethiopia, and later Egypt, where they may have migrated in prehistoric times to a pre-Hellenistic Greece, and hence, the legend of satyrs. If shaggy, red-haired satyrs were actually rare, relict Neanderthals, then it might be possible to mistake a long shaggy mane of red hair coming down the back and dangling down behind the body, as a horse's tail, especially if seen from a distance. Satyrs are always depicted as having hairy, hardy bodies, which is another matching attribute of our Neon folk. It is rather amazing that the satyr called Socrates had such a profound effect upon philosophy in the West. We can recall the death-defying words of Zalmoxis, who said, like this author, and all Yogins and Yoginis . . . that no one ever dies. Zalmoxis and Socrates may have lived close together in time, approximately 700–400 BCE. Thus, we can see a similarity to Zalmoxis, in the spiritual words below.

"Death may be the greatest of all human blessings."

Socrates

In his youth, Socrates was considered a strong man and a fearless warrior. He was short and stout, and he walked with an unusual swagger, swaying to and fro, as he proceeded down the streets of Athens. Plus, he was known for having a rather intimidating stare, with his large, bulging eyes. The shorter Neon people, with their larger eyes, and their relict ancestors have been often considered by anthropologists to likely have had such a swaying gait. It may be difficult for some readers to fully understand and appreciate the nature of a person such as Socrates, who could be both a spiritual philosopher and yet also a fierce warrior when called upon.

Socrates, the Leader of Western Philosophy, was a Hybrid Man.

Is it possible that ancient Neon folk and their hybrid descendants were also both fierce and spiritual? The red-haired Getae-Dacians, with their faith in Zalmoxis, would answer a resounding yes! The concept of the 15–

91

17th century American Indian as a 'Noble Savage' also comes to mind, in citing both spirituality and fierceness. The reader's tendency may be to mentally separate the two seemingly disparate attributes of violence and spirituality, but this is inappropriate. In both ancient and modern days, these two opposing forces intertwine many times. As an illustration, the life of Socrates exhibited both great violence and a deep love of his inner spirit he called his guardian 'Daimon.' We should consider that knowledge of this inner spirit was a large part of what Socrates meant when he famously dictated "Know Thy Self," perhaps alluding to a greater metaphysical presence, larger than the Ego.

In his youth he was called to war on behalf of Athens, his Greek city-state; service was mandatory. As a Hoplite, or Grecian infantryman, he wound up fighting in hand-to-hand combat in three separate battles. During one raging battle scene, Socrates bravely rescued his Grecian Commander-General, the severely wounded Alcibiades, and fiercely repelled the enemy swords and spears as they both retreated to safety. Socrates was seen to be a savage, an odd-looking wild man gone berserk, who wielded a terrible sword in his rage, against the overwhelming numbers of his enemies, while defending his fellow soldier. Alcibiades survived and went on to publicly remark about the great valor of Socrates.

"Then if you care to hear of him in battle – for there also he must have his due – on the day of the fight in which I gained my prize for valor from our commanders, it was he, out of the whole army, who saved my life: I was wounded, and he would not forsake me, but helped me to save both my armor and myself."

Plato, The Symposium

One can imagine a fearless, heroic Socrates, swaggering to and fro in his Hoplite battle gear, his large googly eyes darting from left to right, as he strode into a thicket of enemy troops, courageously saving his commander against overwhelming odds. The enemy, it seems, did not want to engage with the young wild man named Socrates. Who knows how many he killed in his three battle campaigns? No one knows for sure, but hand-to-hand sword and dagger fighting is generally quite lethal.

He must have been an exceptional fighter, as he excelled in his historic rescue.

Later, Xenophon the historian declared this fierce Socrates to be the 'most spiritual person' of all the Greeks. So, the answer is yes; strong, seasoned philosophers can emerge from the challenging battles encountered in the harsh lessons of life—even war. At age seventy, while on trial and awaiting death by the poison of hemlock, Socrates compared his military service to his courtroom troubles, and said anyone on the jury who thinks he ought to retreat from philosophy must also think soldiers should retreat when it seems likely that they will be killed in battle. So, this remarkable hybrid man, who taught of the extreme importance of knowing oneself, went on to influence Plato who wrote, correspondingly, that "Man's Greatest Victory is to Conquer Himself," as the proper modality and technique of gaining such true knowledge. This would imply overcoming one's Ego . . . and then 'Knowing One's True Self.'

Like the fierce, strong Getae-Thracians, living north of Greece, Socrates, living in 500 BCE, may have been a hybrid Neon-Human, based on these observable traits. Perhaps, like the Getae, his Neon DNA percentage was high compared to ours, perhaps 9–12%, as a speculation. But skeptics should know that *speculation is important* here, because, somehow, we have to bridge the gap of the millennia, between our own known 2–4% Neon DNA, and the original crossbreed pairing which produced children that were 50% human, and 50% Neon, perhaps 40,000–50,000 years ago, or more. There are likely thousands of historical figures to choose from, but space is short, and Socrates is an excellent hybrid-hominid candidate, having several notable features.

Rather incredibly, he, a Neon-Sapiens hybrid, who along with Plato, his pupil, are the co-founders of the huge expansive school of thought called Western Philosophy. Socrates is considered far and away as its leading influence, yet now, overly analytical views of academic philosophers greatly diminish the field, which Plato once started 2,500 years ago, as he taught in his school, the Academia, in ancient, sacred groves of trees.

"All of Western civilization is but a series of footnotes to Plato."

Alfred Lord Whitehead

In his day, Socrates was considered a true spiritual leader of the Greek mystery school systems by his friends and followers, yet, he was also seen by the masses as being a bit of an outsider, or even an oddball, to the average Greek. There are several reports of Socrates spontaneously going into standing dreamlike trances for twenty-four hours at a time. Stan Gooch's notion of 'The Dream Culture of the Neanderthal' comes to mind. Socrates' neighbors used to camp out nearby and place bets as to what time he would 'return' from his distant reverie. And Socrates always listened to his spirit Daimon, when it spoke to him.

Those Gentle Voices I hear, Explain it All with a Sigh.

The Moody Blues

Standing trances are also a form of Yogic meditation, as demonstrated in modern times by Yogin Kirpal Singh and his Shabda yoga followers. Indeed, Kirpal's own guru, for instance, made his young disciple stand in knee-deep pond water the entire night, with the aspiring devotee mandated not to move the entire time. Standing trances are a practice that all Yogins and Yoginis should consider, especially late in the night. Socrates acknowledged that he had an inner spiritual presence he called a 'Daimon.' This was his internal voice that activated when necessary and prohibited him from doing certain things or taking certain courses of action. He was constantly being corrected by an active, sentient sense of conscience—this is more than mere philosophy. The implication that he was guided by an inner divinity was seen by his cultural enemies, who favored the traditional outer Greek Gods, as all the more reason for other Athenians to be suspicious of Socrates, the wild-looking man-satyr. By comparison with our Neon-hybrid hypothesis, let's recall that Gooch wrote that Neanderthals, and their hybrid ancestors, often entered into a personal 'dream reality' or even an expansive 'dream culture' as a natural aspect of their larger vision center, and a natural tendency to retreat from the violence of the world. This dream reality sounds a lot like a short, ugly Greek fellow named Socrates, who entered into his own day-long psychic trances. It would be rather remarkable to find his fossils and test them, to confirm that the greatest philosopher of Western Culture . . . was actually a Human-Neon hybrid, with perhaps 9–12% Neanderthal DNA. As the old saying goes, "Truth is often Stranger than Fiction," and perhaps we can include our strange Socrates in the ongoing strangeness of universal truths. Yes, we should 'Know Ourselves,' as he said, and part of that knowing is the revealing knowledge of our true hybrid ancestors.

We can also consider that Plato, or Platon, as he was called, may also show some signs of a hybrid background, although fewer details are present. Neanderthals and their partially human descendants had much larger rib cages and lungs than humans and thus could run faster and generally exert more continuous strength. The name Platon means 'broad-chested' or being large of both body and head. The philosopher was given the name by his wrestling coach. So, Plato himself, like Socrates in his youth, was a strong fellow, being a successful wrestler in his day. Being named for your large body and head might be seen as a possible sign of a hybrid influx, since Neons, and therefore their descendants, had a much larger chest cavity than modern humans. Or, we could simply say that Plato was like us, in that he possessed 2–4% Neon DNA—or perhaps it was slightly higher. Statues of Plato don't reflect facial anomalies such as those found in the busts of Socrates, thus, we'll likely never know more about Plato.

Another possible hybrid-hominid candidate is the Greek Diogenes, the Dog Philosopher, who knew Plato well.

Plato once called Diogenes, "a Socrates gone mad," for the raw approach that Diogenes took towards philosophy. The Dog Philosopher begged for his food and slept in wooden barrels adjacent to the market square, usually with several dogs, whom he felt were trustworthy, compared to the citizens of Athens. While sequestered in his wine barrel, he forced himself to endure the harsh cold winters, having a cold-endurance similar to that of Socrates. Diogenes, interestingly, wrote a tragedy, entitled *The Satyrus*. Like the wise satyrs, Diogenes maintained that all the artificial growths of society were incompatible with true happiness and that morality implies a return to the simplicity of nature. So great was his austerity and simplicity that the Stoics would later claim him to be a "Sophos" or wise man. In his words, *"Humans have complicated every simple gift of the gods."* Could this statement reflect the ever-growing analytical left-brain-dominance of the Greek masses? Like Socrates, who spoke out for truth-telling and against telling lies, Diogenes believed that people must police their thoughts and not allow the negative traits of deceit and falsehoods into the brain. He was very direct in his teaching and famously walked the streets of Athens with a glowing lamp during the day, informing everyone he met that he was looking for an honest man. This reminds that, in Athens, and in our own time, over 90% of humans are left-brain-dominant, to recall the statement of Dr. Sperry. And it's been shown in neuroscience, that *lying* is the trait of the left-brain hemisphere, as a twisted form of its interpretation of the external world. Socrates also advised against lying, but to no avail. We must speak as we think, then we enter into our own synchronicity. Bite your tongue, if it wags to lie.

If you act, as you think, the missing link; Synchronicity.

Synchronicity I, **The Police**

As *Ancient Shock ~ Monsters, Philosophers & Saviors* proceeds through its chapters, looking at twenty or more legendary and historical figures through a new hybrid-hominid lens, the reader may be either stunned or skeptical of several of our claimants, since we are describing past events, without archaeological proof. But, the one thing we can be sure of, and agree upon, is that the slow DNA trickle between the Neons, Sapiens, and their descendants, migrating into and around human cultures over the eons, surely did occur. We are the living proof.

The Roots of the Mixing Pools

In looking for clues to Socrates' potentially hybrid background, there are several opportunities to pursue. First, we should consider that pre-Hellenic Greece was a vastly different, wilder place when contrasted with its later well-known Golden and Classical ages. Over the millennia, there were many migratory waves of differing DNA hominid species that settled into the land of what is called Greece today. Many Neanderthals lived around or near the Mediterranean and Black Seas. In Greece, 35,000-year-old Neanderthal fossils have been found in the Kalamakia cave, on the Mani peninsula.

Did these creatures simply die out, perhaps eliminated by natural conditions or the larger numbers of the Cro-Magnon species, or did they slowly 'mix-out' and disseminate their genes and DNA throughout early human cultures, in prehistoric times? Our hybrid-crossbreed notion favors the mix-out hypothesis. Ancient historical traditions of the Greeks, Egyptians, Phoenicians, and Assyrians, all refer to a hoary pre-existing ancestral culture, spread over a great portion of Africa, Asia and Europe, of which little is known today. The Greeks called this prehistoric culture the Pelasgian race. Only legends and myths remain of their once-powerful presence. The Greeks considered the primitive Pelasgians as their ancestral forebearers. They had been the first to gather together families and tribes, scattered throughout caves, mountains, and forests, to form villages and cities, to found the first organized states, with their own godlike kings. Later, a series of migrating Kurgan peoples from the north, near the Black Sea, likely conquered the existing Pelasgians. Is it possible that the Stone Age Neons, who likely first inhabited Greece, slowly mixed with the incoming tribes of Homo sapiens, and that the early Pelasgians and Kurgans peoples contained a Neon DNA percentage larger than our own today? Many possibilities of DNA exist.

Austrian linguist Julius Pokorny (1887–1970) argued that the word 'Pelasgian' is taken from Pelasgoi from 'pelag-skoi' ("flatland-inhabitants"); specifically, in his words: "inhabitants of the Thessalian plain." This meaning could infer that migrations to the Greek province of Thessaly occurred, from other areas and tribes, possibly those northern Getae-Thracian tribes, or their prehistoric forbearers.

Vladimir I. Georgiev, a Bulgarian linguist, asserted that the Pelasgians spoke an Indo-European language and were, more specifically, related to the Thracians, whom we previously discussed as being hybrid tribes. Georgiev also suggested that the Pelasgians were a sub-group of the Bronze Age Sea Peoples, who often raided the Egypt and the Levant. Gooch wrote that hybrid peoples would tend to in-breed more than normal, as like attracts like; many times. These people were ostracized by more Sapiens-like tribe members.

Born in 470 BCE, Socrates was the son of Sophroniscus, an Athenian stonemason and sculptor, and Phaenarete, a midwife. The bloodline ancestry of his parents is unknown. Little is known other than the mere names of his grandparents. There are no references to either their physical appearance or personality traits. A few scholars, however, have speculated that Socrates' mother's family may have migrated from the northern Thracian area near the Black Sea, which is where the Wild Zana, and the numerous hairy Wild People lived in modern times. This is also the area where the extremely strong, red-haired Getae tribes lived, separated in time. If the Getae had once wandered into Greece from Thrace, then having a Getae-Thracian lineage in his ancestry would be a good genetic explanation for the rough-looking Socrates.

The Egyptian Waves

Although this author favors the ancestry of the strange-looking Socrates as emanating from the Black Sea and Thracian areas, we will note that another likely hybrid-hominid migratory pattern existed between ancient Egypt, Phoenicia and pre-Hellenic Greece, although this seems a hidden or taboo secret in Greek academia. Phoenicia (Lebanon) was an ancient colony of Egypt's for many years, and strong Neanderthal fossil evidence has been found there—perhaps the strongest Neon fossil finds in the world. Today's Jewish people from that area have a larger than average Neon DNA percentage, and we can assume that the percentage was even higher in the past. This Neon DNA would influence any Greek settlements coming from Egyptian and Phoenician prehistoric migrations. Plato, who was secretly initiated under the pyramids by Egyptian priests, wrote of his ancestor Solon in the 6th century BCE, who had also traveled to Egypt for spiritual training. In the excerpt below, taken from Plato's

Timaeus, Solon is advised by an Egyptian priest as to how Athens and the Egyptian city of Sais were settled in prehistoric times, by prehistoric migratory waves, which would have carried a flux of mixed hominid DNA.

The scene begins with a conversation, in Timaeus, between Critias and Amynander, concerning the travels of Solon:

"And what was the tale about, Critias? said Amynander.

About the greatest action which the Athenians ever did, and which

ought to have been the most famous, but, through the lapse of time and

the destruction of the actors, it has not come down to us.

In the Egyptian Delta, at the head of which the river

Nile divides, there is a certain district which is called the district

of Sais, and the great city of the district is also called Sais, and

is the city from which King Amasis came. The citizens have a deity for

their foundress; she is called in the Egyptian tongue Neith, and is

asserted by them to be the same whom the Hellenes call Athene; they

are great lovers of the Athenians, and say that they are in some way

related *to them."*

"To this city came Solon and was received there with great honor; he

asked the priests who were most skillful in such matters, about antiquity,

and made the discovery that neither he nor any other Hellene knew anything worth mentioning about the times of old. One of the priests, who was of a very great age, said: O Solon, Solon, you Hellenes are never anything but children, and there is not an old man among you. Solon in return asked him what he meant. I mean to say, he replied, that in mind you are all young; there is no old opinion handed down among you by ancient tradition, nor any science which is hoary with age. And I will tell you why. There have been, and will be again, many destructions of mankind arising out of many causes; the greatest have been brought about by the agencies of fire and water, and other lesser ones by innumerable other causes. In the first place, you remember a single deluge only, but there were many previous ones; in the next place, you do not know that there formerly dwelt in your land the fairest and noblest race of men which ever lived, and that you and your whole city are descended from a small seed or remnant of them which survived. And this was unknown to you, because, for many generations, the survivors of that destruction died, leaving no written word. For there was a time, Solon, before the great deluge of all, when the city which now is Athens was first in war and in every way the best governed of all cities, is said to have performed the noblest deeds and to have had the fairest constitution of

any of which tradition tells, under the face of heaven.

~

So just who was this ancient 'fairest and noblest race' that existed before modern man? One can imagine, if we take our minds back in time, and slow it down, that many, many Neon and Sapiens DNA migrations occurred during the many ages described above by the Egyptian priest above. The conversation continues:

"Solon marveled at his words, and earnestly requested the priests to

inform him exactly and in order about these former citizens. You are

welcome to hear about them, Solon, said the priest, both for your

own sake and for that of your city, and above all, for the sake of the

goddess who is the common patron and parent and educator of both our

cities. She founded your city a thousand years before ours,

receiving from the Earth and Hephaestus the seed of your race, and

afterwards she founded ours, of which the constitution is recorded

in our sacred registers to be eight thousand years old.

Modern archeology considers that ancient Athens is only about 5,000 years old, whereas the Egyptian Priest in *Timaeus* relates an older age, coming at the time of the 'most recent deluge.' This timing roughly corresponds in history with the melting of the last great Ice Age, 11,000 years ago, which would have corresponded to the vicious, destructive floods that are mentioned. Author Graham Hancock, with his many books concerning ancient civilizations, is perhaps the greatest non-academic person to write about the impact on human culture by the most recent Ice Age, likely caused by comet strikes coming from space, and also of those additional Ice Ages further back in prehistoric times.

As we can see from the Egyptian priests' lengthy words about Athenian and Sais historical relations, there have been several forgotten cultural exchanges between the Greeks and Egyptians in successive generations. It is highly likely we can surmise, or understand, only a small portion of these continuing, shifting changes over the millennia, regardless of academic or independent efforts, yet we must suspect, that these supposedly 'human' migratory patterns would often contain hybrid-hominid individuals from the Levant.

The Hybrid Games

In returning to Socrates as a strong, wild-looking, half-human satyr with bulging eyes, let us consider, of course, that he certainly couldn't be the *only* example of a hybrid-hominid living in Greece around 500 BCE. Nor would we suspect Zalmoxis of being the only Getae mixed breed, living near the time of Socrates. We might expect Socrates to have had perhaps 10–15% Neanderthal DNA in his body, which gave him his very unusual appearance.

It is well known that the ancient Greeks often killed their newly born infants if they were 'misshapen' or deformed. Could crossbreeding between ancient folks of differing Neon-Sapiens DNA admixtures, result in a higher rate of child deformation?

However, as anthropologists and geneticists might anticipate, if deformities from crossbreeding were *not* present, many of the Grecian hybrid-hominid males would likely be stronger, faster, and more muscular than the average Greek man, who was likely born from a more Sapiens bloodline. Thus, the tribes were different. The famous Olympic and Panathenaic games, which drew many Grecian tribes and sects together every four years, likely sported many hybrid-hominid athletes in 500 BCE; this was the approximate time that our Socrates lived and died as a warrior turned philosopher.

The Greeks, including Plato the broad-chested wrestler, believed in whole-body training and focused upon running, weight training and wrestling exercises. Elite athletes could become rich at the Games, as wealthy Grecian patrons handsomely rewarded the winners for their efforts. Gifts of oil, presented in large painted vases called amphora, were provided, along with copious amounts of gold and silver. Yet, could rigorous training alone be the reason the ancient winners won their contests, or was hybrid-hominid DNA a factor? Let's consider the images portrayed on the ancient Greek vase below, commemorating the important Panathenaic Games.

Runners at Panathenaic Games, 530 BCE, Credit: Mathias Kabel; CC 2.5

As we take a look at the large, red-haired stout fellow on the far right, who is winning the race at the games, we note his physique; his unusually large legs, trunk, chest, and head are obviously portrayed in contrast against the poor fellow on the extreme left, who is smaller in every way—and losing. Today's runners, primarily Sapiens, with only 2–4% Neon DNA, are smaller and leaner, like the last runner on the left. Both of the individuals on the right appear stronger and faster than the two trailing behind on the left. Having larger chests and bigger legs would be traits of Neanderthal ancestry. Was this merely artistic license? Was there really that much physical distinction between the many members of the ancient Greek tribes, or were there, instead, select athletes who had a greater Neanderthal DNA amount, a la Socrates, the fierce warrior and philosopher?

If a Greek man, a Sapiens, was pitted against a stronger Neon-Sapiens Greek at the Olympics, who would win the shotput contest? When I was younger, I used to throw it, so I know that strength is the greatest factor, with good technique being second. Thus, the stronger man would usually win, and his training and technique would be secondary factors with the first being hybrid-hominid genetics. As they say today of great athletes— 'It's in the Genes'—and good training, diet and technique are secondary. Some of the sports heroes of the Grecian games *must* have been Neon-Sapiens athletes, who were simply stronger and faster than those coming from the more purely Sapiens Grecian tribes—the slender folks.
The answers from mainstream history are often unclear, however, it remains that we, with our 2–4% Neon DNA, must find ancestral answers hidden in the past, and break new ground as we go.

Tibet and the Sherpas on High

In moving to the East for a moment, to consider new groups of likely hybrid-hominid candidates, we note that first, easily and without question, the remote Sherpas of Nepal are exceptional, extraordinary human beings. The people of the Tibetan plateau are famous for their incredible feats of athleticism; scaling the planet's highest mountain peaks with apparent ease as others succumb to the devastating symptoms of altitude sickness. It's as if they were born for the task.
Amidst the tall, majestic peaks of the Himalayas, over 150,000 Sherpas lived peacefully amongst themselves for centuries in high altitude mountain villages and small towns, trading and tending to their Yak herds, in their old, traditional ways. Then, everything changed in 1953, when Britain's Edmund Hillary came to Nepal to climb Mount Everest—the world's tallest peak, which had never been climbed before.

Hillary's successful attempt was made possible by Tenzing Norway, his Sherpa guide, without whom Hillary would surely have perished. Today, on an annual basis, hundreds of mountain climbers, mainly white folks from the West, struggle to ascend to the top of Everest. Many of the Caucasians die in the attempt, yet their Sherpa guides, like the famous, enduring Kam Rita, can return to the ceiling of the world again and again, like career journeyman-athletes, without serious health issues.

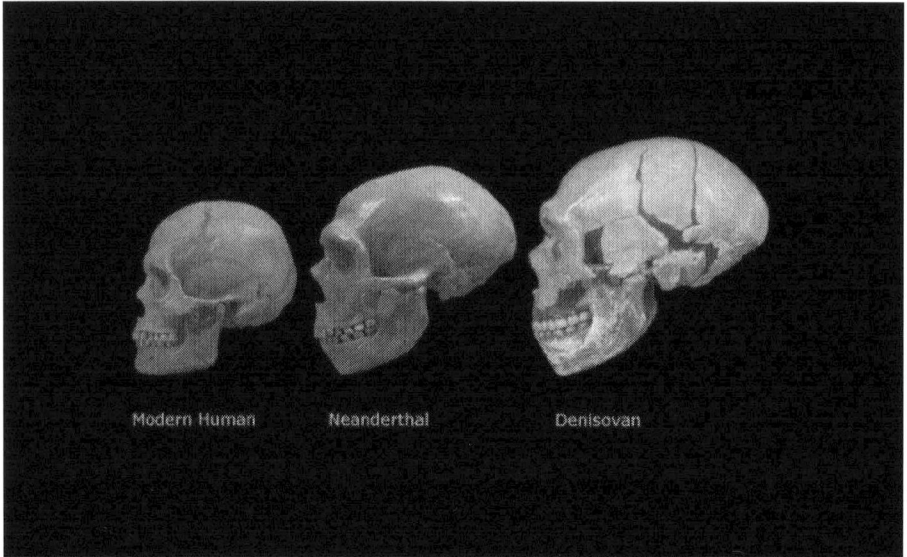

Denisovan skull comparisons Credit: curiosmos.com

In 2008, anthropology, and ancient history were once again upended by the discovery of ancient fossils in the Denisova cave in the Altai mountains of Siberia, by a group of Russian anthropologists. Yet another new humanlike species had been discovered, and named the Denisovans, after the location of the ancient cave. Remarkably, the Denisovan skull case was even larger than the Neanderthal's! The age of the fossils of the new species was placed at 160,000 years by Swedish geneticist Svante Paabo, director of the Max Planck Institute for Evolutionary Anthropology in Leipzig, Germany.

REALLY GET A GRIP

Just as the Neanderthal's FOXP2 gene assisted language development in later humans, another gene, EPAS1, from the Denisovan species, is directly responsible for the high-living Sherpa's unique adaptability to survive, and even thrive in extremely thin mountain air, thus the indigenous Sherpas are the first choice as guides for all foreign mountain climbers in the Himalayas. Scientists recently discovered that the Sherpa mountain culture living today, is related to the ancient Denisovans, and have inherited their metabolic ability to survive on the roof of the world, in the Himalayan mountains. Not only do they have to live in thin air, but they also endure extremely harsh weather conditions and bone-chilling cold, yet, like our barefoot Socrates and the earlier Neons perhaps, the Sherpas have adapted their hard bodies; their metabolism is remarkably different than others. The EPAS1 finding has been labeled by scientists as being the 'super-athlete' gene.

The key to surviving and thriving in their high, mountainous lifestyle is literally in their blood. The Tibetan variant of this gene does a surprising thing—it actually lowers the hemoglobin count in your blood at high altitudes. Hemoglobin is a protein in red blood cells that transports oxygen to the body. Normally our bodies respond to lower oxygen pressures by increasing hemoglobin in our blood, allowing for more O_2 to reach the muscles. It's remarkable that Tibetans would have a lower hemoglobin count at high altitudes, yet this variance allows them to thrive in their mountains.

The Sherpa migrated 600 years ago from the Kham region of Tibet. Tibet has long been considered as a spiritual center of the world. Like the high-climbing Sherpa, the Buddhist monks of Tibet regularly meditate outside in extremely cold weather. As an ascetic practice, the monks are then draped with freezing sheets of wet fabric, which they dry with their body heat. The monks claimed meditation was the key, and it is, but it's important to note that they too appeared genetically predisposed to greater resistance against cold weather.

Long before Buddhism was practiced in the region, there was an ancient folk religion, BON, and an ancient, now-extinct language called Zhang-Zhung. The primary writing of these early people may be prehistoric and is mysteriously entitled 'The **Cavern** of Treasures.' Perhaps, somewhere between 35,000 to 50,000 years ago, the first mating of Sapiens and Denisovans occurred, producing a fully fifty-fifty DNA percentage in the resultant offspring. These were the distant, ancestral cousins of Kam Rita and the Sherpa, and the Dalai Lama and his Buddhist monks of Tibet.

Eons, ago, after roaming through Asia, the Denisovans began to spread out. Aboriginal Australians and Melanesians have up to 5% Denisovan DNA, indicating ancient migrations flowed freely between China and the lands of the south. In speaking of the Denisovan's influence, we note Chad Huff, geneticist; University of Texas:

"The fact that human populations have undergone such strong selection and have such major changes—even if it's only at certain loci—in just the past 15,000 years is remarkable."

And so, we may conclude that Sapiens and Denisovans mated extensively in the distant past, and that numerous human cultures were affected. But we should ask: did this crossbreed mating also produce strange, mysterious children, as we often saw with the Neon-Sapiens matings? As it turns out, as revealed in later chapters, yes, the Sapiens-Denisovans DNA admixtures produced their own special versions of Monsters, Philosophers & Saviors.

The Yeti and the Curious Clan of Shennong

We now move from the relatively tame world of the Sherpas to consider another wild human hybrid, said to live in the high mountains of the Himalayas and elsewhere. The Sherpas were terribly afraid of encountering this monstrous creature, for it meant death had arrived.

Yes, the mysterious Yeti is both famous, and a little infamous. Nearly everyone has heard about the legendary Abdominal Snowman. Hoaxes abound in the vast multi-media realm, forever seeking to catch the public's attention. However, behind the apparent ruses, there is a good trail of hybrid-hominid clues for our pursuit. After researching, however, I found that to properly understand the mysterious Yeti, we must first go back in time to understand an important, ancient tribal culture: the Chinese Clan of Shennong, which was the eastern extension of the vast, prehistoric Yamna culture, which covered most of Eurasia at one time.

The strange legend of China's ancient Shennong Clan is shrouded in shadowy myth, like most of our ancient candidates in our hybrid species theory. This prehistoric clan produced a truly remarkable God-king of the same name. King Shennong, also known as the Red or Flame Emperor, is thought to have lived 5,000 years ago, on the edge of known history; his was the first Chinese dynasty, which was soon followed by the rule of the Yellow Emperor, and the rest of Chinese history. The Shennong Clan is thus considered to be the primitive ancestor of today's Chinese people, and this notion bears further investigation, because it is likely true, based on recent scientific findings.

Shennong: The Odd-Looking King

There are very few extant portrayals and images of King Shennong. He is usually depicted as having a very unusual non-human body and face, which certainly suggests a hybrid, crossbreed presence originally existed in the Shennong Clan. Based upon the known genetic information for this region, we must suspect a Sapiens-Denisovan ancestry for this person, the first King of China.

King Shennong, the Divine-Farmer, by artist Guo Wu, 1503 AD; Public Domain

King Shennong's unusual body appears thicker, stronger, and larger than a normal Chinese man, or any Sapiens' for that matter. The face and eyes also seem larger than those of a Sapiens. Perhaps a pre-Sapiens Chinese look is depicted by the artist, concerning this founding King, who lived over 5,000 years ago.

Oddly, the bumps, or horns, seen on his head may seem shocking at first, but there are at least two explanations. Science is now aware that our Sapiens species, somewhat rarely, actually does produce hard, wart-like protrusions on the skull. Even today, elderly Chinese folks have been found who have wart-horns several inches long on their heads; it's likely this wart-virus has existed in the area for millennia and possibly affected the Shennong Clan too.

Alternatively, we may consider that a plethora of 'horned deities' are symbolically depicted with horns or antlers and are found in many different religions in Europe, Africa, and Asia. Statues of Alexander the

Great, as he migrated from warrior to God-king, sported rams' horns upon his head, which, in his day, represented great wisdom. The presence of these numerous horned gods, may also symbolically indicate a prehistoric awareness by Sapiens of the existence of hybrid crossbreeds in numerous cultures as suggested by Stan Gooch. Thus, the many Horned Gods, including the Satyrs of Egypt, Greece, and India, may stem from confabulations—real semi-lost ancient memories, and thus are not totally mythical.

The name of King Shennong has several possible meanings, according to Chinese scholars: Divine-Husband-Man, Divine-Farmer, and God-Peasant. We note the name of Divine-Husband-Man here, because of its close association as a 'protector' of women, children, and childbirth. These qualities we have also observed in the hybrid named Enkidu and the Egyptian Bes, a thick-faced, stout God who is discussed in an upcoming chapter.

The Divine-Farmer-Healer

Shennong was also called the Divine-Farmer because he is said to have introduced agriculture and the use of herbs to the early peoples of prehistoric China. He is rumored to have eaten hundreds of plants while using his body as a natural laboratory to research the medicinal properties. There is a likely link, scholars consider, between Shennong the ancient King, and the growth of the marvelous modern Chinese medicinal herbal system. King Shennong wrote of over 800 plants, including cannabis, opiates, and psychoactive substances. His writings formed the basis for an early Chinese pharmaceutical system. The Huainanzi Chinese anthology, written in 139 BC, reveals that the people were starving, and were weak, sickly, and diseased, prior to the prehistoric arrival of the Shennong Clan. The Chinese myths also say that he helped people transition from a diet of meat, clams, and wild fruit, to one based on grains and vegetables. The Shennong Clan also taught of the cultivation of tea.

~!~

This Chinese method of quickly 'learning' the properties of hundreds of plants is curiously akin to a process of the Peruvian culture, far away across the Pacific Ocean, possibly suggesting an ancient cultural diffusion and migration. Mythologist Joseph Campbell pointed out, in his book, *The Mythic Image,* that Chinese art patterns have been found in Ecuador and Central America, but mainstream academia cannot yet accept the idea of such cultural diffusion.

Anthropologist Jeremy Narby went to the Pichis Valley in the Peruvian Amazon basin in 1985, to study the shamanistic culture of the ancient Ashaninca Indians. He was interested in the deep shamanistic knowledge of the many thousands of plant species in the rain forest. He wrote a book, *The Cosmic Serpent*, where he noted, in the opening sentence;

"The first time an Ashaninca man told me that he had learned the medicinal properties of plants...by drinking a hallucinogenic brew, I thought he was joking."

In a short time, the anthropologist became convinced that it was possible to learn a great deal from such eventful 'brews,' called Ayahuasca—not only about unknown plants but DNA in general. The reason Narby had asked the question about medicinal knowledge of plants, was because he was wondering how the Peruvian shamans knew of so many. There were nearly 80,000 species, which meant finding a given 'remedy' for an illness would require testing up to three million plant combinations. In considering the similar knowledge of the legendary Shennong Clan, is it possible that a common trans-oceanic shamanistic knowledge existed in prehistoric times? King Shennong would not be so unusual in history, if he too imbibed or consumed hallucinogenic plants.

~!~

One might also consider that the earliest hunter-gatherers, in China and elsewhere, were of a higher crossbreed percentage than our own today, which is generally 2–4%Neon, and 96–98% Sapiens. It is entirely possible that Sapiens, Neanderthals, and Denisovans, all interbred in this region, during the time prior to the arrival of the Shennong Clan 5,000 years ago. *SOUNDS PLAUSIBLE.*

If we call Shennong a God-Peasant, does this indicate others saw him as a God, or that, being consciously aware, he recognized God in himself, and may have taught others in the same vein? This would be the start of an early religion. The nearby ancient Yogas of India, all acknowledge that they too are simply God-men, without fanfare. Just who were these ancient, benevolent Shennong folk?

In the legends, King Shennong taught the prehistoric Sino peoples how to farm and care for themselves. Said to have been born, lived, and died in a cave in the sacred Hua Shan mountains, this benevolent God-king is also credited with the invention of the hoe, plough, axe, water wells, field irrigation, the storing of seeds and the creation of a farmer's market in early China. Sophisticated metal tool works have been found nearby, dating to 3,000 years, indicating an ancient civilization once existed there. Red, the color of fire, was known as 'Yan' in ancient Chinese, thus Shennong, the first Godlike King of China was also called the Yan or Red Emperor, and had various attributes associated with him.

We are especially interested in *why* King Shennong was called the *God of the Wind of Fire* and *why* Shennong was said to have been born to a princess and a divine **dragon**. The subject of dragons is extensive— please see Appendix C: '*The Human Dragons*' for more information on a rather provocative subject. Neanderthal-Sapiens being confused as dragons are also discussed in an upcoming chapter: *Beowulf, Grendel, and the Dragons*. IS THE DRAGON THE EROBORUS?

In his myths, Shennong is sometimes said to have been ox-headed but his artistic images generally show him as a hybrid-crossbreed, perhaps a Wild-Man-King of the mysterious Yandi tribes, also known as the Shennong Clan. His legends also related how he was sharp-horned on his head, with a bronze forehead, and was iron-skulled, which perhaps might be a term that can be used to reflect a thicker, larger, hybrid cranium. The Denisovan skull was actually larger than Neanderthal's.

The Evolving, Revolving, Yamna, Yandi & Yeti Cultures

Where did the Yandi (Shennong) come from?

Generally, in history, there is little information available from 5,000 years ago, the cited date for the origin of the Shennong (Yandi) clan, the clever tribal people who helped to found modern China. But, as the Shennong-Yandi legends suggest, this impressive clan suddenly 'arrived' somehow, in the mainland China area, around 3,000 BCE, where King Shennong is said to have been born in a cave. Who were his migrating parents and clan members? In the legend, as he grew to adulthood, Shennong began teaching the poorer, indigenous people, to improve their lives, both materially and spiritually . . . this was the early founding of a Chinese nation.

We must suspect a Yandi migration from some other, earlier location—most likely outside of China itself. Most readers are familiar with the concept of Indo-European cultures, where Eurasian tribes routinely mixed and migrated for thousands of years. Now, anthropologists are further defining, and refining, the meaning of 6,000-year-old Indo-European cultures, and also the earlier Proto-Indo-Europeans (PIE), and their languages. These ancient folks were also referred to as migrating Indo-Aryans by earlier generations of historians.

Yamna became Yandi

One possible source for the Yandi clan is the ancient migratory Yamna culture, which was in existence, roughly speaking, during the same time. Anthropologists tend to view the older Yamna culture as essentially being slightly differing, multiple waves of interweaving migrations, reaching the vast lands stretching between Ireland all the way to China, many millennia ago. These scholars acknowledge that these migrations produced many different Sapiens (human) DNA admixtures, crossbreeding as they moved along, but they are silent about the nature of Neanderthal-Sapiens or Denisovan-Sapiens hybrids, who had migrations of their own, as they co-existed with their more Sapiens counterparts.

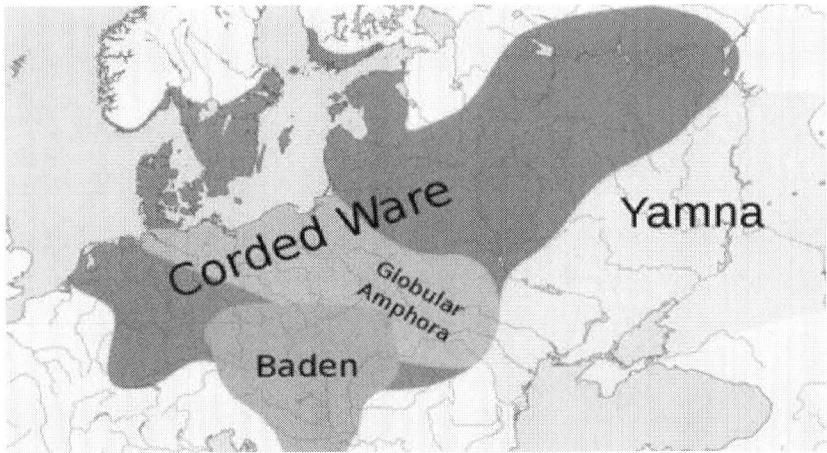

Map of migrating Yamna cultures. credit Wikipedia: CC: SA 3.0

Archaeologists often use their sparse findings of pottery vessels, such as amphora, or 'corded ware' clay jars to give the geographical regions their cultural names. These odd names do not do justice to the attributes of the tribes, however, as the Corded Ware peoples were also called the 'Battle-Axe' folk, many of whom were considered to have been so fierce as to be totally genocidal towards their neighbors. DNA analysis shows that the Corded Ware peoples were remarkably similar to Yamna, and some scholars consider the groups to be one and the same. In the name of Yamna, the reference may be to what these ancient peoples actually called themselves: the Yamna.

This Yamna culture, which may have originated from what is now central Russia, may actually be much older than archeologists currently acknowledge. It is the likely origin of the PIE (proto-Indo-European) linguistics and languages and the known migratory paths, which eventually formed most of the Silk Road, thousands of years later. Scholars consider the Yamna culture as having the early vestiges of a funeral system. These were known as the 'pit-grave' people, who placed their dead in burial mounds, and covered them in reddish-orange magnetic ocher. It's important to note that this practice may have been taken from earlier peoples, the Neanderthals, who were also known to

bury their dead in red ocher hundreds of thousands of years ago.
It is possible that the widespread name of Yama, known as the Lord of the
Pits, and also the Hindu God of death, was associated with this ancient
proto-Indo-European culture, the ancient Yamna, as both the death-
inference and similar phonics suggest.

It's rather curious that the powerful nickname for the Shennong Clan was
'Yandi.' Scholars consider this name as a precursor to the title of the
'Yan' Emperor itself, the first ruler of ancient China.

Shiva & Shennong

Besides the Yamna-Yandi possible connection, there is a possibility of an
ancient Hindu association as well. The religion of Shiva, well known in
India, also penetrated into China in ancient times, although never gaining
large amounts of followers, except in Tibet. Lord Shiva has dozens of
epithets and formal names; a few of those starting with 'S' are Sanatana,
Sarvayoni, and Shambhu—meaning: Eternal Lord, Source of Everything,
and One who brings Luck.

Although overlooked by scholars, there are several noteworthy
similarities between the two characters of Shiva and Shennong.
First, we find that the basic, two-syllable sound of Shennong, if long-
vowel chanted, is also phonically similar to Siva or Shiva. A louder
emphasis, and breath, is given to the first syllable, and a lesser, shorter
sound to the second syllable. The sound is nearly identical.

Shiiiiiiiiiiiiiiiiiiiiii-va
Sheeeeeeeeeeeeee-nuhg

In their respective locations and times, both China's King Shennong and
India's Shiva are considered the 'first teachers' or 'first givers' to
humanity. Both are 'Lords of the Dance'; King Shennong with his
'Plough-Dancing' and Shiva with his dancing Nataraja.
Descending from Godhood, and living upon Mount Kalish in the
Himalayas, India's Shiva was also known as Adi Guru, or the first guru to

DANCE = "AMBULO ERGO SUM". DANCE YOUR WAY
TO THE DREAMTIME, INTERACTION "PLAY". ONE CAN
ONLY DANCE IF ALIVE.

teach the people. The Divine-Teacher Shennong is also noted as the first great teacher of his people, and taught them many different skills, including agriculture, to improve their lives. Thus, there are hints and traces of a migratory path in ancient times, where hybrid DNA, and culture were likely carried over thousands of miles before history began. Legends sprung up over the eons, as the fanciful human mind spun stories and tales around ancient cave campfires and hearths, yet, this author believes someone like Shiva, perhaps also translated as Shennong in China, likely existed.

"In the yogic culture, Shiva is not seen as a God. He was a being who walked this land and lived in the Himalayan region. As the very source of the yogic traditions, his contribution in the making of human consciousness is too phenomenal to be ignored. Every possible way in which you could approach and transform the human mechanism into an ultimate possibility was explored thousands of years ago. The sophistication of it is unbelievable. The question of whether people were so sophisticated at that time is irrelevant because this did not come from a certain civilization or thought process. This came from an inner realization. This had nothing to do with what was happening around him. It was just an outpouring of himself."

Jaggi Vasudev:Sadeguru

Disregarding myth for a moment, we should consider that this human Shiva had mixed hybrid DNA, similar to our own. Going further, can we conceive that Shiva, the Adi Guru, like King Shennong the Divine-Teacher, could be a relict Neanderthal-Sapiens or Denisovan-Sapiens? Stan Gooch remarked several times that Neanderthals, Denisovans and their descendants were the forebearers and givers of spiritual systems to Sapiens humanity. NO ARGUMENTS BUT DNA DOES NOT PASS ON WISDOM. SMART IS SOMETHING YOU DO, NOT BESTOW SOMETHING YOU ARE.

Yeti: The Wild People living outside of Human Society

I recently listened to comparisons of English and Proto-Indo-European language; the rich gutturals and contrasting styles of speech were extremely apparent, so much that I couldn't understand the English words, in PIE form, at all. We have already seen how King Shennong did not present a fully human (Sapiens) countenance. In our hybrid-hominid hypothesis, it's surely not a coincidence that the sound of Yandi is phonically similar to the famous Yeti of old Tibet and the Himalayas.

Like many others, I naively lampooned the Yeti Hoax for years as being a total fake. Although endlessly caricatured in modern media as a huge, snowy cartoon-monster, or possibly mistaken as a huge snow bear by ancient folk, it remains that the word Yeti translates as jungle-man or wild-man, epithets that are obviously applicable to the ancient Yandi in early China. After my hours of research on hybrid-hominids, I saw that there is parsimonious evidence for the Wild People called Yeti, Meti, and Yachi, along with many other names. Yet, now, I believe in the existence of the early Yeti, and their descendants, as strong, long-haired creatures, impervious to the harsh cold, and perhaps, yes, they were often covered with Himalayan snow. The older local Sherpa legends held that *"anyone who sees one dies or is killed"*; this statement was gathered by mountaineer Frank Smythe, in 1937, while discussing the Yeti with a large group of Sherpa mountaineers. Now, with all of the daily mountaineering efforts going on at Mount Everett and other great heights, the modern Sherpas state that the Yeti may have died out twenty years ago, or perhaps moved further away.

British anthropologist Myra Shackley is recognized as a leading international authority on the management of international historic sites. Her significant book, *Wildmen; Yeti, Sasquatch, and the Neanderthal Enigma*, is highly suggestive of a real hybrid-hominid group or wild sub-culture, existing high in the mountains of America and Asia.

We consider here that the early Yeti may have occasionally mated with the Yandi thousands of years ago, who then cross-bred into the early

118

Tibetan and Chinese prehistoric peoples, giving them their Neanderthal or Denisovan genes. Scholars do allow for the migrating Shennong tribes to have once been located in the western-most area of China, the Qin province. In our hybrid-crossbreed scenario, we can suggest that the Shennong people, or their ancestors, were originally living even further to the west, residing in or near the mountains of Tibet, Nepal, and northern India, which is also the home of Shiva; the Ad-Guru.

While media portrayals often depict Yeti as being fictitiously tall, perhaps 9–10 ft high, with glowing red eyes, etc.; the more serious scholars consider them as creatures who are less than six feet in stature, extremely strong, hairy, and aggressive.

The Splay-Foot: There is a remarkable correspondence to the footprints given below, and the unusual feet of King Shennong in the image provided in the beginning of this chapter. Stan Gooch also commented that Neanderthals and their descendants may have splayed toes on their feet.

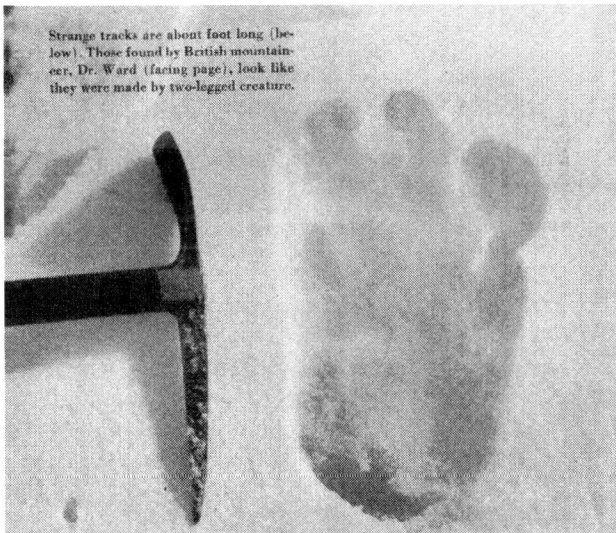

Strange tracks are about foot long (below). Those found by British mountaineer, Dr. Ward (facing page), look like they were made by two-legged creature.

Wikipedia; Yeti image now in Public Domain

In 1953, Sir Edmund Hillary (1919–2008), became the first white man in history to climb Mount Everest. The mountain climber's team took this intriguing photo of a Yeti foot, which appears to have a splayed foot feature, unlike Sapiens, or a large bear, for that matter, which Yetis are often conjectured to be.

Otisk nohy neandertalce nalezene v jeskyni
Tana della Basua v Itälii (odlitek)

Neanderthal footprint in the Natural History Museum in Prague. CC: SA 2.0

One of two Neanderthal footprints in existence, this is a child's foot. One can see a similarity in the feet of the previous two images and the artist's depiction of the feet of King Shennong. A splayed large toe is suggested in all three instances.

Over the years, there were several other Yeti sightings, mainly by mountaineers hiking in extremely remote areas. In 2004, Henry Gee, editor of the journal Nature, mentioned the Yeti as an example of folk belief deserving further study, writing:

"The discovery that Homo Floresiensis survived until so very recently, in geological terms, makes it more likely that stories of other mythical, humanlike creatures such as Yetis are founded on grains of truth."

Yes, if we can shed the myths and hoaxes surrounding the Yeti, we will likely find vestiges of hybrid-hominid creatures in the Himalayas, who are either still alive, or perhaps went extinct within the past few decades. In 2010, a group of Chinese scientists and explorers proposed to renew Yeti searches in the Shennongjia Forestry District of Hubei province, which was the site of similar expeditions in the 1970s and 1980s. This search location, in the Shennong area, is another strong clue of the mysterious connection between the ancient clans of Yandi peoples, who may have been Sapiens-Denisovans or Sapiens-Neanderthals hybrids. The more pure-blooded, truly wild Yeti, living beyond the fence of humanity, may have rejected, or were rejected by the tribes of Sapiens folk, and chose to live in the extremely high wild climes of the Himalayas, where few humans ever go.

~!~

"Anyone who sees One dies or is killed."

Sherpa Legend

In 2019, the Russian government reopened an old mysterious murder case, sixty years after the extremely strange event. In 1959, nine athletic, college-aged hikers and skiers had been terrorized and killed, in a most shocking way, while camping and trekking through the northern Ural Mountains, thousands of miles away from the Himalayas.
On February 1, the group of hikers set out, climbing to Dyatlov Pass, but were believed to have become lost in a snowstorm. When they did not return, their relatives organized a rescue mission. Six days later, the search party found the remains of the hikers' campsite and their bodies. How the nine hikers died has baffled forensic experts and is the stuff of nightmares. Some Soviet researchers, in 1959, suspected wild Yetis may have been disturbed and committed the crime.

When the search team found the remains of the group's tent, it was a bizarre site. The tent had been abandoned, and strangely, was cut open from the inside with the inhabitants' clothing and shoes left behind. As many as nine sets of footprints, some barefoot, some only in socks, one with only one shoe, led away from the tent as if the group had suddenly fled in terror. But from what? A mile from the camp, at the edge of the forest beneath a tree, searchers found the bodies of Yuri Doroshenko and Yuri Krivonischenko, wearing only underwear, next to the remains of a small campfire; they had died of hypothermia. Broken branches suggested the tree had been climbed by one of the hikers, maybe in an effort to spot something far away, or perhaps, the torn branches had been planned as defensive weapons, against whatever force had driven nine young hikers from their tent, in the dead of winter.

Soon after, the search party found three more hikers half buried under the snow. It appeared that these hikers had been with the other two at the forest's edge and died on their way back to the camp, and similarly, weren't dressed for the harsh, brutal weather.

What happened next is a bone-chilling tale. As it turns out, the hikers all died on a Ural elevation curiously known as Dead Mountain. It took over two months to find the bodies of the last four hikers. These hikers died in a deep ravine even further into the forest. Once winter snows began to melt, their bodies were revealed at the bottom of the ravine. Unlike the rest of the group, these four were wearing winter clothing, though not necessarily their own. Even more strange, they had been killed apparently not by exposure to cold, but by *extreme blunt force trauma* that one investigator likened to the violence of a car crash. Lyudmila Dubinina was missing an eye and her tongue. Nikolai Thibeaux-Brignolles had massive skull trauma. The rest had suffered severe chest fractures, but they had no external injuries. It was as if they'd been crushed by severe pressure that left no marks on their skin.

It's of no doubt that five of the group—those found with no clothing—died of hypothermia. But there's little obvious explanation for why they'd flee a tent after cutting it open, then run a mile through the snow with no shoes. A possible scenario follows: The nine hikers fleeing their tent and campsite quickly separated into three groups, each running pell-mell through the darkness, in abject fear.

Soviet authorities had coyly concluded the group had died from a "compelling natural force," adding to an element of mystery. Let us consider this disruptive 'force' could only pursue one of the groups, the four fully-clothed people who ran into the ravine. If this were truly an overpowering wild creature, such as a hybrid-hominid Yeti, we might imagine the Yeti giving a horrible, terrifying scream, as it gave a crushing bear-hug to the hikers' skulls and chests, while also ripping out tongues and eyes of those who had offended it. A Yeti's strong, bone-breaking strength, along with its dazzling speed, would be the reasons why the Sherpas said, if you see one, you will die.

Some researchers have suggested that the Mansi, an indigenous people of the region, attacked the hikers, but there was no sign of struggle around the campsite, nor were there extra footprints. The Discovery Channel sent a film crew to the area in 2014, to conduct research for the documentary: *"Russian Yeti: The Killer Lives."* During the filming, the crew talked to locals who swore they'd seen signs of the mythical beast in the area and heard strange sounds the night of the killings.

Quasimodo, Bes, and Asmodeus

Relief of Bes: Egyptian Hathor Temple, credit Olaf Tausch, CC SA 3.0

BES the NEON God of Ancient Egypt

N
ot all of the ancient hybrid-hominids were aggressive monsters, such as the remote-living Yeti. Before the great dynasties of Egypt first began 5,000 years ago, as recorded by mainstream Egyptology, there were faint traces of an ancient God in the Nile and Phoenician areas, whose name was Bes. Bes, known as the guardian God, became a popular household deity in the early Roman and Persian

Empires. As the reader can see from the image above, the thick-faced, thick-bodied Bes is a good candidate for inclusion in our hybrid Neon-Sapiens hypothesis. The facial representation is not human but more Neanderthal in appearance. Bes was always depicted as being short and very stocky, thus, he was called the dwarf God. As an ancient guardian angel, he came to be regarded as the defender of everything good and the enemy of all that is bad. Like King Shennong and Enkidu, Bes was a protector of mothers, children, and childbirth. We recall that Huwawa the hybrid was actually not an ogre, but a benevolent creature who protected and defended the Cedar Forest and its animals. Yet Bes was also a war God who was a fierce defender, and like the satyrs, he was associated with sexuality, humor, music, and dancing. The prehistoric Bes may arise from an extremely ancient memory of a Human-Neanderthal relation of some sort, where the two species lived harmoniously together, perhaps even assisting each other. As the eons moved along, Bes was caught up in the usual creations of man, being forever caricatured as a whimsical myth. In the ancient Egyptian lore, there is, along with the satyr, a strong element of dwarfism.

"Another possibility is that dwarves are folk memories of the Neanderthals that populated Europe and Asia up to the end of the Neolithic era (dying out approximately 50,000 to 30,000 years ago), coexisting for part of this time with modern humans. This fits rather well into the picture of the dwarf, as Neanderthals were on average shorter but burlier than humans and possessed stronger features (broader noses, more pronounced brow ridges, and so forth), which could be seen by ancient humans as deformities (dwarves are commonly said to be "deformed"). It is also thought that Neanderthal culture revolved more around tool and weapon crafting, explaining why dwarves of legend were known as craftsmen. Finally, Neanderthals (like so many humans) used caves as shelters, thus making them "subterranean" beings. However, this theory depends on the belief that memories of events can become

NBAT

stuck in a culture's psyche and be passed down accurately for many thousands of years. Such things were proposed by Sigmund Freud."

Dwarves; **Wikipedia**

Asmodeus; Prince of Demons

"Nor could I doubt but the Devil, if any Mirth be allow'd him, often laughs at the many frightful Shapes and Figures we dress him up in, and especially to see how willing we are first to paint him as black, and make him appear as ugly as we can, and then stare and start at the Spectrum of our own making."

Political History of the Devil (1726); **Daniel Defoe (1660–1731)**

"The Devil made me do it!"
Old Christian saying

The true 'history' of the Christian Devil, or a Prince of Demons, has a subtle psychological aspect; it underscores the ability of humans to hate and loathe that which is not 'good' or like themselves. When a white author, such as Daniel Defoe, who wrote Robinson Crusoe, writes that 'we are first to paint him as black' in referring to the Devil, we should consider that the author is referring to an unconscious, racist, nationalistic underpinning present in the mind of the public. The bigotry of our species, set against itself by racial skin color and differing culture, is a primary factor in the myth-making that goes into legends; this is true in all corners of the globe. If we add hybrid creatures, such as those already described, we will likely find that the mass of humanity often extends its hatred and fear to them as well, having no shortage. These hybrid creatures likely had a variety of skin colors too, according to several geneticists.

The legendary monsters that Gooch indicated as hybrid-hominids, were likely living outside the boundaries of Sapiens humanity, except for an occasional, lustful tryst, or rape. These creatures, often called trolls, and ogres, were existing in a wide variety of ways, behind the many scenes of history, with varying DNA admixtures and were generally despised, hated, and feared.

Xenophobia, the nationalistic attitude of distrust and hatred of foreign neighbors, would certainly extend to those dangerous, hybrid creatures living in nearby caves. Being like ancient Huwawa and Enkidu, they usually lived beyond the fence of human civilization, which stood in awe of them.

Psychologist Stan Gooch was the first to foster the concept that relict Neanderthals, or hybrid-hominids, were liberally sprinkled throughout human history and were subtly depicted in various legends via certain iconic words: giants, ogres, and trolls.

In this chapter, we can add the words demon, devil, succubus, and incubus to the list, for Asmodeus, the Judean/Christian Prince of Demons is a likely candidate for inclusion into our ancestral hybrid ranks, along with his 'family.' The traits and signs are there. In his book, *The Dream Culture of the Neanderthal*, Gooch strongly emphasizes that the sexual drive in Neons and their hybrid descendants was truly prodigious. Thus, we find that the name of Asmodeus roughly translates as the Lord of Lust. This creature, called a half-breed 'Cambion,' according to the Jewish Kabbalah lore, was the supposed offspring of the Bible's King David and a 'succubus,' whose name was Agrat bat Mahlat. In the Rabbinic literature of Yalḵuṭ Ḥadash, Asmodeus' mother was depicted as a 'roof-dancing' demon, who gyrated and performed wildly while Asmodeus' grandmother roared and howled from the ground, disturbing the desert nighttime silence, and the humans in their huts. While we might suspect only portions of this old tale to be possible, the scene still hints at another crossbreed hominid mating, somewhere in the distant past. Asmodeus, like a Neon remnant creature, was considered strong and powerful, and perhaps did force his way into relations with humans when his sex drive became overwhelming.

I Want You...I Want You So Bad, its driving me Mad.

I Want You; **The Beatles**

He was also rumored by some legends to be a satirical genius, and was said to have been quite revengeful against the human species in general. If so, one might expect the attitude of revenge to be based upon social ostracization, meaning unsightly hybrid-hominids were forced outside of the fences and gates of civilized living, created by more typical humans such as ourselves today. Perhaps a female creature, similar to our previously mentioned Zana, the red-haired Wild Woman, who mated with several human males and produced offspring, also mated with an ancient, primitive King, away from the city gates, in the dark caves of the eastern Levant, where Neanderthal bones have been found, alongside Cro-Magnon's fossils. The rest is, say, not mainstream history, but rather the stuff of legends. Over in nearby Arabia, the demon Asmodeus was known as a 'sakyr,' which we will take as a close approximation of 'satyr,' although scholars may not agree. We recall that satyr was also a basic physical description for the wise Socrates, by both himself and his fellow Greeks. Asmodeus was also referred to as the 'King of the Jinn' or Genies by those desert peoples. In the general legends concerning the sexual intercourse involving humans, succubus and/or incubus, it was commonly reported that deformed children were the resultant offspring; we might consider the crossbreed admixture of DNA to be the cause.

Since it is obvious, even without question, that a certain number of our distant ancestors had a larger Neon DNA percentage than ours, it seems possible, or even probable, that the stories of Asmodeus, King David, and Agrat, are really the faint remembrances of an ancient sexual experience, and perhaps not true legends at all. At least in the misty beginning, for an ugly, hairy baby later named Asmodeus. With the potential, dreary aspect of cross-hybrid mating resulting in deformed, or malformed children, we might consider that most of these young ones died, or that if they survived, their gross appearance was so dreadful that the human mother, or father, might have killed it, since the ancient Greeks, Arabs and other cultures were known to practice infanticide, perhaps for this, and other reasons. Thus, the fate of many a hybrid child was either stillborn death or miscarriage, or infanticide, or, if it was lucky, merely ostracized beyond humankind, to forever lurk in the nearby woods and caves. Somehow, Neon's DNA survived a torturous human world, thus we still carry 2–4% of Neanderthal DNA today.

Quasimodo, the Gentle Giant

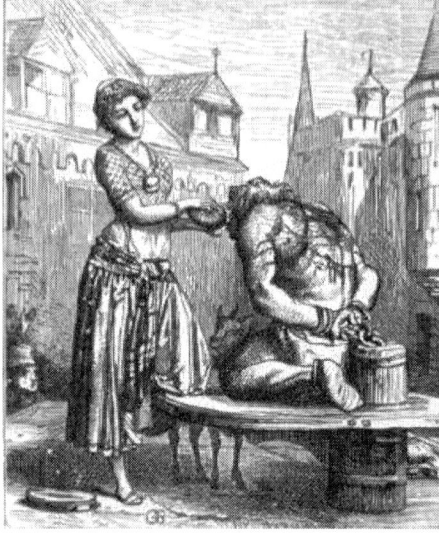

Esmeralda gives a drink to Quasimodo: Gustave Brion (1877) Public Domain

Hybrid humans are also found depicted in literature. One good example is the French Gothic novel by Victor Hugo, *The Hunchback of Notre Dame*, published in 1831. The plot depicts Notre Dame in the fourteenth century. Quasimodo, the gentle giant, is the main protagonist and is feared by the people around Notre Dame as a sort of monster. Found as an abandoned baby on the doorsteps of the huge cathedral, Quasimodo is depicted as being hideously deformed from birth, having only one good eye and is hunchbacked. Like Socrates and other hybrid-hominids, Quasimodo is bow-legged. He is taught by a kindly church father to ring the bells of the tower to earn his keep. So, in Victor Hugo's brilliant mind, in observing what he called a 'cusp of a relationship between two separate cultures,' he created a hybrid-monster who delivered the sweet sound of ringing bells to call the faithful to worship, yet those same maddening folk were his downfall, as they turned against an innocent, deformed, possibly slightly hybrid man, who was trying to defend a kind, beautiful woman,

Esmerelda, from the sexual ravages of the so-called priests of Notre Dame. The hunchback was a true hero in yet another story about a beauty and a beast. The entire plot was thought to be completely fiction, but researchers later found records that show, during Hugo's time, that there really was a hunchback at the huge religious site, and that he was actually a foreman in charge of restorations. Perhaps the sight of the hunchback working at his trade inspired certain portions of the novel. As for Esmerelda and the hunchback, Hugo posited, and perhaps thought, that kind *and* beautiful women, were . . . as rare as hunchbacks. She was his only love. Victor Hugo may not have considered the hunchbacks, both in his novel, and the one he saw at Notre Dame, as hybrid creatures, yet it is quite possible that they were, and not mere human deformities. Since we have 2–4% Neanderthal DNA in our bodies, someone in history, or in created fiction, such as Quasimodo, eventually has to be seen, or suspected, as having a greater crossbreed DNA mix than ourselves. In Victor Hugo's savvy view of human society, Quasimodo, the courageous heart beneath a grotesque exterior, was not a monster at all, rather it was the maddening crowd.

Merlin the Magician

The story of Merlin's unholy birth as told in Merlin. A prose version illumination by Jean Colombe (c. 1480–1485). Wiki: Public Domain

Most readers are vaguely familiar with the Welsh and Arthurian legends about Merlin the Magician, but like many iconic figures in history, Merlin's image has changed and sweetened over time, to where he is depicted, in modern days, as a wise, white, Welsh wizard, even handsome. This convenient portrayal, like the European depiction of Jesus Christ as an Anglo-Saxon, is another of history's lies, in recalling Voltaire's words.

So, just who was this enchanting fellow, this mysterious wizard, as he was called? The poignant answer is another shocker for the reader, for we find that Merlin too, if we just dig a bit deeper into our hybrid-hominin hypothesis . . . was a Wildman.

There' a Wildman-Wizard hiding in me, illuminating my Mind.

Taxi, **Harry Chapin**

The modern English name of Merlin is derived from the Welsh language, where our character was known as "Myrddin Wyllt," which translates as "Merlin the Wild." Another important name for Merlin, as strange as it seems, was "Merlin Ambrosius." Although many differing scholarly interpretations have been made of Merlin and King Arthur with his Knights of the Round Table, we will break new ground with an emerging hybrid-hominid view of a nearly forgotten Merlin.

This cave, below Tintagel Castle in Cornwall, is said to have been the birthplace and residence for Merlin the Magician, linked to the legend of King Arthur.
Credit Wikipedia ~ Public domain

The standard depiction of Merlin first appears in Geoffrey of Monmouth's Historia Regum Britanniae, written c. 1136. Geoffrey is thought to have created an amalgamated Merlin and based his writing upon previous historical and legendary figures, such as Myrddin Wyllt, and a 5th century Romano-British war leader with a curious name; Ambrosius Aurelianus. Thus, it is said, that Geoffrey's pen created the character known as Merlin Ambrosius, or Merlin Ambrose. But, is there a hidden pattern here, concealed in the naming conventions? And what of Merlin's relationship with King Arthur?

Merlin's strange, mysterious birth is also of interest to us here and segues into the strange names. Merlin's traditional biography casts him as a half-human, half-animal cambion, which, as we recall, was the exact, same description used by the Kabbalists to describe Asmodeus, the so-called Prince of Demons. One of Merlin's many titles was 'Son of the Devil.' Notice the phonetic similarities between Asmodeus and Ambrosius. Both the sound and meaning of these two words are nearly identical, which is usually sufficient to indicate an ancient link.

Merlin the baby; born rough and grisly

The birth of baby Merlin, in the partially true, clue-lending legends, was very unusual, if not extreme. The moment the infant was born he was *HOMO SAPIE* described as appearing 'rough and grisly,' so we can suspect a non-human child was delivered, perhaps carrying more Neanderthal DNA than the other peoples in Wales. There is always the possibility of cultural diffusion from the Middle East as well, as stories of cambions carried well as conversation upon the roads and campfires of early Europe and the Levant.

In the New Muse Series book, *The Vikings Secret Yoga – The Supreme Adventure,* it is revealed that a purposeful, poetic encryption concealed the true, hidden spiritual meaning of the Norse poems, known as the Poetic Edda.

Like the 10th century Poetic Edda, the various British literatures of Merlin and King Arthur, are also possibly encrypted, and may also be an admixture of both historical record, and allegorical story, as we shall see. Truth is always stranger than fiction . . . and our inaccurate historical stories.

Geoffrey of Monmouth often contradicted himself with differing portrayals of Merlin in his history of Britain and also in his strange, playful biography of the wizard; *Vita Merlina*. Thus, there are so many meaningful conflicts in Geoffrey's writings, as well as that of many other writers on Myrddin the Wild Man, and King Arthur, that we are reduced to considering only a few noteworthy items for our hybrid-hominid hypothesis. After being born 'rough and grisly,' Geoffrey often depicts

Merlin as being humpbacked, which we may suspect as a deformity of a mixed-breed parenting. So, the question begs: just who were the parents of the child born 'rough and grisly?' There are widely differing reports of Merlin's folks in the various Welsh and British myths. In one story, Myrddin the Wild is said to have had a father, Morvrn, who sired twins, and also having a daughter named Gwendydd. The other two parental 'explanations' are a closer match to our hybrid-hominid notion. Geoffrey states that Myriddin the Wildman was born without a father, meaning no one knows who the father was. In another writing, Myriddin is said to have had an insatiable incubus for his papa, who impregnated a mortal woman, and that the wizard gained both his mental powers and his madness from his non-human progenitor. Towards the end of his life, the maddened, or at least extremely different Myrddin, retreats into the forest caves, where he was born and raised. Finally, another hybrid-hominid hint lies in the story of King Arthur, who was said to have been born under the magic of Myrddin, who later became the young ruler's mentor. Arthur's father was, rather curiously, named Pendragon, which normally translates as 'Chief Dragon.' (Please consult Appendix 'The Human Dragons' for a more detailed account of humans-as-dragons.)

For now, let us consider that the English word for dragon derives from Old English and Old French, which stems from the earlier Greek 'drakon,' usually translated as 'dragon.'

EYESIGHT OR INSIGHT.

However, the word 'drakon' translates more correctly as 'I see,' or perhaps 'sharp-sighted one,' which may reflect the keen eyesight of the Neanderthal hybrids we have been discussing. Thus, the 'Chief Drakon,' as King Arthur's father, seems another hint from the pen of the old scribes, such as Geoffrey. Besides King Arthur, we have already witnessed how King Shennong was also the son of a dragon (drakon), and there are many more examples of the drakon-born in upcoming chapters. In returning to the curious name of Ambrosius Aurelianus, he was reported historically as a war hero of the Romano-British tribes, yet, eventually, given the misty myths of time, he was transformed into the uncle of King Arthur, the brother of Arthur's father Uther Pendragon. Thus, we have clues of both half-man-half-animal cambions and drakons being seen in these legends, and many other cloaked names.

135

If Ambrosius Aurelianus was a hybrid-hominid without deformities, he would likely have, perhaps like the fierce, overwhelming Getae tribes, greater speed, strength, and agility than a mere Sapiens warrior. This would help to explain his great feats in battle, as a war hero.

Merlin's many legends are often caught up in the mysterious Stonehenge monument, which is so famous as to not need introduction, yet incredibly we introduce here a suggestion that it was constructed in a way we don't currently understand, by our hybrid-hominid ancestors.
After a decisive battle against the powerful, invading Saxons, King Ambrosius-Aurelius decided to create a monument to the fallen. According to Geoffrey, the wizard Merlin, suggests that the King should create a stone circle like one in Ireland known as the 'Dance of the Giants.' We recall that Gooch insisted on portraying hybrid-hominids in various legends under anomalous names, such as giant, ogre, troll, etc. Thus, we can accept another clue from both Gooch and Geoffrey that hybrid humanity was indeed about, and perhaps danced in the stone circles that they constructed. Stonehenge is simply the largest and most impressive of the many stone circles in Britannia with cosmological implications as astronomical observatories.

In British elegies like "The Wanderer" such curious windswept piles of stones are referred to as "the old work of giants, standing abandoned." It is truly remarkable that the modern account of the construction of Stonehenge is reflected in Geoffrey of Monmouth's 12th century legendary history, which claimed the rocks of the Giant's Dance were foreign to Salisbury Plain, almost 900 years before modern science identified the source

Similar to Geoffrey's depictions, in the 12th century Norman literature called Roman De Brut, a French version of Merlin and Arthur's exploits are given. In the colorful manuscript, which contained images, King Arthur meets a *large-faced, red-haired giant* roasting a pig in the deep woods. Is this an old image of a hybrid-hominid, mere folklore, or a hint of both? The manuscript also contains the earliest known image of Stonehenge. The chronicle relates that King Ambrosius Aurelius desired to create a victory monument to the fallen British fighters killed by the invading Saxons. Thus, the King enlists a great number of men with various engineering and construction skills, but they are not capable of erecting anything deemed worthy of their fallen brothers. Merlin suggests they consider bringing a special set of stones, which were placed in a circle called 'The Dance of the Giants' from nearby Ireland, to use in the construction of the monument. King Ambrosius gives his blessing, and Merlin leads the British men to Ireland:

"Merlin, who was in their company,
led them to a mountain
where they found the dance of the giants,
which they had been searching for."

Roman de Brut

Once they arrived at Ireland's Dance of the Giants, the King's men struggle mightily trying to move the great stones, to take them to England to erect the monument to the dead Britons. When human effort fails, Merlin the Wise One, performs a levitation magic to allow them to be picked up and carried to the waiting ships. Merlin was known as the 'Enchanter,' which may infer that he was a sound-shaman, or a chanter of mysterious sounds. Since we are always dealing with the incredulous, and there are reports of Buddhist monks using sound-horns to move stones, in their own secret fashion, could Merlin and the Tibetans, and several other ancient groups not mentioned here due to space, be using an ancient knowledge of acoustic-levitation, which was only recently re-discovered by modern science? Merlin's brain, and vocal capabilities, were likely quite different from ours, if the clues in the legends hold true. Perhaps he was 15–25% Neanderthal, as a speculation. *LEAVE THE BRAIN OUT OF IT.*

Strangely akin to scenes previously observed in The Story of King Gilgamesh, an old British fable called 'Lailoken and Kentigern' depicts a Saint Kentigern who meets in a remote location, with a naked, hairy madman named Lailoken, who is said to be 'Merlynum' or Merlin. Lailoken declares that he has been condemned for his sins against humanity, to wander in the company of beasts.

Finally, as we depart from our focus on Myrddin, the Wizard-Wildman, who was said to be so helpful at Stonehenge, it's appropriate to note that, over 175,000 years ago, the Neanderthals were making stone rings, or circles, in the depths of their caves, using broken pieces of stalactites. Somehow, perhaps, these early Neon rings were a distant forebear of the great and mysterious Stonehenge itself, and other ancient stone monuments. There certainly are a lot of subtle hybrid-hominid clues lying about—both in the puzzling names, and in the ancient stones.

"Truth is stranger than fiction.

Literature is the faint remembrance of ancient experience."

Beowulf, Grendel, and the Dragons

In the ancient British Isles, there are tales in both England and Ireland that have stories that indicate the presence of hybrid creatures. The Irish Wildman, Cu-ChulainnDenisovan the Hound, is a good example, with his dark, matted hair, and extreme battle frenzy, and is sometimes described as a 'unrecognizable monster.'

As I was writing on hybrid ancestors (which we all have), my research led me to a related story, about a modern journalist, James Fallows, who was writing about the DNA of Neanderthals, and was informed by a genetic scientist that the writer himself had a whopping 5% Neanderthal DNA, a rather large anomaly. The journalist's story follows below, excerpted from his own article posted in TheAtlantic.com, where the DNA specialist is informing the journalist:

"You do have an abnormally high percentage Neanderthal component, and I wonder if that's connected to the unusual genetics of your mother. I see contact with Neanderthals as having been ephemeral and primarily a result of rape by Neanderthal males of AMH (anatomically modern human) women and that the locus of that interaction happened halfway up the Red Sea coast on the eastern shore. Your mother's DNA may be showing the most ancient European line still extant, isolated as it was in Scotland."

James Fallows then made a remarkable observation about himself, about which this author, Colin Wilson, and Stan Gooch would certainly agree:

"At 5% Neanderthal, you are an outlier, and perhaps it's time to reconsider Beowulf's Grendel and the implications of that story on our genetics. It makes no sense for a cold adapted animal, like Neanderthals, to be naked. I think they were heavily furred, and the stories of yetis, sasquatch, snowmen, and Grendel (and Gilgamesh's Huwawa also), are ancient memories, passed on in the oral tradition, of a time when we shared the earth with furry hominids.

THE GENETICS HOWEVER DO NOT INFLUENCE THE "HUMAN" GREAT HUMANS ARE "WISE" HOMO SAPIEN WISE HUMANS

139

My thought has been that we only interbred with Neanderthals (or more accurately, Neanderthal-AMH hybrids) only once, soon after the exodus from Africa, when the aboriginal population was very small so that Neanderthal genes could be spread among all descendants. There was an AMH population living with Neanderthals in the Levant as early as 90,000 years ago, who are not ancestral to us, but who could have spread Neanderthal genes to us."

James Fallows is likely correct about Grendel the Monster in the legend of Beowulf. There are several noteworthy clues that indicate we can treat the story as part-fiction, with hints of evidence for our hybrid-hominid hypothesis.

A thousand years ago, when anonymous Viking authors were compiling spiritual secrets into their mysterious Poetic Edda (See New Muse Book: *The Vikings Secret Yoga – The Supreme Adventure*), anonymous Anglo-Saxon poets were assembling one of the greatest pieces of Old English literature: The Legend of Beowulf.

The curious myth is set in Scandinavia, where Beowulf is an extremely strong hero of the tribal Geats, who are likely related to the strong, red-haired *Getae* folk mentioned earlier, as a likely hybrid-hominid group, with perhaps 8–15% Neanderthal DNA. The long meandering plot, which is engulfed with poetic aggrandizement and symbolism, also contains a hidden encryption. Beowulf, while likely a strong Prince, is exaggerated to have the 'strength of thirty men.' The poetic legend is peppered with such exaggerations, yet there are many interesting hybrid-hominid clues in this tale, as seen below in the English translation by Strafford Riggs (1901–1968), in 1933.

~!~

The Beowulf Saga

ONCE upon a time, in the far north of what is now called Europe, there was a kingdom known as Geatsland, and its ruler was named Hygelac. It was a harsh country, with high mountains and narrow valleys, and it had

*a long seacoast with many harbors and inlets, and the men who lived
there were famous for their bravery, on both sea and land.
Like their neighbors the Danes and the Frisians, the Geats were warlike,
and for the greater part of every year Hygelac and his warriors were
engaged in fierce battles with various tribes, who would enter the
territory of the Geats, to steal cattle and lay waste the fields of grain, and
burn the farms of his retainers. There were other foes, too, to be dealt
with. The great caves along the coast were inhabited by all manner of evil
monsters that lived partly in the sea and partly upon the land, huge
serpents with scales of brass, that patrolled the coast and devoured
fishermen when they could be taken by surprise at their nets.*

*In Geatsland were vast forests where loathsome beasts made their homes
in the hollow trunks of dead trees and prowled only by night, feeding
upon sleeping pigs and young rabbits and other innocent animals. It was
not safe to travel in those woods after dark, and the wandering minstrels
who went from place to place in the countryside were careful not to be
caught in their ghostly depths.*

*But for the most part the sea-monsters and the forest terrors kept to their
own lairs and seldom invaded the more populous districts. Only when an
incautious farmer or fisherman had been foully killed by one of them did
the lords of Geatsland wage war upon the strange inhabitants of the
coastal caves and the forest fastnesses.*

*Now, for many years Hygelac ruled over his people with a stern but kind
hand. Beside him was his queen, named Hygd, and called the Wise and
Fair. About the king and queen were gathered the finest lords of the land.
All were valiant warriors whose courage had been tried in many battles.
They were tall like the trees of their forests, and broad like the stout
beams of their boats, and each man had the strength of ten. They were
yellow of hair; their eyes were deep-set and burned blue like the sea; on
their arms and around their necks were great circlets of beaten gold; and
upon their heads they wore helmets decorated with the horns of bulls or
the black wings of ravens. When they gathered in the great drinking-hall
of the King, the minstrels would come among them after they had eaten;*

*and with horns of ale passing from hand to hand, these lords of Geatsland would listen to songs of other lands and to news of the world which lay beyond their own frontiers. They heard the stirring story of Sigmund (Sigurd), that great hero; and learned how this king was warring with a terrible **dragon** that had destroyed a whole army of brave fighters."*

~!~

Moving forward into the lengthy saga, we find that Prince Beowulf and fourteen of his best fighters travel by sea, and come to the aid of Hrothgar, the King of the Danes, whose kingdom has come under attack by a monster known as Grendel. For twelve years, the hideous Grendel has systematically killed, and eaten, most of the young men in Hrothgar's kingdom. The very use of the description 'monster' may itself reflect upon a man-creature, or 'man-ster,' a hybrid man-beast. It's important to note that Grendel the Beast-Man was considered as being descended from the biblical Cain, whom we also depict in subsequent chapters as being a hybrid-hominid creature; believe it or not, as Mr. Ripley said. It's beginning to look like the myth-shrouded connection is true, and that we have been chaining together a long saga of monsters, philosophers, and saviors all the while. Monsters predate written history, and the academic study of the particular cultural notions expressed in a society's ideas of monsters is known as 'monstrophy,' or the study of monstrosities—yet this study has not yielded the pattern that is observed here in this book. Biblical and Jewish history provide evidence that Grendel's descent from Cain is just a small part of the descendants of the monsters and giants known as the Cain Tradition, although the curious list of creatures is too long to discuss here. This Jewish 'tradition,' is likely another confirmation of Stan Gooch's observations that hybrid-hominids, especially if they had a higher level of Neanderthal DNA, were often called trolls, giants, ogres, monsters, etc.

Grendel is also referred to as a 'sceadugenga'—a shadow walker, or night prowler. The monster was repeatedly described to be in the shroud of darkness, likely because he, like his mother, was hideous to look at, and normally stayed beyond the human village and its fences. Gooch considered that Neanderthals and their hybrid descendants were likely moon-loving, nocturnal creatures, such as Grendel's family, whereas Cro-Magnons, as early humans, moved about more freely during the day, under the rays of the sun.

Author-poet Seamus Heaney, in his translation of Beowulf, writes in lines 1351–1355 that Grendel is vaguely human in shape, though much larger:
... the other, warped

in the shape of a man, moves beyond the pale

bigger than any man, an unnatural birth

called Grendel by the country people

in former days.

Having an unnatural birth and being bigger and stronger than humans fits the pattern of our Neon hybrid-hominid understanding.

There are several (5) disputed references in the Legend of Beowulf that seem to refer to both Beowulf and Grendel as a 'āglǣca,' a word which can be interpreted as, strangely, either monster or hero and means 'strong, hard fighter.' Beowulf, whose name may be interpreted as 'bear-wolf,' is thus also indicated as a partial hybrid. As part of the northern Geats tribe, he may be possibly related to the strong, red-haired southern Thracian tribe of the Getae, which we previously observed. Thus, both Beowulf and Grendel may be implicated as having moderate to larger amounts of Neanderthal DNA than today's human. They are both āglǣca; tough warriors; Hero and Monster, as different forms of hybrid-hominid DNA expression.

In the British saga, like the biblical Cain before him, who attacked and killed Abel because he was overcome with joy at being chosen by the Lord, Grendel viciously attacks the King of the Danes and his men because they are engaged in a joyous pastime in their mead hall, singing and making merry. The loud sound of joy is too much for the unfortunate, maddened, creature.

Almost, but not quite human because of ancient crossbreed matings, Cain and Grendel, postulated as real creatures in ancient, misty history, may have terribly resented their awkward position beyond the outer fences of human society, and so resorted to violence, in their pained, deformed condition. Grendel both killed and devoured his foes, as an early implication of cannibalism in the small, hidden, hybrid-hominid colonies of history. Thus, the legend of Beowulf and Grendel can be seen as an intense, early form of social inequality, in an extremely raw form, based upon differences in DNA, and not necessarily skin color. This social imbalance and ostracization, is also likely in several other, if not all, of our hybrid creatures, as a primitive aspect of Colin Wilson's Outsider theme.

Paleo-anthropologists today, in evaluating Neanderthal fossilized teeth, recognize that a wide variety of diets existed—there were vegetarians, animal meat-eaters, omnivores, and likely a portion of them were cannibals; all four patterns are also seen in the history of Homo sapiens.

The Tales from The Wanderer

The unknown author of the Legend of Beowulf introduces the unfolding plot via a character known as 'The Wanderer,' who sings songs and wonderous tales, and then explains the dire plight of the Danes, terrorized by Grendel, the Monster.

The Beowulf Saga continues;

"My brothers," spoke the king, "there is among us this night one who has come a long way over the sea and the land. He brings, he says, a wondrous song for you to hear. It is long since we have had word from the North, and this man's harp is a sweet one. Sing to us, Wanderer, that we may have your news and your entertainment."
Then the minstrel came forward with his harp. He was a tall rugged man, with a beard streaked with gray. He had the air of one who had traveled long distances, and his blue eyes were wide and fixed like one used to watching the horizon of the wide world.

Around him was wrapped a cloak of deep blue, held together by a curious clasp of gold. Beowulf, noting the clasp, thought it resembled a coiled snake, for there were two green stones set in it which glittered. This man, Beowulf thought, has been in far-away places. He will chant us a good song.

Then the Wanderer (for so he was called) sat down upon a wooden stool, threw back the cloak from about his arms, and with long thin fingers struck the resounding strings of his harp. He sang in a sharp voice that was like the crying of birds on the gray sea, but there was a sweetness in it at the same time which held his hearers, and the lords of Geatsland leaned forward on their benches in eagerness to catch every word.

He sang of the vast and frozen North, where winter lay upon the land for many, many months, and men fought in the gloomy light of the night-burning sun.
He sang of endless forests stretching black and forbidding in a sea of snow; of mountains higher and bleaker than the highest mountains of Geatsland; of the strange and fearful demons that inhabited this ghostly region. He sang of dragons that had no blood in them, but which, when they fought in bitter combat among themselves, oozed a white liquid so cold that even the fir trees withered where it fell.

He sang of the limitless gray sea and the green-white icebergs floating treacherously, and of the sirens who lived in caves upon them, and whose bodies were clothed in blue fish scales and whose hair was swaying seaweed. He sang of the monsters of the deep, strange wormlike creatures with brazen heads and tails like the tails of serpents

Then the tune of the Wanderer changed. His voice fell to a lower note, and he sang of Hrothgar who was King of the Danes, that country not far from Geatsland, across the water.

He told a sad story of desolation and despair in Hrothgar's land, because of a beast which had struck mortal fear into the hearts of the lords of Daneland. For on one cruel night, twelve years before, there had come to

Heorot—which was the great drinking-hall of Hrothgar—a monster, part animal, part man, part bird. The lords of Daneland were sleeping soundly in Heorot, and the monster, who was called Grendel, had forced open the solid doors of the king's hall and carried away in their sleep thirty of the greatest earls of the Danes.

There had been lamentation throughout the land, and many were the attempts to slay Grendel, but none had succeeded. And Hrothgar and his councilors no longer dared to sleep in Heorot, since for twelve long years Grendel repeatedly visited the king's hall and wrought destruction there. Yet Heorot had been well built by Hrothgar and for twelve years it had withstood the monster's onslaught, but in those twelve long years the valiant young warriors of the king had not withstood so well the nightly visitations, and now the land was despoiled of its youthful strength, and there remained to the king only those fighters whose early vigor had long since passed, and Daneland had become a country of old men and defenseless women.

The Wanderer sang of the fear that was in the Heart of Hrothgar the King and in the hearts of all his vassals and retainers, of the sorrowing of the women who were the wives or mothers or sisters of the slain warriors. He told of Unferth, who was Hrothgar's beloved companion, and how Unferth had not once offered to meet Grendel in combat, because the fear in his breast was greater than his love for his master. And at this a scornful murmur ran through the company that listened, and the lords of Geatsland condemned Unferth for a black coward.

Now, all the while that the Wanderer was singing, Beowulf sat as one bewitched. Those about him paid no heed to his rapid breathing, and failed to notice the light that had sprung into his blue eyes.

He leaned forward upon the table, his arms folded under his still beardless chin, his eyes fixed upon the minstrel. Now and again he lifted his head and shook out the fair hair that hung beneath the golden band encircling his wide white forehead. The huge bracelets that weighted his wrists gleamed like his eyes, and the jeweled collar about his throat was tight because of the swelling veins of his neck. The thoughts that ran through his head were confused, but one idea held sway over all others. He would seek out this monster Grendel and slay him—yes! Slay him with bare hands, these very hands that gripped each other now upon the table until they showed white beneath the pressure of the fingers. His muscles under the armlets of beaten gold rippled like water ruffled by a breeze. He saw himself face to face with the monster Grendel, and suddenly a wild cry broke from his lips and he leaped from his seat. "Lords of Geatsland and Earls of Hygelac," he shouted, as the minstrel finished the song, "I am the son of Ecgtheow and of Hygelac's sister, and in olden times this Hrothgar was a war-brother of my father. Therefore, I claim kinship to him, and I will go to the land of the Danes and serve their king. **I will slay this Grendel***!"*

~!~

The scene ends with the Geats mead hall erupting into chaos; everyone is shocked at the young upstart's bravado. The King commends Beowulf, again stating that his nephew has the strength of thirty men, but also, that if he doesn't kill Grendel, he must never return to the land of the Geats, and so the medieval stage is set for a huge do-or-die monstrous conflict.

The First and Second Battles:

In the Legend of Beowulf, the Getae hero has three primary battles, all of which are extremely revealing to our hybrid creature theory, as each battle of Beowulf's is against a crossbred human. After traveling to the land of the Danes by sea, accompanied by fourteen of his best earls, Prince Beowulf is greeted by a Guardian of the Beach.

~!~

The Beowulf Saga continues:

"Welcome, O Beowulf, to these sad shores," the Guardian cried. "Our king will better receive you than it is in my poor power to do. Leave your ship in my care. I will see that no harm comes to it. But I dread beholding such a fine company of young men coming on this fell business. For the fiend Grendel, who has robbed Hrothgar of his rightful estate, and destroyed so many proud young warriors of our kingdom, is terrible beyond words to describe." But Beowulf cut his discourse short and begged the Guardian of the Beach to direct them to the hall of Hrothgar, that they might make themselves known to the king, and rest themselves after their long, tiring day at sea. Then the old man took them a little way into the forest, and pointed out a path to follow, and bade them farewell. And Beowulf and his earls set out at last upon their great adventure in the land of the Danes."

~!~

The Geatan group of warriors treks for hours through swampland and finally arrive at Heorot, the Dane King's great mead hall, where Grendel has often been known to attack. The Geatans are met cordially by an aged King Hrothgar, and a group of elderly, white-haired, warriors, in full battle armor. Beowulf quickly assesses the situation; all of the young men are dead—eaten by Grendel. After their long journey, the Geatan warriors rested, and then a great banquet was held in Heorot, for the first time in twelve years, since the monster Grendel had begun his terror.

The Beowulf Saga continues:

"The tables were spread with viands such as warriors crave and there was much mead in great cups. The drinking-horns were passed from hand to hand, and many healths were drunk that evening to Beowulf and his earls, and many cups were raised to the destruction of Grendel. Beowulf sat in the place of honor at Hrothgar's feet. He was clothed in scarlet and gold, with gold bracelets upon his mighty arms, a golden wire necklet of

his king's giving about his throat. To his right sat Aescher, the close companion and trusted counselor of Hrothgar. He wore a blue mantle over his broad shoulders and costly jewels glinted on his breast.

On Beowulf's left was **Unferth**, the king's favorite, of whom the Wanderer had sung in no uncertain terms concerning his lack of bravery. He was lean and black of hair, with a black divided beard, and he was dressed from head to foot in black and silver.

Aescher leaned toward Beowulf and engaged him in deep converse, enjoying his company, and praising him for his valor. But Unferth, the black son of Ecglaf, sat moody in his place, **scarcely touching the meats before him, and drinking only lightly of the mead** as it was passed to him.

A gloom hung over the vast hall, and only the noble lords of Geatsland were gay in that sad company. They talked a great deal, and praised everything about them, especially the hall of Heorot with its gold-bright roof, a hall larger and more magnificent than anything they had ever seen before.

Then they fell to boasting of their leader Beowulf and spoke pridefully of his strength and virtue. In this they were upheld by Aescher, who had heard of Beowulf's feats of strength. And while they talked and toasted one another in the bright ale, Unferth the Black lapsed more and more into sullen silence, and offered no word of praise to Beowulf, and never once lifted his beaker to the lord of Geatsland.

Beowulf noticed this presently, and turning to Unferth said, "You are very silent, O valiant son of Ecglaf. Come, let us hear your deeds of valor, that we may in turn praise you. Speak, friend Unferth, that I may drink from your cup with you."

Then Unferth, the son of Ecglaf, rose in his place, and his look was blacker than the night which hung over the land of the Danes. The torches *flaming against the walls flickered on his cheeks, which were paler than the cheeks of a dead man.*

"Beowulf!" he cried, and there was scornful anger in his tones, "Beowulf! Look you, my noble earls of Daneland, at this stripling who comes so proudly among us, saying that he will deliver us from Grendel's toils and spells!

"Who is this boy, beardless and white of skin, that he should come over the sea-fields in a boat with his fourteen thanes? Where are his vaunted courage and strength, I ask?"

~!~

The disruptive scene ends with Beowulf and Unferth exchanging stinging insults; the Danish King steps in to make peace in the mead hall, and a final toast to the fifteen Geatan heroes is made. Then the King and his entourage quickly leave Heorot, and the young warriors are left to their own wares, bedding down in the dark night, waiting uneasily for Grendel to arrive, as The Beowulf Saga moves forward, towards the first battle:

"THE fires were burnt out on the hearths when the last of Hrothgar's train had departed. Then Beowulf and his companions set themselves to fastening tightly the door of the hall. They secured it with wooden bolts and tied it with leathern thongs, and so strong was it that no mortal could have passed through. Then the warriors of Geatsland unfolded their cloaks upon the benches and laid themselves down to slumber, and Beowulf stretched his great length upon the dais of the king and resolved that through the long night he would never once close his eyes. Near the door lay the young Hondscio, Beowulf's favorite earl, who swore that if any one broke through the door of Heorot he would be the first to give the intruder battle. Silence crept over the shrouded forms where they lay upon the floor and benches, and there was no sound save their steady breathing and the faint sighing of the night-wind in the trees about the hall. Beowulf, upon his couch, lay still as death, but his eyes moved here

150

*and there in the deepening gloom of the hall, and his breast rose and fell
evenly with his breathing. Outside, a fog was creeping up from the sea,
obscuring the moon in milky eclipse, and at last there was not even the
sound of the wind in the trees. To Beowulf the deep silence seemed full of
moving things invisible to human eyes. Gradually there came over him a
kind of drowsiness that he fought to ward off. His eyelids fluttered against
his eyes, and then he swooned with a sleep that lay upon his weary limbs
like a heavy garment. And the fog thickened and wound itself about the
vast mead-hall in thick veils of damp gloom. The moon faded in the fog's
depth, and the trees dripped with moisture, and the sound of this dripping
was the only sound that came through the night. But suddenly there was a
rustling among the wet trees, and a noise like the deep grunt of a pig, but
soft and low, startled the fog-bound night, and the drops of mist-water on
the trees fell sharply to the ground like heavy rain. Then the fog parted
evenly, and in the wide path it made through the night a Shadow loomed
gigantic in all that was left of moonlight. Slowly, slowly it neared the
great hall of Heorot, and the night shuddered at its coming, and behind it,
as it moved, the fog closed again with a sucking sound. And the Shadow
stood before the great door of the hall, and swayed hideously in the
ghastly light. Within Heorot there was a deep stillness, and Beowulf and
the Geatish earls slept soundly, with no knowledge of what stood so evilly
beyond the door. For the monstrous Shadow was the fiend Grendel and
standing there in the fog-strewn night he placed a spell upon those who
slept in Heorot, and the spell he wove was a spell to make sleep more
soundly those who already slept. But Beowulf hung between sleeping and
waking, and while the spell did not completely deaden his senses, it so
ensnared his waking dream that he fought desperately against it in his
half-sleep and was not quite overpowered. This Grendel did not know as
he placed his great shoulder to the door of Heorot, while Beowulf on his
couch tossed in the nightmare that possessed him. Little by little the
thongs that secured the door gave way, and the huge wooden bolts
yielded under the pressure that was strained against them, but no sound
broke upon the silent struggle that went on between Grendel and the
door. Beowulf tossed and turned in waking, but the other earls of*

151

Geatsland fell deeper and deeper into the swooning sleep.

Then with a rush, the door flew wide, and the fog and salt-smelling night swept in and filled Heorot with strange odors. And in the doorway, swaying this way and that, stood Grendel, huge and dark against the dark night, the fog weaving about him in white veils, and the door of the hall limp on its hinges.

*And Beowulf came out of his dream-spell and saw what stood so vast and evil in the doorway. But his eyes were heavy with the spell that clung to him as the wisps of fog clung about the body of Grendel, and only slowly was he able to distinguish the monster. Through his nightmare, now, there came the sense of what had befallen him, and he strove to cast the last remnant of the magic from him as he saw the great form of Grendel swoop down upon the innocent form of young Hondscio, catch him up in enormous hands, and tear him limb from sleeping limb. And Beowulf struggled, and on the earthen floor of Heorot Grendel swayed with his prey. And now at last Beowulf saw what manner of thing this Grendel was. His legs were like the trunks of trees and they were covered with a kind of **gray dry scale that made a noise like paper** as the fiend moved this way and that. The body of the beast was shaped like that of a man, but such a man as no mortal eyes had ever before beheld, and the size and shape of it were something to be marveled at.*

*The head was the head neither of beast or man, yet had something of the features of both, and the great jaw was filled with blunt fangs that ground the bones of the unhappy Hondscio to pulp. Shaggy matted hair hung over the low forehead, and the eyes in the face of Grendel were the **color of milk**. Horror-struck upon his couch, Beowulf felt his limbs in thrall and could move neither leg nor arm to raise himself as Grendel devoured the body of the young Hondscio. And when Grendel had finished his horrid meal, the beast straightened a little his vast form and looked now to the left, now to the right, until his gaze fell upon the length of Beowulf. Then the milk-white eyes burned with a dull light that was like the light of the moon, and slowly, slowly Grendel moved toward the dais. But Beowulf, stung with loathing, leaped from his bed. Silently they fought in the fog-*

152

strewn hall of Heorot. Silently their bodies twisted and bent, this way and that, and Beowulf kept Grendel's huge hands with their long claws of sharp bone from him, and Grendel in turn sought to tear apart the quick body that slipped so easily through his arms and legs.

All about them lay the sleeping earls, and not one moved in the deep magic of his slumber as the two fought that silent fight. Their bodies wove in and out among the sleepers, and Beowulf felt the hot reek of Grendel's breath upon his cheek, and the sweat stood out on Beowulf's broad brow and ran down into his eyes and blinded him. And Grendel's huge hands sought over and over again to clasp his opponent's head, to crush it in their iron grip. Then the fight became a deadly struggle in one far corner of the hall, and neither one gained any advantage over the other. Then Beowulf slipped. On the earthen floor of Heorot they fell together, and the force of their fall made the earth tremble, as when two giants fight in mortal combat. But Grendel's hold lessened, and fear smote the heart of the fiend. He strove only to free himself from Beowulf's grasp and flee into the night, away from this white youth whose strength was the strength of thirty men. And now Beowulf had the upper hand, and flew at the giant's throat. But here his hands clutched at thick scales upon which he could get no grip. Grendel nearly took the advantage, but before he could seize Beowulf, the lord of Geatsland had fastened both mighty hands upon the monster's arm, and with a sudden twist that forced a groan of agony from Grendel's lips, leaped behind him, forcing the imprisoned arm high up Grendel's back, and the beast fell prone on the floor. Now came the final struggle, and sweat poured from Beowulf, while from Grendel there oozed a slimy sap that smelled like vinegar, and sickened Beowulf. But he clung to the monster's arm, and slowly, slowly he felt its great muscles and sinews give way, and as his foot found Grendel's neck, he prayed to all the gods for help, and called upon his father, 'Ecgtheow' for strength to sustain him in this desperate effort. And the mighty arm of Grendel gave way in the terrible hands of Beowulf, and, with a piercing shriek that shook the gilded rafters of Heorot, Grendel stumbled forward, leaving in Beowulf's hands the gory arm. At that very moment the spell that lay upon

153

*the sleeping warriors of Geatsland was broken, and the thirteen
remaining earls struggled, as Beowulf had lately struggled, with the
nightmare that was in their eyes, and swam out of sleep into waking.
Beowulf fell back upon the dais, the bleeding arm of Grendel in his hands.
And Grendel, with a prolonged and ghastly wail, his blunt fangs gnashing
together in dumb fury, stumbled toward the door, and before Beowulf
could recover, the fiend was away into the fog which swallowed him as
surely and completely as though he had plunged into the everlasting sea.
And Beowulf, his magic-dazed companions crowding and babbling
behind him in the doorway of Heorot, looked out into the fog-wet night,
and the only sound that came to their dulled ears was the steady drip,
drip, drip of the mist from the black trees."*

~!~

The scene of the gory first battle ends with the Geat warriors hoisting
Grendel's great, hairy arm from the branches of the Hall's great tree,
hanging it for all to see; the monster had been defeated. The Danish
people arrive, along with the King and Queen, and are delirious with joy,
but happiness is short-lived. The Mother of Grendel, enraged at the grave
mauling of her son, launches her own lethal attack upon the Danes, killing
and eating Aescher, one of the King's favorite earls, who had recently
befriended Beowulf at the Mead Hall.

Beowulf sets out once again to kill a monster; he and his companions
track the hideous Mother of Grendel to a large lake, where, in the
embellished story line, Beowulf goes below the deep lake to do battle
with the female demon, where she has a cave, complete with a fire-
burning hearth. Is it possible, in an ancient and dim, misty reality, that a
hybrid creature once lived behind a waterfall of such a lake, in a small
cave recess, completely hidden from human view, where no one ever
went, and the legend of a demon living below the deep lake was simply a
bit of sprouted folklore, along with her Medusa-like hair of snakes?
Once deep below the lake (or under the waterfall) Beowulf is ambushed
by Grendel's mother, as The Beowulf Saga proceeds to describe the

hero's great second battle:

*"Her great **claw-fingers** sank into his flesh, his skin crept with the sickening touch of her, and they struggled there at the bottom of the world, in a cave under the water, and the great heart of Beowulf smothered him in his breast with a fear that was like nothing he had ever felt. Sweat poured from him, his legs melted under him like wax, there was a spell upon him that drained him of all strength.*

He managed to draw his sword, Hrunting, but so protected by magic was that mother of Grendel that try as he would Hrunting would not pierce her body and at last clattered to the floor from his numb hand. The fiend twisted this way and that, and with each twist the horrible hands reached nearer and nearer to his throat, and he grew weaker and weaker, and shorter and faster came his stifled breath. He managed to lock his leg round one of the monster's, and then with all his fast-fleeing strength he seized the hag and threw her. But in falling she fell upon him, and now the loathsome, grinning jaws were close above his face, and the sharp claws found his throat. But for a moment, the smallest moment in the world, she relaxed her hold, so sure was she of her prey, and in that little moment the magic was lifted, and Beowulf with a great cry hurled her from him. Once more on his feet, he staggered to the wall of the cave, and found, suddenly, in his grasp, the hilt of an old sword which was driven deep into the wall. But the fiend was on him again now with a strangled cry of terror. Beowulf clutched the old sword with both hands, and with a great heave drew it from the wall, and so great was the force of the blow he struck Grendel's mother that he cut clean through her body."

A brief commentary on the first and second hybrid battles

Grendel and his dear mother, whose body was severely bent over with a serious hunchback, since, if truly crossbreeds, likely had a plethora of deformities and ailments. Grendel's 'milky white eyes' could be a sign of serious ocular ailments; humans today can develop milky-eyes from a variety of serious untreated medical causes. The half-monster's 'claws of

155

bone,' may really have been large, thick, gross, misshapen, uncut fingernails, which may appear as bone during a fight, and/or the 'claws' were embellished or misreported in legend. Long hardened fingernails might appear as nails of bone and be nearly as lethal. When Beowulf attacked Grendel and later his mother, he found that they were covered with protective armor, where daggers and swords would not pierce the monsters. These statements may not be totally myth, for today, in the subarctic regions, the tribal folks still use stiff moose hides, and other thick, layered leathers, as a natural body armor. They cut the tough hide into thick plates to cover the legs, body and neck, which are quite capable of stopping arrows and stabbing instruments, so this part of the highly embellished legend may have a hint of truth hidden underneath the fabrication. These would be the 'smooth, gliding plates,' placed upon the stout legs, that made a noise like paper, as the beast Grendel walked into the hall.

Dark Unferth

There is a hint of a subplot in Beowulf, concerning the dark Unferth, who is considered a coward for never offering to fight Grendel. Every other able-bodied Danish earl has bravely offered . . . and died. But is cowardice and fear really the black Unferth's motivation? In the mead hall before the battle with Grendel, the anonymous author of the Beowulf epic writes into the plot that, during the heavy Geatan and Danish drinking and feasting in the hall of Heorot, Unferth the Dark One barely touched his meal and drink, and perhaps not at all. Later, after the heavy partying, the Danes leave, and the Geat earls fall into a strangely deep slumber, much deeper than normal. Why? Then, when Grendel silently approaches and breaks down the door, only Beowulf is partially awake, staring in horror as Grendel approaches while the others sleep on. This is no mere drunken hangover from the feast; the Prince is paralyzed, unable to move his arms and legs, and watches his favorite warrior killed and eaten by the monster.

Now, the hidden scribe of the tale informs us that Grendel himself *'cast a spell,'* but this may be embellishment, or an intended ruse by the unknown scribe, as is discussed later.

Beowulf overcomes the hybrid by grabbing Grendel's great arm, and then placing his strong boots against the neck and trunk of Grendel, while the ogre is prone and accosted by Beowulf's men, who have since awoken. With a superior man's strength, as such is reputed for Beowulf, it is entirely possible, somewhere in the remote past, that a man and his companion actually did fight an overwhelming crossbreed . . . and really did rip its arm off, when knives and daggers didn't penetrate the 'skin,' which we consider is really a leathery armor plate, as suggested earlier. In the mead hall, before the beginning of the first battle, Unferth alone, tries to sway the Danes into rejecting Beowulf and his company, as unsuitable fighters. There may be another hidden motivation here. Later, after Grendel is mortally wounded, and Beowulf prepares to attack Grendel's mum, Unferth mumbles an apology to Beowulf and, in apparent goodwill, gives him his own sword, seemingly a strong weapon, to kill the female monster. When Beowulf and Grendel's mum square off in a ferocious back and forth battle, Unferth's sword breaks easily and proves worthless. Beowulf only succeeds by luckily finding another kingly sword in the dank cave, and it cuts entirely though the female ogre, slicing her in half. So, the suspicion here is that the author of the Beowulf tale purposely placed a hidden plot inside the outer tale. Consider the clues associated with Unferth;

1: Being a coward and never fighting Grendel; perhaps he wasn't afraid but secretly concerned for the beast. If so, why?

2: Insulting the new fighters; trying to get them to go away.

3: Not drinking or eating at the meal, perhaps because the mead is drugged. The Beowulf author purposely points this out, as a clue. Why?

4: Cannily giving a sword to Beowulf, perhaps knowing it won't work and that he will be killed as a result by the female hybrid.

The Father of Grendel?

Looking at these little clues, laced together, one can construct a view that leans towards Unferth not being cowardly, but actually being secretively sympathetic towards the hideous monster. If so, why? A strange explanation could be given that Unferth the Dark One once 'bumped hips' with Grendel's young mum, somewhere in a dark cave, like so many other hybrid, near-bestial stories we have seen . . . and the rest is untold, forgotten history, hiding in a riotous chorus of embellishments, created by the anonymous bard, for purposes of his own, as he silently winked at his readers. Unferth may have been the human father of Grendel, or we can just, yawn, and accept an old fable as merely a child's tale. But, was it? In the legend, before Beowulf's arrival, Grendel is said to have killed thirty men at a time, and perhaps killed many thousands in toto. Killing thirty men in one fell swoop also suggests that the brave men were drugged, as we have seen, and taken away one by one, back to the creature's lair, which likely existed in remote, untold history, and stacked the bodies like cordwood meals, for his later dinners. Given what we have seen, if Grendel had encountered thirty warriors at once, he would likely have been quickly defeated, so drugging and human support are possible reasons his murderous, macabre campaigns were so successful. He was simply being fed human food and being assisted by his human father, Unferth, in our speculation, since everyone, of a necessity must have a father. So, in our hybrid-humanity hypothesis, Grendel, along with his mother, are both DNA outcasts from the 'cleaner' social order. This situation, we shall see, is also repeated in the upcoming chapter involving Cain, the third 'human.'

The saga of the Geat King may have had some representation in truth, beyond merely being scary tales for children, which Beowulf has become, in our modern age.

Victorious, Beowulf and his happy troupe of earls return home to Geatland (Götaland in modern Sweden). The Prince later becomes King of the Geats, because of his feats, and a long peace reigns in the Geat kingdom. However, after a period of fifty years has passed, reports of a large dragon terrorizing the countryside require an aging Beowulf to arise and enter into his third and final battle, with yet another hybrid-hominid.

The Third Battle: Enter the Dragon

The Beowulf Saga continues, with Beowulf encountering his fiercest foe; a legendary, fire-breathing dragon, or was it something else? The Beowulf Saga continues. ..

~!~

"ONE night, when the winter was at its deepest, and the king sat in his mead-hall with all his lords about him, there came a knocking at the door. When the servants opened to the knocking, there entered the shabbiest visitor that had ever crossed that noble threshold.

The servants would have thrown the stranger out again, so disgraceful was his attire, had not Wiglaf, son of Weohstan, called to them to let the visitor remain, for there was something in the man's face that caught the earl's interest.

"Who are you?" demanded Wiglaf. "Whence come you? Speak, and do not fear, for no one will harm you. I see your knees shaking with fright and cold, and your eyes are wild with want of sleep and strange things that you have seen. Come and eat, my good man, and then you shall tell your story to the king."

But the stranger made a sign with his head that Wiglaf took for a denial, and so led him, a little roughly, before Beowulf.

"This fellow," the noble Wiglaf said, "will not say his name or whence he comes. But to you, my dear lord, he will speak, I know."

Then Beowulf bent on him his kindly-strong gaze and bade the visitor have no fear. The man fell on his knees before the king and spoke in a high voice:

"Great king, I have no name and am but a poor escaped slave from a Frankish galley, and I am seeking my own home in the Northland. Early this morning, faint from cold and hunger and want of rest, I came upon a deep barrow in which I discovered, sleeping, the hugest dragon, surely, in all the wide world. At first, I was so overcome with fear that I fled from the place. But after a while, when I got back my breath, I was taken with a burning curiosity, and when my hair had lain down again upon my head, I returned, and there I saw, heaped round and about the sleeping dragon, the lordliest treasure that ever man beheld in one place together. Gold and jewels"—the slave raised his arms high and wide—*"so much that twenty cart-loads would make no diminishment that the eye could see."*

Beowulf leaned forward in his great chair, his vast hands gripping the carven arms. "Slave," he cried in a loud voice, "if you lie, I will have you first beaten like a dog and then torn limb from limb until you are dead!" But the stranger did not flinch under the blue fire of the king's glance. Instead, he drew from beneath his tattered cloak a wondrous jeweled cup, set about with a hundred brilliants of all the rainbow's colors, and standing upon a base of purest gold, most delicately carved. "Lord," he replied simply, "I do not lie."
The court crowded about, better to see this marvel of workmanship and worth. Beowulf handled it lovingly and held it to the firelight. But at this point the escaped slave was seen to totter in a faint and quickly he was led away to be given food and warm clothes and a bench to lie upon. Then Beowulf the king stood up in his place and said to the assembled company:

"My friends, you have heard this man's tale, and you see that he is no idle spinner of yarns who would obtain food and shelter on a bitter winter's night, for he has shown us this wondrous cup of gold and jewels. Surely there is no fairer goblet on earth, and this slave says that whence this came there is more and still more treasure. My comrades, eleven men I want, who will follow me to the foul dragon's lair. This grave menace must be destroyed before he wakens and finds that he has been discovered and plundered. Eleven of you, then, to my side. There will be deeds of bravery for all, and of treasure more than each man can dream."

160

Then Wiglaf, the son of Weohstan, the best beloved of Beowulf's earls, stepped forward, but as he opened his lips to swear allegiance to his king, the night was shattered by a roar that shook the roof of the hall and made the earth tremble underfoot.

The warriors, having laid aside their armor and swords, rushed to secure the door, but as confusion spread among them and women screamed, the roar persisted in its clangor and at the entrance door blue flames began to lick along the sill. Then Beowulf cried in a loud voice to the court that they must escape from the monster until they could assume their weapons and armor, and secure the women against the hot anger of the furious dragon. So, in orderly manner, the company followed their king through a back way, leaving the vast hall in emptiness, the benches overturned, the fire on the hearths burning low."

~!~

We can pause here and notice that, thus far, the unseen dragon has only roared and breathed fire under the doorway, and not flown in the sky as is commonly seen in the media portrayals today. This dragon has his feet on the ground, as we shall see. The King plots his next strategy, as The Beowulf Saga continues:

"DAWN came slowly over the snows lying heavy about the house of Wiglaf, and the wife of Beowulf's favorite earl was ordering her servants in their early tasks when Wiglaf burst in upon the family hearth. His face was drawn with rage and fear, and he embraced his wife with such impetuousness that the good lady became instantly consumed with the darkest of thoughts and forebodings.

"My lord," she cried, "what dread errand brings you hither at this hour from the king? Speak! Some disaster has befallen the world, that you should look so distraught."

And she hastened to relieve him of his great cloak. But he put her away from him, and cried out in anguish: "Dear lady, gather together all that

161

*we have of value which the servants can carry upon swift horses, for this
night a dragon, the vastest dragon in all the world, has come upon our
Geatsland, and even as I speak pursues his hideous way across the snow
toward this our home. Already the mead-hall of the king is naught but a
heap of smoldering ashes, and the granaries and storehouses of our
people are hiding the sun from the world with the smoke of their burning.
Make haste, I pray you, my lady, and fetch me the biggest of my swords
and the stoutest of my armor. Then get you gone to the caves by the
Whale's Headland while we pursue this hellish demon to his lair.*

*"I go at once to my king. There is such death and destruction abroad this
morn as never man has beheld, and the ruins of our fairest farms and
halls are dotting the white land with sorrow and woeful suffering."*

*Then Wiglaf's wife brought him his great broadsword and his stoutest
armor and embraced him tenderly ere he strode to the door.*

*Even now the sky was brown with dense smoke, and a vast and sinister
rumbling was heard upon the air, proclaiming the steady and awful
approach of the dragon. Gathered together in the depths of the great
forest, Beowulf and his band of eleven trusted warriors held a council of
war.
There arose a warm debate concerning how the dragon should be fought.
Some thought they should attempt to slay him while he wrought
destruction. Others, again, would lure him, if possible, to a high cliff, and
force him into the boiling sea below. Yet others were in favor of letting
him wreak his vengeance at will upon the countryside until such time
should come when, sated in his lust for killing, he might fall into an
exhausted sleep and become fair game for their sharp swords.
Then Beowulf spoke:*

*"My lords, each of these three plans has excellent reasons for pursuing it.
But it is my opinion that none of them is sufficient for our dear purpose.
For, in the first instance, if we attack the dragon while he is yet roaring
through the land, the creature will be able to retreat in any direction. In
the second instance, it is not likely that he will permit himself to be forced*

over a cliff into the sea, for by all tokens he is a wily dragon and the treasure is close to his heart. And in the third instance, we cannot permit him to continue his depredations throughout the countryside, and further impoverish our people. Therefore, hear you what I have to say: It is necessary that we track this vile enemy to his very lair, there to slay him. For when he finds that Beowulf and his noble earls are gone to his barrow, then will he leave our halls and farms and seek to defend his heart's treasure. Let us away forthwith, for soon enough will he discover our ruse."

And Beowulf was right, for, even as he spoke, the dragon, writhing his way from the desolation or the king's country, **was informed, by magic,** *of the plans that were being made for his destruction, and switching his scaly tail so that twenty stout trees fell at its movement, and snapping gigantic jaws in horrid rage, the creature hastened to protect that which he had guarded during three hundred years of sleepless vigilance. NIGHT was coming down when at last Beowulf and his eleven earls approached the dragon's barrow. It lay deep in a dark and gloomy forest, and the only light was the reflection of the dead day upon the ground-snow. The tall trees stood naked in their places, and all about hung a cold stillness which was broken only by the trampling of the adventurers upon the crunching snow. It was quite dark now, as they neared the spot, and through the dim night they beheld in the distance a reddish glow. Nearer they came, until, peering through the dense wood, they saw a broad clear space among the trees. At one side was an old burial-mound, and at its entrance there issued in hissing gusts the red steam of the dragon's hot breathing. All about the place, the snow was trampled by huge feet and the tree trunks were blackened and scorched. Then brave Beowulf drew his earls about him and said to them:*

"I go alone to engage this dragon. You shall remain here at the clearing's edge in readiness to stand by me in case I fail. For I am an old man now, and it comes to me, as in a dream, that this will be my last adventure, my final fight."

Then gripping his vast shield of iron surely in his left hand, and in his right the noble sword Naegling, Beowulf advanced to meet the dragon.

163

But his earls, all those trusted earls, save only that faithful and loving lord Wiglaf, were seized with a sudden fear, and fled away into the darkness of the night and the shelter of the encircling forests. King Beowulf did not see their fleeing, as his eyes were upon the mouth of the barrow, and his ears were dimmed by the noise of the dragon's breathing and the swish-swish of the angry body within the cave's fastness. Then Beowulf cried out in a ringing voice:

"Come out, O most foul fiend, for Beowulf, King of Geatsland, Prince of Weders, and son of great Ecgtheow, stands without and calls you to battle. Come out, I say, arch-dragon, and pit your vaunted strength against my strength, which is the greatest known in all this cold Northland!"
And Wiglaf, standing ready and alone at the circle's edge, laughed a clarion challenge to the dragon's undoing.

For a moment there was a death-like stillness in the night. No sound came from the cave, and no steamy breath, and no dull glare of fire. Then with sudden roaring that caused the night to splinter and the earth to quiver in horrified response, the lordliest dragon in all the world rushed from its lair.

Over ten ells in length it measured, from the proud head to the poisoned tail-tip, and its vast body was covered with **scales of brass as big as plates and thicker, each, than three fingers.** *Its forefeet were armed with* **six-inch claws of razor edge** *and helped support a* **head so large and terrible** *that Beowulf marveled for a moment at the size. Its* **eyes were of green fire**, *its wide* **nostrils belched red flame and steam**, *and the* **immense jaws dripped livid ooze** *as they snapped in hideous savagery. So great was the issuing heat that Beowulf held up his shield, else he would have perished upon the spot. Again, came a moment's pause while the two antagonists stood firm and eyed each other, each gaging his own strength and that of his adversary.*

Battle came upon them with the swiftness of lightning. The still forest was filled with the clamor of their combat. Beowulf slashed out bravely, but

164

his good sword Naegling glanced helplessly against the brazen scales of the dragon's armor, and so great was the heat of the creature's breath that Beowulf was forced to resort to cunning in an attempt both to wear out his enemy and keep himself from being burned to death.

*He wove this way and that, feinting now here, now there, until the dragon was so bewildered with this wonderful display of agility that his roaring grew louder and more terrible, and the violent swing of his huge body grew wider and wilder. **Trees fell to earth at the flick of his tail**, the snow melted beneath his breath, and his green eyes bit through the steam clouds of his breathing. And always Beowulf fought for the advantage of a well-placed thrust of his sword, for he knew that every dragon has its vulnerable spot, and this he sought to find.*

Back and forth over the hard ground they raged. Now the dragon seemed the victor and Beowulf spent and weakening—but only to renew his attack. And time stood still in the black night, and the stars in their courses stayed to watch this struggle of giants. Beowulf's breath came short and stifled, his arms grew weak from the weight of his great sword and shield, and this last grew so hot that it no longer served to protect him from the living furnace which he fought. His strong legs shook beneath him, and short cries were wrung from his throat. The encircling trees swam before his faltering eyes, the heavens seemed to close down upon him. Then at last to his aid came Wiglaf the faithful, and Beowulf's ears were gladdened by the sound of his dear friend's shout, and new strength streamed through his veins. Together they fought, side by side, and the dragon gave way to their onslaught.

*But in one wide **sweep of the dragon's tail** Beowulf was caught, and he sank to the ground broken, at last, in body. But Wiglaf, fresh in the fray, with a great cry of rage, found the **weak spot in the dragon's armor**, and into the heart of the beast sank his good sword to the hilt. No sound came from the dragon. But he rose to his full and terrible height in great majesty of dying and fell prone beside Beowulf. Then there went up a shout from the cowardly earls who had hidden in the forest to watch the* *fight in safety, and they crowded about their dying king. But Wiglaf drove them away, saying:*

"Away, wretches of faithlessness! Not for you the honors of a battle you feared to engage in. Away, cowards! Our king is done to death in a noble adventure, to save you and your foul breed from the dragon's wrath."

Then turning to Beowulf, he knelt at his side, took him dying into his arms, and loosened the helmet from his brow. "O my dear master," he cried over him, "leave us not in your hour of triumph!"

"Nay," answered Beowulf, "'tis not my triumph but that of a faithful friend, my Wiglaf. Take the treasure, do what you will with it. But . . . but let me have one piece of it about me as I die. For I die soon, my friend . . . so haste you . . . haste . . ."

Then Wiglaf went into the dragon's barrow and beheld there the greatest treasure, surely, in all the wide world. And he selected from the heaped-up gold and jewels a wondrous crown of glittering gems, and this he placed upon the brow of his king.

"I die," whispered Beowulf, "and I forgive those others—those foolish ones who deserted me in my hour. Farewell, good Wiglaf, my own true friend. Make a barrow for me upon the Whale's Headland. Farewell, and now I shall sleep . . . the longest sleep."

THUS, passed to his own gods Beowulf, King of Geatsland, in the North.

~!~

As he fought his drakon (dragon), Beowulf was astounded at the size of the creature's head; this would be a good match for the larger skull case of Neanderthals and their hybrid offspring.

And so, as The Beowulf Saga comes to a close, the Geats warriors dragged the great body of the dragon to a cliff, and pushed it off with a great shout, to flail and fall far below and become engulfed by white waves and the gray ocean depths. A great funeral pyre was held for King Beowulf, and his bravest warriors—first and foremost good and brave Wiglaf—marched around the dancing flames for the entire night, in their final farewell to their hero. Thus, ends the legend of Beowulf, Grendel and the Dragon, with commentary below.

What's all this Talk about Dragons?

A Commentary on Dragons and the Third Battle of Beowulf

In the Welsh saga, Beowulf is casually stated to have fought 'little dragons' in his youth, but no detail is given of their appearance or behavior. As we recall from the earlier chapter on the Shennong Clan, the English word 'dragon' was taken from the Greek, 'drakon,' which largely focuses on keen eyesight. Further below, we will explain the nature of a dragon's ability to fly, its armored body, and its curious ability to breathe fire. Let us quickly list the historical and legendary figures that are figured in our 'drakon' theory as hybrid-hominid:

In China, King Shennong was born of a mortal woman and a dragon (drakon) father.

In an upcoming chapter, we note that the founder of the clan of the Buddha and his family, was reputed to be the son of a male dragon (drakon) and a mortal woman, whereas Buddha himself was born of a mortal mother and a 'white-elephant' father, which also appears to be a hybrid-hominid, in disguise.

Merlin the Magician, or the Wildman called Myrddin Wyllt, was born 'without a father' or by an incubus-father, which we too may take as akin to a drakon. Merlin was considered a 'cambion,' or half-man and half-animal; the words cambion and dragon are somewhat similar phonetically, when slowly drawn out, as in a long-vowel chant:

Caaaaaaaaa-bion

Draaaaaaaaa-gon

These two words may have been slightly misinterpreted over the many migratory routes in Eurasia in past times, so we may consider them as one and the same, with similar meaning and sound.

Merlin was deeply linked to King Arthur, whose father was Pendragon (chief dragon), and whose uncle was also a Pendragon.

Today, in modern psychological terms, dragons are considered mythical fixations of the human mind. They are often depicted in Western media culture as being huge, flying, scale-covered, flame-throwing beasts. This portrayal, however, is entirely mythical. The stereotypical, public view of what makes a dragon must be totally dismantled, as it is an obstacle of itself in seeing a deeper truth. While the marvelous prehistoric Chinese story of King Shennong and the others having a dragon (drakon) for a father initially smacks of being totally myth, it turns out that there may be a way to understand how one's parents could be both human and dragon. As we recall, the early, nearly uncivilized humans were struck dumb with fear when they encountered an overwhelming foe. Anthropologist David E. Jones has revealed that belief in dragons was extremely widespread among ancient cultures because evolution slowly created an innate fear of predators in the human mind. Just as monkeys have been shown to exhibit a fear of snakes and large cats, Jones considers that the trait of fearing large predators such as pythons, large birds of prey, elephants, lions, bears, and other fearful animals, has been permanently imbedded in the subconscious mind of all Sapiens. In more recent times, he argues, these 'universal fears' have been frequently combined in folklore and created the myth of the dragon. Might we, like Gooch, include our large-eyed Neons and their hybrid offspring in the list of terrifying creatures—those ancient dragons (drakons) of the past?

"I SEE YOU."

Avatar, the Movie

~!~

In returning to Beowulf and his battles with hybrids, we note that Peter Dickinson, author and winner of two Carnegie Medals, cannily wrote, as a shrewd guess, that Grendel, of the first battle, may have been a *bipedal dragon,* and now we will not argue with him; yes, a bipedal drakon.
We are getting closer to realization that dragons are really Neon-Sapiens hominids, in such a remarkable, unusual way, not discussed before.

We have seen how the word 'dragon' is mythically misunderstood, and how 'drakon' truly referred, historically, to a creature with tremendous strength and great eyesight; now we will turn to the drakon's armor, fire-breathing, and his remarkable flying.

Occam's Razor*, with its notion of simplicity being the best solution to a complex problem, is at play here; the reader is strongly advised to drop old notions of dragons and keep an **open mind**, for we are about to get real . . . and amazingly simple.*

The Scaly Armor: A dragon's legendary scales are the easiest part of a dragon to explain. In ancient caves, hybrid-hominids, using skills developed over many thousands of years, simply used incredibly tough animal hides, such as moose leather, by cutting them into protective pieces or plates and stitching them together with leather cords. Ancient Chinese warriors also wore moose-hide armor, with coins covering the hide, which gives the armor a brass color and appearance. When seen in the dark, dim recesses of a cave by a fearful human, this drakon body armor likely developed into a mythical illusion later, both in the 'impenetrable skin' of Grendel and his vicious mother, and also in the 'scales' of the dragon in the third battle. It's entirely possible, from what we have seen of Neons and their descendants, that the history of man's evolving military body armor was another 'gift' from our hybrid ancestors, along with rock spear heads and obsidian-glass knife blades. Thick Moose 'scales' or fashioned leather hides, are still in use today in the subarctic tribes, and they do indeed stop sharp objects.

169

Grendel's mother attacked Beowulf with extremely powerful hands whose fingers were described as being extremely hard and bonelike. Is it possible that hybrid-hominids, such as Grendel and his dear mum, had perhaps 10—20% Neanderthal DNA in them, and that their fingernails were gross and misshapen, appearing hard as bone?

The Flame and the Flair Fights: As we recall from The Story of King Gilgamesh, Huwawa the monster-guardian in the Cedar Forest, was said to have 'flaming breath.' Then, in Beowulf, a human being is attacked by an ancient hybrid, a 'drakon,' who also has flaming breath. Is this entirely folklore, or have historians overlooked the obvious, and there really were creatures that could 'breathe flame' but they were (and are) hybrid-hominids? Today's humans, in a circus arena, can project a deadly flame, using a simple white substance such as liquid cornstarch, well over twenty feet.
Now, for an additional insight into a hybrid-hominid fire-breathing drakon, let's do a brief thought experiment.

You and I, are ancient, brave warriors—just the two of us, sneaking into a dark cave to kill a 'drakon.' We hear its great roaring around a campfire, see the fire glow on a wall up ahead; then the sound abruptly stops . . . the drakon has heard us, with its large ears and superior hearing.

With fear held down in our throats, we approach slowly, helmeted, swords drawn, shields at the ready. In the near total darkness of the cave niches, we are suddenly surprised by a large, hairy man-beast, who is perched ten feet above us on a large boulder, well beyond the reach of our swords. The beast is holding a lit firebrand in its hairy claw. Suddenly, the creature leans forward and spits a white fluid down upon us which instantly catches fire as the drakon activates the deadly substance with his fire stick. Our thick clothing catches fire; the creature spits his flame breath once more. We die, flaming in agony. The creature peers down at the burning enemies, and begins to roar continuously, in victory celebration.
This simple thought experiment shows just how easy it would be to have primordial fire-breathing, used as a weapon of war in ancient times. It's a

rather excellent form of cave defense, but today fire-breathing is only performed at the circus.

Now, in this talk of dragon's breath, we should certainly consider the hoary, primordial origin of human fire-breathing, as seen below. A man, dimly seen at the far bottom of the image, is also using a white, flammable substance held in his mouth, and blows a powerful, deadly flame upon a ceiling.

A human flame-blowing technique called 'The Dragons Breath'
Credit Wikipedia ~ Public domain

"Literature is the faint remembrance of Experience."

"HISTORY"

SAK

LITERATURE CREATES DREAMSCAPES

The very same situation may have been revealed in The Story of King Gilgamesh, where Enkidu reports:

Huwawa—his roar was a whirlwind,

Flame in his jaws, and his very breath Death!

Now, imagine being in an ancient cave, when you are surprised and badly burned by a fire-breathing Neon descendant. One must ask, just when did hominid fire-breathing begin? Its birth is certainly in the prehistoric time-period, long before today's circus performers, who are quite good at their fire-blowing craft.

In Beowulf, it is mentioned when the Wanderer is spilling his tales, that, when the dragons fought and killed each other, the dead ones *oozed a white substance*, perhaps from their mouth, or perhaps from carrying containers held close to the body. When the Wanderer, in telling his tale, says that 'dragons have no blood,' this may be a legendary offshoot of such ancient observations of defeated dragons (drakons), as dead hybrids, with mouths open, and oozing a white, flammable substance therefrom, seemingly having no blood. The drakon died, unable to release and shoot his last fire-breath. Perhaps he was engulfed in flame, or clubbed from behind; we'll never know all, or even many, of the sordid details of such ancient cave battles, as flaming flair fights.

If an ancient outsider, as a hybrid-hominid, began interacting with humans in a deadly way, the human community would respond by sending in large groups of armed men in retaliation, to eliminate the threat. In Beowulf, it states that a dragon killed thirty men or more; a small army. While seemingly only a myth, this lethalness may have been possible in a distant past. Using a simple thought experiment again, let's imagine thirty men with torches, swords and shields, spreading out in single file, moving slowly into a vast European cave. They are being silently watched by not one, but three or more hybrids—the clan that lives in the cave. All of them have great strength, eyesight, and fire-breathing skills, and possibly armored animal-hide plating, as surmised of Grendel and the dragon (drakon). They hide in dark shadows as the humans approach, and then ambush and attack the invading warriors, repeatedly spewing and blowing out a deadly fire. The warriors die horrible, fiery deaths. One horribly burnt man escapes, and lives to tell the tale—from his limited point of view of the dim, rocky pathway into the vast cave complex, of how a single dragon killed thirty of his comrades. This postulated scenario could easily have occurred, somewhere back in time, as a faint remembrance of an ancient experience. Occam might agree. In a strange twist today, there are websites that promote how to 'blow like a dragon,' using a simple white cornstarch liquid or another propellant. If today's circus fire-blowers desired to kill someone, they have an excellent weapon; the principle is basically the same as our Neon descendants, who essentially weaponized fire-breathing somewhere in the distant past.

The Deadly Tail: In his third and final battle with a large dragon, the King is finally felled by a 'swoop of the dragon's tail,' which is reported by our ancient poet, as being able to 'fell twenty trees' with one deadly swish. Our purpose here is to further distill the clues and hints of real creatures in a hidden hybrid history, from the graceful, bard-like exaggerations in literature.

Neuropsychologists know today that our left brains are responsible for confabulation, or corruption of one's memory. The left brain basically makes up its own story, in an attempt to understand the nearly unfathomable.

Is it possible, beyond the embellishments, that the hybrid creature, the dragon (drakon), had a swinging weapon, which became a 'tail' in the dim light and the memories of any survivors of such an encounter? In the nearby Irish tales of the fatherless Cu-Chulainn the Hound, yet another likely Wildman (hybrid-hominid), there are reports of his using weapons such as deadly foot-spears, called the Gae Bolga, and also sling-stones. Further, it is possible to think of the sweeping 'tail' as a drakon weapon, which could simply be a flexible, strong, 5–10 ft vine or rope, tied on one end to a large stone, and which could certainly kill in one blow, and would also make for great cave defense against animals, etc. Such a weapon would be similar to today's tribal usage of a bola; a rock and rope weapon which is thrown at enemies or animals. Or perhaps the dragon's tail was really simply a long, heavy tree branch, which, if swung with hybrid force, in the dim light, was quite capable of killing a man. In the darkness of the cave shadows, who can see well, except for the Neon-hybrids? Since there really isn't any tail on the mythicized dragon, we can play along with the silliness of the tale, or perhaps consider lethal swinging weapons, which were later fabricated into a vicious tail, and even claws of the feet, by perhaps unreliable witnesses, to a real event, entering myth, but not history, in some dark cave, long, long ago.

"Once you eliminate the impossible,

whatever remains, no matter how improbable,

must be the truth."

Sherlock Holmes

The Flight of the Drakon: Over the centuries, it is our confabulating left brain that has greatly morphed and exaggerated all notions of the mythical dragon, as marvelously and playfully depicted in modern times, in examples such as the popular Game of Thrones. The flight of the dragon is actually a flight of the mind, yet many myths abound.
Joseph Campbell, in his book, 'The Mythic Image,' relates a humorous Buddhist tale about flying animals:

"There is an old myth about elephants, telling how once upon a time they could fly and change shape like clouds. One day, however, a great flock alighted on the branch of a prodigious tree, beneath which an ascetic named Long Austerity was teaching. The branch broke and killed a number of his pupils, and the Yogi cursed the entire race, dooming them to the loss of their powers...so that today, elephants are actually clouds condemned to walk the Earth."

However, aside from funky myth-making, in our alternative portrayal of ancient hybrid drakons flying through the air, a much deeper portrayal is required, which necessitates having an open mind.
While the cultural idea of angels has been around in literature for thousands of years, their common artistic portrayal as having large

beautiful wings began only recently, in Europe's 15th century.

In ancient times, sorcerers, such as Milarepa in Tibet, were routinely reported to fly over the countryside; what the layfolk never understood is that this ability is somewhat rare.

Today, leaving the body and traveling (flying) in consciousness has been dubbed 'remote viewing' by several governments, including the United States, which has used it for military reconnaissance and espionage for over twenty years.

> *There's a place down in Mexico,*
>
> *where a man can fly over mountains*
>
> *and hills...*
>
> Hypnotized, **Fleetwood Mac**

In considering the flights of dragons as a developed, misunderstood myth in ancient times, *the flight of the mind* is a much better substitute, although certainly not flashy!

Not all of the drakons were monsters—some of them may have had cordial relations with humans, as suggested by the presence of King Arthur's father, Pendragon (chief dragon) and Merlin the Wild Man. The entire premise of this book is that some hybrid-hominids were indeed monsters, while others were more philosophical, and even spiritual in their thoughts and behavior. As we look around in modern society today, the song remains the same for us, with our 2–4% Neon DNA; our Sapiens species routinely produces a bevy of Monsters, Philosophers and Saviors. As we saw with paleo-psychologist Stan Gooch's suggestion, Neons and their hybrid descendants, with their superior rear braincase, were likely also superior with their aspects of eyesight, imagination, dreaming, and even psychic movement, as in '**out of the body**' experiences and movements of consciousness. Such OBEs, as they are called, often involve close calls at death known as near death experiences (NDEs) and other purposeful projections, known as clairvoyance, remote viewing, or the Siddhi powers of Raja Yoga. This may also have been true with Neons' descendants, some of whom became known as dragons (drakons). One classic OBE/NDE example is in Plato's story of 'The Myth of Er,' where a severely wounded Greek soldier named Er is thrown upon a stack of dead bodies and left for dead. However, he is not dead, and has an OBE experience that lasts for days, with great marvelous visions of his heavenly experiences, which are well described by Socrates' narrative.

It would be easy for a primitive Sapiens to misunderstand the difficult concept of 'flying' in such ways. The common folklore of a dragon flying overhead is a gross misinterpretation of an ancient creature, who may have had extended psychic capabilities, or, if the reader prefers, we can return to the simplicity of modern, mythical dragon folklore.

The Dragon Slayers: There are dozens of mythical and historical hero-figures that are said to have killed dragons (drakons). In looking back over 4,000 years, we find Cadmus, Heracles, St. George and Sigurd atop the lengthy list. The romantic notion of 'rescuing a damsel in distress' may have roots of truth, if a lustful hybrid ogre, or monster was attacking and raping the Sapiens womenfolk, as was widely reported.

Although truly now swallowed in myth, the 'Golden Legend' of St. George and the Dragon, is worth noting for our hybrid discussion. The saint intervenes, in the 11th century saga, in a town where a drakon (dragon) is demanding human sacrifices; it eats humans, as did Grendel. St. George confronts and charges the beast on horseback, and severely wounds it with his lance.

The creature then has a noose tied around its head, and is led back into town, where it is killed. Most of the fictitious paintings of St. George portray him, with artistic license, as fighting winged dragons with tails, an image still common today, but notably, there are a few 10th century paintings that show him *stabbing a humanlike figure,* which would be our hybrid-hominid, called a dragon in the lore.

Sigurd, or Siegfried is a legend of Germanic mythology; his name is mentioned in dozens of Northern poems where one of his most famous feats was slaying a terrifying dragon. Sigurd was in Germany; St. George was in Greece. In between the two dragon slayer stories, geographically, there lies the ancient Dragon-Hole of Austria. To the north, Beowulf was in Sweden. If European caves held creatures that were an admixture of Neanderthal and human DNA, there could have been hundreds of such drakon cavern populations. Human interactions with these populations likely produced either hybrid babies . . . or death, on both sides. The many migrating waves of hybrid and 'normal' humanity crisscrossed each other many times in prehistoric and historic times; like the many ripples of a stone tossed into a pond. To the East, in Tibet, India and China, there are reports of terrifying Yeti, which likely were the Yandi hybrid tribe, but there are no widespread reports of dragon slayers, as in the Western lore.

In Beowulf, the hero dies fighting his last dragon, who may have been the largest hybrid of his kind, back in the shrouded days of mist and myth. More information on dragons is found in Appendix C: The Human Dragons.

PART IV ~ The Hidden History of Monsters, Saviors and Kings

The images of Jesus in art have been heavily influenced by cultural settings. Credit: Wikipedia: Public Domain

The most common depiction of Jesus Christ is that of a delicate, decidedly white, tall man, created by Europeans more than a thousand years after the death of Jesus.

Truth is stranger than Fiction.

Jesus, the Humpback Christ

"It has served us well, this myth of Christ."

Pope Leo X

Could it be true that the Neanderthal DNA percentages in the historical figure known as Jesus the Christ, were higher than normal? Shockingly, after investigation, this appears so. Based upon his appearance and other information, we consider Jesus, and his mother, Mary, as possibly having 9–15% Neanderthal genes.

Perhaps the greatest legend of all time, in our known history, is that of the church-spawned myth of Jesus Their Christ. In my youth, I was raised under the auspices of the Baptist and Methodist churches, but quickly departed for deeper pastures, leaving the pastors and preachers, some good, some not, in my wake. What is revealed below is an alternative view of who and what Jesus really was, supported by numerous, credible ancient historians, who portray Jesus as being separate and far, far apart from the usual churchy misunderstanding of Jesus as the white European-looking Savior. Nothing could be further from the truth. The following information is not for deeply convicted Christians nor the fainthearted, but rather, the open-minded, courageous, and responsible. These are the few who step past outdated, common myths, especially the big doozy, the monstrous curiosity called *Churchiosity*, which comes in many flavors and varieties. They are a slowly dying force, as most Western folks simply no longer accept the extreme incorrectness, nor the blatant plagiarism found in the teachings of their Bible. For some evangelical, religious readers, it might be time to close this book, because an extremely iconoclastic view will be presented of the unusual birth, life, and teachings of Jesus.

Those millions of followers of the American churches, on both continents, north and south, extend tremendous influence, and money, upon their respective governments and cultures.

The religious influence and politics of the United States, in particular, is so strong as to nearly dominate the world; however, the USA is a last

AMERICANS ARE FOCUSED ON RIGHTEOUSNESS
THE "RIGHT" ARE ENTITLED.

bastion of a dying faith. Because Christianity is beginning to fail, somewhat due to the strong emergence of the physical sciences, which spawned the Information Age, it might be time, once again, to reconstruct the Christian faith, in hopes of building upon a firmer foundation. Christianity, and its churches, have a long history of reformation in their dreamlike Theology. Thus, Christianity is a rolling stone, like all religions are, operating under the crushing necessity of the eons of time. This author, with his own view, has no issue with the more in-depth secret teachings of Yeshua, as Jesus was originally called. A hidden, Yogic meaning can be seen in his poetic messages, such as 'The Father and Son are One.' However, many conservative Christians, still to this day, become shocked and big-eyed when informed, for the first time, that Jesus's name was really Yeshua, and that it is a derivative of Joshua. Yeshua means healer. The modern church's distorted view contains only remnants of his truth and being. Some authors, such as Sam Harris, have even suggested that Jesus is a pure caricature, quirkily originated by the church fathers, and that Jesus never existed. Many biblical scholars believe that when Yeshua lived and died, he had attracted only a small entourage of roughly twenty followers, consisting of his immediate family, friends, and disciples, yet this, and many other biblical claims are likely untrue. The creative church authors really embellished the life of Jesus, in their Bible, to suit their own ideas and psychological needs. So, in a limited space, let's have a new look at Jesus as a hybrid-hominid candidate, while we keep an open mind.

"Buckle your seatbelt, Dorothy, 'cause Kansas is goin' Bye Bye."

The Matrix

Author Colin Wilson (1931–2013), the Eternal Outsider, was the first to draw my attention to one of the best kept secrets in the Western world. During his life, Wilson served society as a literary 'pilot wave'; he was forever ahead, out in front of his academic critics; his many books of new ideas provided many new insights to a fading, jaded view of history and humanity. One of Wilson's special interests was in the unusual history of criminals. As he researched, he discovered that **the Romans had issued**

an arrest warrant, and poster for Yeshua, our hybrid candidate, at the time of his biblical tribulations, trial, and supposed crucifixion. On the poster, which still exists, possibly now in the recesses of the Vatican, Jesus the Christ is described as short, about *four foot six inches tall,* which is roughly a full foot shorter than the Roman soldiers who came to arrest him, in his dirty, ragged clothing. The iconoclastic poster also described him as *swarthy, bald-headed and humpbacked*, which of course forever destroys the image of the handsome, white, Euro-American Jesus depicted in artwork today and during the past several centuries. Thus, Yeshua was an anomaly and was physically and psychologically different from those around him in ancient Israel. And there's more.

Author Riaan Booysen also realized the sleuth and truth of Colin Wilson's investigations, and was inspired to embark upon a deep research path with a focus on a hidden Jesus. He produced a remarkable book entitled, *Barbelo, The Story of Jesus ChristBeowulf*, which thoroughly destroys many of the errant views of the mighty empire of Christian Churches.

Since the mystical pillar of the modern, fading church is obviously threatened, the sole bastion of its goodness lies in the ability of its members to provide charity to others, as it continually reforms (deforms) over the next several centuries.

The so-called life of Jesus Christ, as touted by endless theologians in infinite flavors, are all complete fictions. Sigmund Freud once commented that religion is a type of insanity, and perhaps it is, but, if we look around, we can extend that sentiment, as people often do, and say that the entire world . . . is crazy. *Hmmm?* It's enough to drive a soul inside, both Sapiens and Neanderthals!

Booysen, a non-academic with a career in advanced electrical engineering, placed his scintillating gaze upon many esoteric, but highly accurate, tiny pieces of history concerning Jesus, the humpbacked Christ. Scouring the many ancient biblical, Jewish, Greek, and Arabic sources of literature produced near or during the time of Jesus, Booysen's research

181

and writings revealed the dark, unknown underbelly of the story of Jesus the Christ. The results are absolutely astounding. In the revealing *Barbelo*, a convincing case is made, that not only was Yeshua a short humpbacked fellow, but Saint Paul was as well. This has tremendous implications, since most theologians believe that St. Paul was the actual progenitor of the early Christian faith, as he offered the teachings of Jesus, and caused the early movement to grow. *TRUE*

Riaan Booysen also produced a 2014 condensed, online version of *Barbelo*, which he called *The Physical Appearances of Jesus and Paul* which is available online as a PDF.

Below, we list excerpts of his article. Booysen quickly lists his poignant points concerning both the image and behavior of the diminutive Yeshua, who may have disguised himself as Paul. Truth is Stranger than Fiction.

~!~

The Physical Appearances of Jesus and Paul

THE ROMAN POSTER ~ THE ACTS OF PAUL and THECLA:

"A key turning point in my research came when I was stunned by a remark by Colin Wilson":
"The Romans issued a wanted poster for Jesus, which still survives, describing him as short (about four foot six), bald-headed, and humpbacked." *HAS HE SEEN THE POSTER. SAYING IT EXIST. DOESN'T MEAN IT DOES*
This description of Christ appears to somewhat *match* the description of Paul in the apocryphal books, The Acts of Paul and Thecla:

A man of small stature, with a bald head and crooked legs, in a good state of body, with eyebrows meeting and nose somewhat hooked.

Could Jesus and Paul have been the same person? One of the greatest mysteries associated with modern theories about Christ is—if accepting that he had survived his crucifixion—the question of what had become of him afterwards. If Christ had indeed survived his crucifixion, he would

182

not have gone through such an ordeal only to vanish into obscurity. He could hardly have continued to be around as "Jesus," since he was supposed to have been taken up into heaven forty days after his resurrection. In *Barbelo*, it is shown that following his recovery from the crucifixion, Christ continued leading his revolution and building up his forces **under the guise** of the biblical Paul of Tarsus.

Josephus knew him very well but referred to him as the Egyptian who led a failed uprising against the Romans, an accusation brought against Paul during his final arrest.

Another great misconception about Christ is that he was a strikingly handsome and imposing figure, as typically depicted. Nothing could be further from the truth. In this article I will only point out the physical similarities between Paul and Christ, and some unique events that were common to both.

To begin with, in the Halosis of Josephus, Christ is described as:
NOT EXTANT

...a man of simple appearance, mature age, dark skin, small stature, three cubits high, hunchbacked, with a long face, long nose, and meeting eyebrows, so that they who see him might be affrighted, with scanty hair (but) having a line in the middle of the head after the fashion of the Nazireans and with an undeveloped beard.

A similar description of Paul is given in The Acts of Paul and Thecla, ?.
[Paul]...a man of small stature, with a bald head and crooked legs, in a good state of body, with eyebrows meeting and nose somewhat hooked.

Another version of The Acts of Paul and Thecla reads:
Quite small, bald-headed, bow-legged, with knees far apart, with meeting eyebrows, large eyes, a long nose and a red, florid face.

Historian Pseudo-Chrysostom describes Paul as *'the man of three cubits'* (4 feet 4.7 inches), matching the height of Christ as given in the Halosis of Josephus.

183

Robert Eisler, the renowned scholar, and Jewish polymath, recognizes the resemblance between Christ and Paul:

*A glance at the personal description of Paul already given shows at once that the tradition has come down to us in a form exactly corresponding to the one found in the iconismus (imagery) of Jesus . . . this **resemblance of Paul to Jesus.***

However, despite a lengthy rationalization, this intelligent man fails to consider the most logical of conclusions, that Christ and Paul of Tarsus must have been, or at least could have been, one and the same person. I'll next list additional physical descriptions of Christ and Paul as presented by the fathers and critics of the early church.

Of Christ . . .

According to Hierosolymitanus, as well as John of Damascus, 'the Jew Josephus' recorded that Christ "was seen having connate eyebrows, goodly eyes, long-faced, crooked, well-grown."

Nicephorus Callistus also claims that Josephus had described Christ as having been seven spans (5 feet 1.5 inches) tall, with beautiful eyes, a long nose, tawny hair, black eyebrows and his neck gently bent "so that the carriage of his body was not quite upright and rigid," i.e. hunchbacked.

In a letter of certain bishops to the Emperor Theophilus, Christ's height is described by the epithet tripechus (three cubits) which translates to a height of 1.34 m (4 feet 4.7 inches).

Tertullian, Celsus, and the 'Acta Johannis Leucii', all agree that Christ was below medium height.

Ephrem Syrus (320–379 CE) describes Christ as "God took human form and appeared in the form of three human ells; he came down to us small of stature."

Zaccheus had to climb into a tree to see Christ, because he (Christ) was small and was being dwarfed by his followers.

Theodore of Mopsuhestia likewise records "Thy appearance, O Christ, was smaller than that of the children of Jacob."

Tertullian, another early Christian writer, describes Christ in very unflattering terms:

Let us compare with Scripture the rest of His dispensation. Whatever that poor despised body may be, because it was an object of touch and sight, it shall be my Christ, be He inglorious, be He ignoble, be He dishonoured; for such was it announced that He should be, both in bodily condition and aspect. Isaiah comes to our help again. According to the same prophet, however, He is in bodily condition 'a very worm', and no man; a reproach of men, and an outcast of the people.
As when they said, whence has this man this wisdom and these mighty works? Thus, spoke even they who despised His outward form. His body did not reach even to human beauty, to say nothing of heavenly glory. Had the prophets given us no information whatever concerning His ignoble appearance? His very sufferings and the very contumely He endured bespeak it all.

According to Irenaeus, Christ was described as weak, unattractive and afflicted:
Some of them, moreover—[when they predicted that] as a weak and inglorious man, and as one who knew what it was to bear infirmity.

Celsus describes the physique of Christ as "little (small), ill-favoured (ugly, hideous), and ignoble (shameful, dishonourable, mean)."

In The Acts of Peter we read:
Him [Christ] who is great and quite small, comely and ugly: small for the ignorant, great to those who know him, comely to the understanding and ugly to the ignorant, youthful and aged…glorious but amongst us appearing lowly and ill-favoured.

According to The Acts of John, John wrote of Christ:
He (Christ) appeared to me again as rather bald-headed but with a thick flowing beard.…But he sometimes appeared to me as a small man with no good looks.
Saint Augustine states that Christ "appeared ugly (foedus, meaning 'horrible, abominable') to his persecutors."
Tertullian, denying that the appearance of Christ had any beauty, goes as far as stating that:

The ignominy of the face (of Jesus) would roar (as a witness against the heretics) if it could.
In the Koran, Christ is described as an "amazing thing" brought forth by Mary.
Mandaean and Gnostic texts describe Christ as "something that was created in the womb of Mary," and she had given birth to, causing her to grieve at the sight of its imperfection. In another text this birth is further described as "something came out of her that was imperfect and different in appearance from her, for she had produced it **without her partner**. It did not resemble its mother and was misshapen."
Paul would later describe himself as *"one abnormally born"*
(1 Cor 15:8), matching the descriptions presented above.

In *The History of the Contending of Saint Paul*, he is described as having a countenance that was "ruddy with the ruddiness of the skin of a pomegranate," and his cheeks were full, and bearded, and of the colour of a rose, matching Christ's reddish complexion.
A description of Paul as recorded in *The Passion of Paul* reads:
And he was easily recognizable, having a crooked body, a black beard and a bald head.

Paul and Christ; the same person

It is not only their physical appearances that match, but also their actions and legends about them:
Scholars have long identified Paul with Simon Magus, and in *Barbelo* it is shown that Christ and Simon Magus were one and the same person. Paul and Christ were therefore the same person.
A remark in The Acts of Paul and Thecla, that Thecla *"saw the Lord sitting in the form of Paul,"* suggests that they were indeed the same person.

In The Acts of Saint Peter, John and Peter have doubts about Paul:
And I, Peter, held converse with my brother John secretly, for we were marvelling at the act of Paul, and wondering whether Simon the magician

186

(having heard the rumour of us) had appeared unto us in the form of Paul…

This remark in turn suggests that Simon Magus and Paul were the same person, thereby linking Simon Magus to Christ through Paul.
A sect called the Cathars maintained that *"Jesus was not ever in this world except spiritually in the body of Paul."* In other words, Jesus was Paul.

Following Paul's arrest, he was accused of being *"the man who teaches all men everywhere against our people and our law and this place,' and 'who had brought Greeks into the temple area and had defiled that holy place."* Christ was the one who turned Judea upside down with his teachings and who stormed the temple with 310 of his savages, robbing it of all its holy items.

Paul was also accused of being the Egyptian who started a revolt and led four thousand terrorists into the wilderness. Several scholars have identified this Egyptian as Simon Magus, confirming that Christ, earlier identified as Simon Magus, was also the same person as Paul. Christ fed four thousand of his followers in the desert.

Felix and his wife Drusilla frequently sent for Paul to talk to him, while Simon Magus convinced Drusilla to marry Felix. Simon Magus and Paul are therefore linked to Felix and Drusilla in the same setting, confirming that they must have been one and the same person.
Given the evidence presented above, those with an open mind should come to only one conclusion, namely that Christ and Paul must have been **one and the same person."**

End; Physical Appearances of Jesus & Paul; Riaan Booysen

~!~

And so, thanks to Riaan Booysen, Colin Wilson, and many ancient historians, we have a remarkable new insight into the slightly deformed

WELL MAYBE AN INTERESTING CONJECTURE!

187

hybrid-hominid that Yeshua most likely was. But now, we must turn to an especially important question: Who were the parents of this little, holy fellow? What follows is just as astounding as Booysen's work. The first thing we must do is toss out the unnecessary church story of Jesus' divine birth—it is a complete fabrication.

The Rape of the Panther and the Birth of Jesus

So, where do the divine birth stories of Jesus come from? Remarkably, from just a few influential persons, whom are little known today.

Early Christian scholars continuously rewrote their 'Biblia,' which means 'collection of small books'; these eventually became famously known as the Bible. There used to be dozens of versions of the Gospels. Origen and Irenaeus were influential figures in reducing the Bible to the canonical version of Matthew, Luke, Mark and John. To this day, each gospel still contradicts the others, concerning the adventurous life of Yeshua, the devout little Jewish man. Origen also was influential in crafting the Christian divine birth narrative, where Mary is impregnated by God. However, an old Jewish story stood in the way. The premise of the tale, as a short revelation, related how a Roman officer named Panthera raped or seduced young Mary, who gave birth to Jesus. This story would be pivotal in separating the Jews and the early Christians, since it was impossible for the Jewish folk to see Yeshua as the anticipated Messiah, given his known parentage of Panthera and Mary. This was a sensitive subject, to say the least. Origen was queried by his scribal peers as to what the Jewish people of the time would think and believe—the tale of Pantera or of Divine Birth? Origen coyly responded by saying that the *rumored story of divine birth was simply irresistible*, and so another lie was placed into the Bible and thus the history books . . . this one was a great, big whopper. Yes, the Bible, as the Christians say, is the Greatest Story Ever Told.
Thomas Jefferson, the great American statesmen, intuited that large portions of the Bible were untrue, and used to cut up his Bible into small pieces and placed them into his own book. He kept only those chapters and verse that he felt were essential teachings of Jesus; this small book became known as Jefferson's Bible.

So, who was Panthera the Roman Panther? Let's hear from Wiki:

"Tiberius Julius Abdes Pantera (22 BC–AD 40) was a Roman soldier whose tombstone was found in Bingerbrück, Germany, in 1859.
A historical connection from this soldier to Jesus has long been hypothesized by numerous scholars, based on the claim of the ancient Greek philosopher Celsus, who, according to Christian writer Origen in his Contra Celsum ("Against Celsus"), was the author of a work entitled 'The True Word.'
Celsus' work was lost, but in Origen's account of it, Jesus was depicted as the result of an affair between his mother Mary and a Roman soldier. He said she was "convicted of adultery and had a child by a certain soldier named Pantera." Tiberius Pantera could have been serving in the region at the time of Jesus's conception. Both the ancient Talmud and medieval Jewish writings and sayings reinforced this notion, referring "Yeshu ben Pantera," which some scholars believe should be translated as "Jesus, son of Pantera."

Pantera; **Wikipedia**

Although Origen knows that Celsus, using Jewish sources, calls Mary an adulteress, it is more likely, as was common in ancient warfare, that invading soldiers routinely raped the indigenous females of the lands they conquered, as a spoil of war. It's also quite possible that she was bribed for her sex, as is another common practice with soldiers in war. In this case, Mary may have exchanged favors with Panthera, her Panther, as a common form of ancient prostitution. Scholars consider that Panthera was possibly of Phoenician (Lebanese) origin, due to his formal assignment of long Roman names, thus he was granted Roman citizenship for his good military service. Panthera's parents are unknown to history, but we have a hint of a clue with Mary's lineage, which is related to how Jesus got his humpback.

Mary

The Bitter One

Before we begin with an astounding, hidden portrayal of the Mother of Jesus, let us recall, from an earlier chapter, how journalist James Fallows was informed of his unusually high (5%) Neanderthal DNA, by a geneticist:

*"You do have an abnormally high percentage Neanderthal component, and I wonder if that's connected to the unusual genetics of your mother. I see contact with Neanderthals as having been ephemeral and primarily a result of **rape** by Neanderthal males of AMH (anatomically modern human) women and that the locus of that interaction happened **halfway up the Red Sea coast** on the eastern shore. Your mother's DNA may be showing the most ancient European line still extant, isolated as it was in **Scotland**."*

The Atlantic.com

The geneticist is suggesting that James Fallows' ancestry was not merely Scottish, but rather also descended and extended from the Levant, likely in the caves where either Neanderthals, or their hybrid-hominid descendants appear to have lived for many thousands of years. When the shrewd geneticist states that Neanderthals and their descendants likely raped the human women in the Levant, we can tie-in the old Jewish stories about incubus creatures attacking and raping the Jewish females.

Mary, Mirian, or Maryan as Jesus' mother was known, has a curious name. One of the primary translations is 'bitter,' which requires a bit of an explanation, as we explain our hybrid-hominid hypothesis, as strange as it is. Today, the Jewish people in Israel have an extremely high Neanderthal DNA percentage, compared to other peoples in the world. There are several large caves on the coasts of the Levant, meaning modern Israel and Lebanon, where good Neanderthal fossil evidence has been found, alongside the Sapiens bones.

The premise here is that Mary and her ancestral family, may have had hoary links to those living Neanderthals and their hybrid-hominid descendants, in such ancient caves for thousands of years, as the geneticist suggested. We don't have good physical descriptions for Panthera or Mary, but based upon Jesus' likely known physical appearance, it's probable his body was influenced by his mother's DNA. In the Bible, Mary, the Bitter One's parents were named Joachim and Hannah (also known as Anna). The father is of no interest here, but Anna . . . well, she became Saint Anna in the church. And just who impregnated Saint Anna, if we are to relieve the Deity of the task?

According to various Jewish stories as well as the Bible, Ann was a sterile woman who could not conceive, so she prayed in earnest to God for a child. The biblical concoction is that she became marvelously pregnant with Mary, like a happy ending in a movie. When she saw her husband Joachim coming with his flocks;

"Anna ran and wrapped herself around his neck, saying, 'Now I know that the Lord God has blessed me greatly. See, the widow is no longer a widow and the childless woman has conceived in her womb.'" (IGJ 4:9)

This curious line is somewhat untrue and wouldn't be the first time that a human being lied to their mate about having a relationship, just to keep the peace. At any rate, the church fosters many mistruths such as this, in order to keep peace, in their own relations with their flocks. Everyone in the churches must toe the Bible line of rather remarkable beliefs, including those telling of great 'divine births.'

And so, Anne gave birth to a daughter, Miriam, or Mary, the Bitter One. Continuing in the mainstream, biblical storyline, when Mary was three years old, her parents brought her to the Temple of Jerusalem, in fulfillment of their promise, where they left her to be brought up. Alternatively, might we consider a hybrid-hominid, slightly misshapen toddler was dropped off, to become an orphaned child; a ward of the Temple? Scholars have long pondered the name of Mary as the Bitter, and have proffered up weak suggestions such as 'life was hard for her,' or that her family was bitter against Egyptian authorities, etc. However, normally, babies are named at birth, and for a hidden reason—Mary was

191

seen as something bitter, unusual. Perhaps that was the real reason she was orphaned to the church at age three. The English words 'mar' and 'marred' stem from Indo-European language roots that are thousands of years old and refer to something malformed or defaced. Could the ancient name of 'Mar-y' actually be related to being marred or deformed? That would certainly account for her also being called 'the bitter.' We must stay on track if we are to investigate the probable cause for Jesus' own physical deformities and reputed ugliness, as reported by many ancient historians.

God or Incubus?

But did God really impregnate Saint Anna, or can we toss that made-up church story into the trash? Let's consider an alternative hypothesis. In Saint Anna's story, it is said that she 'visited' the temple and met with the priest, as part of her process of interacting with God and finally getting her long-desired-for baby. So far, we have developed several possible options for Mary's birth: divine insemination, priestly insemination, and let us add a third, that of a possible hybrid-hominid insemination, as an unknown incubus lying with Anna, and thus being Mary's true papa. Many of the incubus and succubus stories, where *strange creatures raped or had sex with humans*, are derived from ancient Jewish Mysticism and legendary traditions, which may have faint roots of truth. As we shall see, the Bible reported that Israel's twelve clans had several 'unclean tribes,' called the 'Gog-MaGog,' which were eventually driven away. These tribes are discussed in an upcoming chapter.

It is possible, even likely, that the members of these unclean tribes had a larger Neon DNA percentage. Truly, if hybrid-hominid creatures were in the Jewish land for thousands of years, co-existing alongside humans or Sapiens, one can't entirely rule out that the priest himself was one, and perhaps took care of others like himself, not unlike the hidden relation of Grendel the Monster, and his potential father, Unferth the black one, who may have protected the monster, in The Beowulf Saga.

Startingly, the description of the Jewish Incubus mating with humans, happens to match the observation of the geneticist who informed James Fallows of his 5 % Neanderthal DNA, although he thought he was simply

Scottish! The many unknown hybrid-hominid migrations in ancient times must have crossed paths with, and interbred with many migrating Sapiens groups, further sprinkling Neon DNA amongst humans. The large Ashkenazi Jewish sect, for example, once thought to hail from the Levant area, has now been shown by DNA testing to have migrated from Southern Europe two thousand years ago, to further compound the admixtures of the Neon and Sapiens species, which eventually evolved into we humans today, with our 2–5% Neon DNA.

To extend Gooch's theory of hybrid-hominids being giants, ogres, demons, and trolls, we should strongly consider that Mary's unknown papa, while called an incubus; was a hybrid creature of some sort. Being named 'Bitter' (Mary) is somewhat akin to Merlin being called 'rough and grisly' at birth. Being dropped off as a helpless three-year-old may have been a torturous experience for her, given the long history of the church. The goodly church fathers, such as Origen, would routinely clean-up and sanitize the rougher stories of the central characters in the Bible, finally producing a most macabre series of fables that really don't resemble ancient history.

The story of Anna, the mother of Mary, bears a close similarity to that of the much older, Old Testament version of the conception and birth of Samuel, whose mother, also named Hannah, had also been sterile and childless. Hannah had also gone to a temple, the Tabernacle at Shiloh, and acted very strangely. Eli the priest actually accused her of being quite drunk! However, her prayers for a child were ultimately 'blessed' by the priest Eli. Either Eli had a 'good time' blessing Hannah, or, as a second option, a hidden creature was involved, to segue back into the well-known Jewish stories about the incubus and succubus having secret sex, with the Jewish tribespeople, even killing or raping them. Hannah gave birth to Samuel, and 'offered him to God's service,' meaning, as with her daughter Anna, she dropped him off at the temple, to await his fate. Later, Samuel would be known as 'The Seer,' which is strangely remindful of Merlin, who also prophesied. Other miraculous births to *once-sterile* mothers include Isaac's birth from Sarah, Samson's birth to his parents, and John the Baptist's birth from Elizabeth. Is it possible that the Jewish stories of incubus and succubus in the caves of the Levant were hybrid-matings, which were later either sterilized, misreported, or misunderstood by the church scribes? The case of Samson is especially appealing, with his prodigious strength, and his relationship with Delilah—the myth is likely another Beauty and the Beast story.

~!~

Jesus the humpback; Traveling Abroad

We return to the legend of Jesus the Humpback Christ to briefly depict a scenario of how the young child's life developed. In following the Jewish story of a love or lust connection between a hybrid-hominid Mary, and the Phoenician-Roman soldier, Panthera, and the resultant humpback, nearly dwarf child, we can conclude a certain few things. The Jewish folks have been seen as extremely xenophobic throughout their history, distrusting, and loathing the invading Romans. Thus, what social chances would an ugly, half-breed like young Yeshua have, with his Roman father, and a slightly deformed mother, in such a hostile environment? Joseph was an older man with trailing children; his earlier wife had died and so he coupled with Mary the Bitter. The temple authorities are reported to have released her to go with him. It's important to note that the Bible reports Joseph's family, including Jesus, left for Egypt, and then, shortly thereafter, the Bible falls strangely silent about Jesus, around age twelve. He is never heard from again . . . until he suddenly reappears around age thirty. The Christian faith is entirely mute on this subject; their great Savior's life is largely unaccounted for. But, are there more clues in history about Jesus's life? Yes.

Childhood rejection may have been a serious factor in the young humpback boy's life, especially with a Roman papa. There are several books entitled, *The Lost Years of Jesus*, perhaps the most notable one written by the brilliant Russian author Nicolas Notovich in 1887. In this esoteric lore, Notovich wrote extensively about how Jesus traveled to India and lived there during his 'unknown' years. The government of India also publishes scholarly documentation supporting Notovich's claim. The suggestion here is that Jesus was inclined towards spirituality and studied Yoga, possibly in Kashmir.

194

The unknown years of Jesus (also called his silent years, lost years, or missing years) generally refers to the period of Jesus's life between his childhood and the beginning of his ministry, a period not described in the New Testament.

*In the late medieval period, there appeared Arthurian legends that the young Jesus had been in Britain. In the 19th and 20th centuries theories began to emerge that between the ages of 12 and 29 Jesus had visited Kashmir or had studied with the Essenes in the Judea desert. Modern mainstream Christian scholarship has generally rejected these theories and holds that **nothing is known** about this time period in the life of Jesus.*

The Unknown Years of Jesus; Wikipedia

One might easily argue, on the other hand, that the various church authorities, with their own macabre concoctions, are the ones who know nothing, or extraordinarily little, about their own Savior.

It's very noteworthy that the modern government of India, a country of more than a billion people, strongly endorses many documentaries and literatures concerning Yeshua's long stay in Kashmir, while the Western Christian Theologians simply apply more and more dry, wood railings to their 'corral' of self-induced, limited, outdated knowledge. This is why the blind church is the bastion of ignorance, while the Information Age is swirling all around it, informing the world of the church's ongoing mistakes . . . and many cover-ups. Many of its more open-minded, courageous, and responsible leaders are already aware of the failures of the various churches, yet they stay quietly on the outskirts of Christianity, watching its slow demise. Eventually, the concocted corral will burn, and the ailing church will fall to its place in history, as a garbled hybrid admixture of strangeness, not unlike the physical body of its ancient leader, Yeshua, the Healer.

This religious criticism of the churches is not meant to diminish the great Yogic message of Jesus, as a world spiritual traveler, whom we will also depict as a stealthy Paul the Humpback, the founder of early Christianity. His in-depth teachings of God, consciousness, life, and death are remarkably similar, in some ways, to those of Plato, and even the

195

Egyptians, of the olden times. We must keep an open mind, in charting a new path of understanding, into the hidden histories of our past.

History records, possibly correctly this time, that Pythagoras, Plato, Jesus (Paul), and a great number of Greek and Jewish folks traveled to Egypt for secret teachings and initiation, when she finally opened her spiritual doors to the outside world around 700 BCE. Previously, Egypt had kept her sacred secrets to herself, for more than five thousand years.
The great, timeless teaching of Deity being mysteriously contained in the marvelous human body (HA), which releases its spirit at death is the quintessential element of the Egyptian teachings. Further, the joining of the KA (mind) and BA (soul) is required in order to overcome the Ego element of Set, the Egyptian God of personal resistance; the Opposer.

This is Egyptian Yoga, according to Dr. Muata Ashby, who has written prolifically upon esoteric Kemitic Egyptology.
Later, this internal personal opposer, SET the Adversary, became the negative devil-God of Christianity as SATAN (Set-an), which also means opposer or adversary. There are of course, many myths that swirl endlessly about poor old Set, who was morphed into a horned red devil by the Christian masses, as directed by their priests.

Pythagoras and other Greeks spent years traveling to Egypt and India for wisdom, in 500 BCE. We may hypothesize that the young Jewish hybrid, traveling as either Yeshua or later Paul, went to many lands during his life. In Egypt, India, Arabia, and Britannica he learned much, and thus became a Yogin, likely teaching and preaching as he went. He found a way to prosper spiritually, and rose above his physical ailment, perhaps as Merlin the Wise also did. Both men are said to have performed miracles, which may have to do with an unusual brain configuration. Yeshua may have developed extremely strong beliefs, where doubt is never a factor, after the proper Yogic training, where miracles are referred to as Siddhi powers. The title of Father, as God, was heavily used in ancient religions to indicate an inward spiritual authority. Thus, The Father and Son, as Yeshua stated are indeed one, where, in Egyptian terms, the mortal mind (KA) finally recognizes its source (BA) and joins with it. St. Augustine,

196

one of the pillars of the early Catholic church, went so far as to state that the 'Christ' was actually more than 10,000 years old, meaning, that he too, believed in the old ways of Egypt, in some limited regard. When a seasoned Yeshua returned from India to Israel, he got himself into a world of trouble, because he was teaching Yoga to the Jewish folk, which horrified the Pharisees and the Sadducees, the local temple authorities, who desired for the Romans to step in and quiet the little wild man. And so they did.

Another example of considerable mistranslation is that of Matthew 11:29–30 in the Christian New Testament, where Jesus (Yeshua) is informing his audience:

MIND & BODY — YOKED — YOGA

*Take my **yoke** upon you and learn from me, for I am gentle and humble in heart, and you will find rest for your souls. For my **yoke** is easy and my burden is light.*

When I was younger and being taught by my mother and her pastors in the Christian ways, I was puzzled, like many others, about what this cryptic verse could possibly mean—taking Jesus' yoke upon oneself. I simply didn't understand, nor did anyone else, it seemed.

Years later I happened upon an amazing scientific explanation, which again, was based on the issues of cultural diffusion. Here's the inside story: A fledgling Christianity and its devolving and evolving Bible soon passed from the Middle East into Italy, where the Catholic Vatican was being established. After much priestly scrutiny, all of the accepted biblical manuscripts were copied into the Vaticanus, the new Bible of the young Catholic faith. All the scripting and translating monks were well trained in classical Greek, as the language of choice; the Hebrew and Arabic languages were discarded, even loathed. The words of Jesus concerning his yoke were curious to many but went unchallenged by all in the West; the phrase was one of those in the Bible that one just subconsciously skims over without understanding it. A few thousand years went by. Then, fairly recently, a new, insightful understanding of the languages and dialects that were used and spoken in the Middle East during Yeshua's life and time came into focus. Key to the new understanding was the resurgent idea that Yeshua and those living near him in Palestine

197

two thousand years ago actually spoke a trilingual combination of Greek, Hebrew, and Arabic. This cultural arrangement later became known to scholars as "Koine" Greek. It was accepted as the necessary lingua franca of its day, as Greeks, Romans, Hebrews, Jews, and Arabs all populated the area where Yeshua spoke his teachings. In the majority of Christian institutions today, artificial pronunciations are used in an attempt to recreate the true ancient sounds. Armed with the new insight of Koine Greek, we can return to Yeshua's words about his mysterious yoke, and a more advanced understanding and rendering of his words can be attained.

*Take my **yoga** upon you and learn from me, for I am gentle and humble in heart, and you will find rest for your souls. For my **yoga** is easy and my burden is light*

This change of wording has tremendous meaning and implications. Both yoke and yoga mean "to connect" and are phonetically very similar. In the simpler, utilitarian sense, we would expect to yoke a cart to a horse or oxen, whereas in the deepest spiritual sense of Yoga, one connects with his or her innermost being, which we should construe as necessarily residing in our brains, our hearts, the internal regions. To look outside our minds for answers is a large, erroneous modality, although most do not understand the subtleness of this inner directive. As the Jewish guru said, "My kingdom is not of this world." There is also a deep, inward, brain-hemisphere connection implied when Yeshua states in the Bible that "*The Father and Son are one.*" This is the true meaning of Yeshua's words, as we see the Yogic insight into his original meaning; the sentences suddenly become alive, and the truer meaning snaps into place. After understanding these mistranslations, we shouldn't bother with oxen yokes and a Father-in-the sky figure; while waiting for an eventual return of a white-guy Jesus; those are the disruptions of understanding and give no answer to the puzzles of modern Christianity. Most Christians, and even their priests, heavily believe in such external notions, including their Cross and the Bible, but the discussion must be turned inward if we are to accept Yoga as the spiritual system of Jesus.

The cartoonlike situation with the Bible is strangely analogous to the wild, misunderstood myths of the Viking folks, which are called the

Poetic Edda. As revealed in the book, *The Vikings Secret Yoga; The Supreme Adventure*, the true meaning of Odin is all about an inward development via Yoga. Regardless of name or culture, an inward path is always suggested, in the better spiritual systems, regardless of culture. With his simple Yoga, which Yeshua is suggesting to those who will listen, we have the same meaning as Socrates suggested in his "Know thy Self" maxim. Simply, the little self, the conscious Ego, relaxes, and the much larger self, as the Eternal Muse, comes upon the scene as extended awareness. Thus, Socrates knew his own self by recognizing his own personal traits, while also connecting with, and listening to, the quiet, nearly silent traits of his inner spirit, his knowing Daimon.

The right brain hemisphere doesn't, and cannot directly speak, but it gives great hints to the listening brain that can, over there in left field. This intuitive knowledge was widespread in ancient times.

TACK ABOUT NONSENSE — LISTENING BRAIN? TALKING BRAIN? THE BRAIN HAS NOTHING TO DO WITH SPEECH OR HEARING. THE BODY HEARS AND THE BODY SPEAKS MIND IS EMBODIED.

"He who knows does not speak. He who speaks, does not know."

The Tao Te Ching. **Lao Tzu**

The intense conflict of spiritual values and cultures between India's Yoga and Israel's Judaism are quite obvious. In India, it is widely accepted that the senior, sincere Yogin can experience, and even become God, deep inside of the heart center. This is when 'The Father and Son are One.' In Israel, we have an opposing view, of 'Who is like God?' to quote a popular Jewish saying. Thus, Raja Yoga, the actual teaching of Jesus, was, and is, simply not allowed in the Jewish faith.

There is an extremely important similarity in the teachings of Jesus-Paul and Plato, who were both trained in Egyptian spirituality. When Plato relates that 'Man's greatest Victory is over his own Self' and that 'Life is but Practice for Dying,' it is exactly the same course of action that Jesus-Paul famously prescribed when he stated, 'I Die Daily.' How else does one seriously practice? This is also one of the great messages, contained in the unusual monument of the Great Sphinx, as described in the New Muse book; *The Deeper Mysteries*.

Humans are their own worst problems, not something found outside in 'the world.' Humans, both men and woman, have many enemies in life but the biggest are death, and the devil-self—the biggest enemy of them all because it's within them, located in the left hemisphere. Modern neuroscience now clinically refers to the entity in the left brain as the 'Self Module,' which we will also consider as SET. Overcome your vices and your anger, which are mainly found in the left hemisphere, and you will be on your way to your Divine Self. This is the old teaching, still hidden as glimpses in outdated religions.

Moving to the East for a moment, did not Prince Siddhartha Gautama experience great trauma, and then Nirvana, and thus create Buddhism? What does Nirvana mean? It's a surprise for those in the West because Nirvana also means, as the Egyptians and Greeks observed, intense personal death, the great crushing of the ever-thinking personal Ego, only *after* which a great enlightenment occurs. The story of the Phoenix that rises from the ashes is our story; the endless story of life, death, and deity. The Eternal Mystery changes into the slow-moving manifest Everlasting, as the Eternal Changeling moves through its Universe, like a Rolling Stone. This is why all spiritual systems have a core underpinning, which is related to our neural, electromagnetic Wisdom Body; even if you're a short, humpbacked person.

"All is True."
Shakespeare

Several scholars have written of the *'swoon hypothesis,'* which states that Jesus, the small humpbacked fellow, did not die and ascend to Heaven while on the Cross, as stated by the church story. Rather, in this alternative view, Yeshua was drugged by his friends and followers, appeared dead to everyone, including the Romans, and was taken down from the wooden tree, and then recovered and secretly continued his life and traveled abroad, hiding under the pretense of being St. Paul. This alternative, more likely story of Jesus' life appears hidden in plain sight. The public mind is entirely fooled by, or wary of, the church's ruse.

In concluding Jesus; The Humpback Christ, it's rather remarkable that a severely challenged hybrid-hominid individual such as he, could overcome such extreme adversity, and while having a revengeful, violent streak at times, could also achieve great spiritual experiences, having been taught by unknown Yogic teachers in his life. It was India's people who accepted him for what he was, unlike the Romans and the Jewish folk.

Thus, Yeshua truly was a great teacher in his own way, as all great teachings are of the Soul, and not the body. As Stan Gooch said, humanity received its spiritual systems from the Neanderthals and their descendants, as unusual as it seems, in the murky depths of a Neon-Sapiens history.

"Literature is the faint remembrance of Experience."

SAK

Cain: The Third Human, or a Wild Man?

After describing the many alternative stories of Jesus, Mary, and their possible hybrid bloodline, we can continue with the famous story told in the Old Testament, written more than a thousand years earlier.

Cain, the so-called third human, and first son of Adam & Eve, was also not as he seems, for his story is also laced with clues about his truly being a hybrid-hominid; a Neanderthal-Sapiens mix.

We must first drop the romantic Christian notion of a lovely, nearly naked Eve reaching up into a primordial apple tree, where the snake awaits. In the New Muse Series, especially in *The Colors of Mind in Ancient Times*, it is repeatedly shown that all organized religions actually spring from prehistoric times, and that Egypt, Phoenicia, India, and Greece all strongly informed early Christianity, which is hardly an original religion, and which is so disconnected from modern times. The myths of Adam, Eve, Cain, and Abel shouldn't be considered as original stories, but rather as ancient allegories collected from the Levant. Yet, our purpose here is to show that there are definite hints and clues in these stories, of crossbreed mating in the dim past.

Everyone is familiar with the Bible story of Adam and Eve in the Garden of Eden, who then are expelled to *wander* after eating of the fruit of knowledge. LET'S NOT GET TOO EXCITED ABOUT EXPULSION FOR TASTING KNOWLEDGE. OBVIOUSLY THIS WAS AN ALLEGORICAL TALE

*"Adam and Eve, according to the creation myth of the Abrahamic religions, were the **first man and woman.** They are central to the belief that humanity is in essence a single family, with everyone descended from a single pair of original ancestors. It also provides the basis for the doctrines of the fall of man and original sin that are important beliefs in Christianity, although not held in Judaism or Islam."*

TALK ABOUT CHRISTIAN "VIRTICAL INTEGRATION"

Adam and Eve; **Wikipedia**

Let us contrast the Christian notion of 'first man and woman' by providing an update; a News Flash: **There were no 'first humans'**

METAPHYSICAL FRUIT WILL NOT SUSTAIN THE HOMINID, SO YOU WILL SURELY DIE or early Cro-Magnons, as pure 100% Homo sapiens. The evolutionary DNA swirl is further back than we can imagine, in our hominid bloodlines, going on for millions of years. All creatures, including our ancestors and ourselves, are in a state of constant genetic change, as observed by the science of Epigenetics.

The religious idea of a 'first man and woman,' like the stories of divine birth, must take a backseat here, as outdated notions to be discarded.
SURELY IT WAS NEVER INTENDED TO INDICATE A SPECIFIC COUPLE,
These biblical fictions not necessary. All hominid species, including our current genetic admixture of Neanderthal-Sapiens, are in a constant state of universal fluctuation.

> *"No man ever steps in the same river twice,*
>
> *for it's not the same river and he's not the same man."*

Heraclitus

In this book, the reader can quickly see that the genetic evolution of humanity is once again incompatible with outdated, incorrect, religious theory. The story of Adam and Eve is often considered to be an allegory. There is no physical evidence that Adam and Eve ever existed; we should consider that scientific findings in hybrid genetics are incompatible with GOOD the idea of there ever having been a 'first pair of human beings.' Rather, POINT there has been a slow DNA admixture developing between Neanderthals and Sapiens for many thousands of years, especially in the Levant. The religious notion of the 'first human beings,' is akin to the ancient joke: *"Which came first, the chicken or the egg?"*

As we shall see, the issue of evolutionary genetics is not yet fully understood by academia, concerning the obvious hybrid-hominid development on this planet, from which we have all descended.
HOMINIDS NOT SAPIENS
In the Jewish legend of the first humans, Sapiens named Adam and Eve, embark on a long journey to a remote cavern location in the Levant. This story is revealed in an ancient script named *The Syriac Cave of Treasures*,

which, curiously, contained a horde of gold, frankincense and myrrh, strangely reminiscent of the large cache of gold found in the dragon (drakon) caves we discussed earlier in Beowulf. Could it be, in the very dim mists of history, that not only did strange, outcast hybrid creatures we call Incubus, Cambion, or drakon, rape humans, but also took their precious valuables back to their own caves? It would certainly make sense, as the same modus operandi is still in play today, if we consult today's police, who encounter such tactics on a daily basis around the world. So, rape and thievery have always gone hand in hand, in both ancient and modern times. Thus, we might conjecture, the 'dragon's gold' was really just stolen from the nearby humans, a small portion of whom would have been wealthy enough to keep gold, Frankincense, and jewelry in their homes.

Adam was not Cain's Father

Now, as related in the literature of the old Jewish tradition, let us consider that, in this particular cave of 'treasures,' Eve mates with 'someone,' not Adam, and that someone is a hybrid creature whom Jewish folks are calling Satan or Samael, who could also be called an incubus. After Eve mates with this unusual creature, a hybrid-hominid named Cain is born into the world. The Jewish plots twists, in the various Rabbinical literature, where it is said that Eve proclaimed of Cain; *DON'T MAKE THESE STORIES INTO HISTORY*

> *"I have gotten a man from the Lord."*

This statement is remarkably similar, if not identical to the earlier words of Saint Ann. Further, the name of Samael translates as 'bitter beverage or drug,' a name somewhat similar to Mary the Bitter. Perhaps he was, in our own terms, a bitter pillow to swallow. To recall St. Anne's words:

> *"Now I know that the Lord God has blessed me greatly. See, the widow is no longer a widow and the childless woman has conceived in her womb."*
> *(IGJ 4:9)*

HARDLY SURPRISING, THAT THERE WOULD BE INTERBREEDING

And so, Anne gave birth to a daughter, MiriamBuddh, or Mary, the Bitter One, a possible hybrid person, who later gave birth to a small humpback child later known as the wandering Yeshua the Healer (Jesus).

To recap, there are strong reports from the Jewish literature concerning incubus and succubus 'mythical' creatures, who may have been hybrid-hominids, living in the caves of the Levant in the distant past. These creatures were often reported to have sex, possibly violent, with the Jewish folk in the area. This 'Neanderthal-raping humans' premise is also considered in genetic theory, as noted before, in the case of James Fallows' own ancestry, which stemmed from the Levant to Scotland.

Our first clue about Cain as a hybrid-hominid, comes to us from the Jewish legends where there is an ancestral line referred to as the 'Cain Tradition,' which refers to Cain and his unusual line of descendants. In this scenario, Eve bumps hips, not with Adam, but rather someone representing Satan, or the lustful semi-archangel Samael, and Cain is thus brought into the world, without a human daddy.

I embrace, the many-colored beast

Four and Twenty; **Crosby, Stills and Nash**

After mating with Samael/Satan, Eve then mates with someone of her own kind, Sapiens, Adam, and Abel is born.
In the Jewish lore, in a scene where Cain and Able both give offerings to the 'Lord' and the God-Father favors Abel's gift, Cain responds by taking his younger weaker, brother, who has Adam for a father, and is fully human, out into the woods and viciously kills him with a jawbone of an animal. Choosing a jawbone as the symbolic weapon of death may subtly refer to a possibility that Abel, being fully human, could talk, but Cain, being a hybrid, perhaps had speech problems. It's likewise been reported that the extremely strong Samson, another likely hybrid candidate, also used a jawbone of an ass to kill many of his enemies.
As stated earlier, Biblical and Jewish history provides evidence that Grendel's descent from Cain is just a small part of the descendants of the monsters and giants known as the Cain Tradition, although the curious list

of creatures is too long to discuss here. This 'tradition' is likely another confirmation of Stan Gooch's observation that hybrid-hominids, with a higher level of Neanderthal DNA, were often called trolls, giants, ogres, monsters, etc. We can add cambion, drakon, and incubus to the list of unusual names, as they likely all refer to hybrid-hominids of the past, lurking on the outskirts of humanity.

Grendel, in Beowulf, descended from the Cain Tradition, attacked humans because he couldn't stand the sound of men being happy and making joy. Similarly, as a speculation, the younger, more Sapiens child, Abel, would likely be overjoyed at his offering being favored. An older, hybrid Cain became furiously jealous of a father's love, and killed his younger human brother. Cain became known as The Father of Murder. The legend of Cain continues with God expelling the hybrid fellow to 'the Land of Nod,' which translates to the 'Land of Wandering.' We note that God the Expeller had also previously forced Adam and Eve from the Garden of Eden, to wander as well. And so, now it gets interesting. To where did they wander?

Scholars consider that the name of Cain translates as 'to get' or perhaps just 'Get.' In the ancient literature, it states that Cain entered, or wandered, into the Land of Nod, and eventually prospered, and built a city. But where? There are very curious patterns of etymology at play here. If an outcast hybrid creature whose name was 'Get,' began wandering northward, then it becomes noticeable that we encounter the red-haired, extremely strong tribe in lower Europe around Romania, named the 'Getae.' This tribal name is extremely close to Cain's original meaning of Get and suggests they may be ancestors to him. In the Cain Tradition, we also see that Beowulf's tribe is called 'Geat,' virtually synonymous with Get (Cain). Also, the approximate name of Cain can be seen in the word 'cambion' (cain-bion), which also designates a hybrid half-breed. Let us recap our notes about cambions and dragons from earlier chapters:

Merlin the Magician, or the Wildman called Myrddin Wyllt, was born, according to different stories, either 'without a father' or by an incubus-father, which, in other words, we may take as akin to a drakon. Merlin was considered a 'cambion,' or half-man and half-animal; the words cambion and dragon are somewhat similar phonetically, when slowly drawn out, as in a long-vowel chant:

Caaaaaaaaa-bion

Draaaaaaaaa-gon

These two words may have been slightly misinterpreted over the many migratory routes in Eurasia, in past times, so we may consider them as one and the same, with similar meaning and sound.

It is possible that Merlin is descended from the Cain Tradition too. Hopefully, historians of the future will accept this interesting, alternative link to the past, or portions of it, because, it is a logical necessity that some hybrid creatures in our distant past must have contributed to our modern admixture of 2–4% Neon, and 96–98% Sapiens, hominid DNA.

Seth

According to the stories in the biblical Genesis, a young Seth was the third son of Adam and Eve. He was born after Cain had murdered Abel and is said to have lived to the ripe old age of 912. The bible's line of descent, from Adam to Noah, is reckoned through Seth, and he was considered the 'founder of the world.'
However, the Rabbinical lore states that, after the expulsion from paradise, Seth was the first of Adam's children who **had the face and form of man**, and that Adam's earlier post-expulsion progeny, e.g., Cain, had the shapes of **demons and apes**. We may deduce a fair amount of Neanderthal-Sapiens crossbreeding was naturally occurring during these challenging moments, in the ancient caves and seashore of the Levant. In the Bible, two major streams of progeny separately developed. Seth's descendants, dating down to Noah, likely had more Sapiens DNA than those in the Cain Tradition, who were probably outcasts wherever they wandered.

~!~

Adam's Lifetime: 31 or 930 years?

As a brief aside, let's consider the unusual extreme ages given in the Bible to folks such as Adam (930 years) and Seth (912 years). In considering these excessive lifespans as misunderstood math and myth, let us propose a fresher idea, and suggest that, somewhere in the distant past of the Levant, prehistoric tribal scribes used notational methods, and wrote specific calendar 'marks' upon either wooden stick or stones. These marks describe the daily movement of the sun and the monthly cycles of the moon, which we may consider as a 30:1 calendar ratio. If later scribes misunderstood, or mistakenly transposed the markings for the sun and moon, they may have created the excessive lifespans of which we speak, by confusing the daily solar and monthly lunar aspects. If so, it's rather remarkable, and likely not coincidence, that dividing Adams age (930) by 30 days (of the lunar cycle) would result in a much truer, believable age of 31 years. This age is remarkably similar to the anthropologists anticipated lifespans of the ancient primitive man in the Levant; a normal life span was 30–40 years of age. If we accept that a simple, prehistoric scribal misunderstanding occurred, we can close the case and conclude no one was 930 years old!

DNA IS IMPORTANT TO HOMINIDS, OR CROSS BRED HOMINIDS. HAS NOTHING TO DO WITH HUMANS

In the Bible, when Cain was condemned for murder and expelled to wander in the Land of Nod, it was said that he was extremely afraid of others in that, he thought, or stated, *'whoever finds me shall slay me.'* Cain, after viciously killing his younger, weaker Sapiens half-brother, became a wandering DNA anomaly. He was a Wildman, not unlike Enkidu, and thus likely lived beyond the fence of humanity, like his descendants, the monster Grendel and his mum, and those Incubus/Succubus creatures mentioned in the ancient Jewish lore. The Jewish Cain Tradition also includes the Bible's King David, who mated with a succubus, Agrat bat Mahlat, and produced Asmodeus, the Prince of Demons, a hybrid admixture. The questionable biblical archangel, Samael, known as the 'Poison of God,' the 'Bitter Beverage' is reported in other Jewish stories, and is also said to have mated with Agrat bat Mahlat, with the result being a likely hybrid-hominid. Beyond the ongoing swirl and endless overlay of different ancient stories, the hybrid-hominid origins of humanity can still faintly be seen. Truly, even as Beowulf, the Geat King, we are all slightly influenced, and descended from, Cain, Enkidu, or any of the many hybrid persons named in this book, if we consider, as did James Fallows, our extremely remote, paleo-ancestry.

Jeremiah

SPELLS ARE INCANTATIONS.

In the historical lore of ancient Ireland, its noted that Jeremiah, of ancient biblical fame, is said to have traveled and lived there, around 600 BCE. Curiously, he was said to be, like Merlin our hybrid wizard, 'Mighty of Spells.' Jeremiah's name has undergone several renderings over the millennia; he was once called Yeremiah, and it's very telling that one of his earliest, and primary names was 'Caie,' nearly identical with 'Cain.' The magical Jeremiah, or Caie, hailing from the Levant, seems another example of how a hidden tribal culture of hybrid-hominids that the Jewish scholars refer to as the Cain Tradition, eventually migrated into various parts of Europe.

The Jewish legend of Tubal-Cain

Another strong example of a hybrid-hominid presence in the ancient Levant lies in the Jewish legend of Tubal-Cain. Tubal-Cain developed the ancient craft of blacksmithing; his name infers 'smith-getter,' or smith-obtainer.' He was a seventh-generation descendant of Cain himself, in the Cain Tradition. We observe a quality of great hybrid-hominid strength in Tubal-Cain.

"Tubal exceeded all men in strength and was very expert

and famous in martial performances."

Antiquities of the Jews, **Josephus the Historian**

In the Jewish lore, Tubal and his sister Naamah were born into the Cain lineage by their parents Lamach and Zillich. The cultural reference to 'Cainite' and the ancient land of Canaan are apparently related; an association now accepted by many Jewish and Biblical scholars.

Canaan was the land of Cain's descendants, before they started their many migrations over the centuries. In the Book of Joshua, Canaanites, seen as a low caste perhaps, are included in a list of nations to exterminate, and later described as a group which the Israelites had annihilated, or driven off. The land of Canaan was also known as Philistine, who with their Goliath, were enemies of the early Hebrews.

More importantly, the ancient, far-traveling Phoenicians also lived for many thousands of years in this piece of the Levant before the Jewish folk settled there.

A Cain In Spain

At some unknown date Tubal-Cain and his tribe migrated from the Levant to Iberia, now modern Spain. Jewish historian Josephus (1st century AD), wrote of the ethnicity of the current inhabitants:

"Tubal gave rise to the Thobeles, who are now called Iberes."

Thobeles is obviously a misspelling of Tubal, which sounds similar, and the Iberes are a reference to Iber, a son of Tubal's.

Joesphus' observation was echoed by other historians, such as Patriarch Eustathius of Antioch, Bishop Theodoret, and others. However, Jerome, Isidore of Seville, Welsh historian Nennius, and other writers stated yet another tradition—that Tubal was ancestor to not only Iberians, but also the Italians; he must have been a lustful fellow!

Basque historian Andrés de Poza (16th century) also named Tubal-Cain as the ancestor of the Basques, and by extension, the Iberians. Author Augustin Chaho (19th century) published 'The Legend of Aitor,' asserting that the common patriarch of the Basques was Aitor, a descendant of Tubal.
According to Catalan legend, Tubal is said to have sailed from Jaffa in the Levant with his family and arrived at the Francolí river of the Iberian Peninsula in 2157 BC, where he founded a city named after his son. Thus, the presence of a strong, lusty, hybrid Cain in Spain seems rather well substantiated.

The Strange Story of the Rape of the Sabines

We move to ancient Italy now, to discuss the rape, or abduction of the Sabine Women, which is a well-accepted piece of Roman mythology, and was a frequent subject of Renaissance-era artists and sculptors. This abduction myth, however, has its roots in a hybrid-hominid truth. Josippon the historian (c950) and the Chronicles of Jerahmeel both relate how Tubal-Cain's descendants, known as the Sapines, built a city called 'Sabino' near Tuscany, on one side of the Tiber River, while another tribe, the Kittim, ancestors to the early Romans, lived on the other. When the Kittim began to cross the river to steal the Sabine women for the purposes of lust or matrimony, a war soon broke out between Tubal-Cain's descendants and the earliest, pre-Roman settlement. It's noteworthy that another nearby tribe, called the Caeninenses from Caenina was outraged at the Kittim-Roman rape of the Sabines and also attacked the Kittim. Surely the name of Cain can be seen in Caen-ina, as another ancient reference to the earliest ancestor, of the quickly spreading Cain Tradition, which began in the Levant.

Strangely, the fierce war was only ended when the captured Sapiens-Kittim mothers, hateful of war, displayed great courage by hurling themselves, while carrying their children, between the flying spears and battle-axes of the two groups of fighting men. Livy, the Roman historian, described the scene:

"They, from the outrage on whom the war originated, with hair disheveled and garments rent, the timidity of their sex being overcome by such dreadful scenes, had the courage to throw themselves amid the flying weapons, and making a rush across, to part the incensed armies, and assuage their fury; imploring their fathers on the one side, their husbands on the other, "that as fathers-in-law and sons-in-law they would not contaminate each other with impious blood, nor stain their offspring with parricide, the one their grandchildren, the other their children. If you are dissatisfied with the affinity between you, if with our marriages, turn your resentment against us; we are the cause of war, we of wounds and of bloodshed to our husbands and parents. It were better that we perish than live widowed or fatherless without one or other of you."

The abducted females had formed a female line of protest, and the fierce fighting suddenly stopped, for fear of harming the Sapine women, who then showed their Sapine-Kittim children to the Sabines, the descendants of Tubal, who could then see their mutual progeny. Perhaps these children appeared similar to the Sabines, having a mother of one tribe, and a father of another, for the conflict ended, with both sides living more peacefully, each on their own side of the Tiber River, near modern-day Rome. Later the tribes would merge, and Romulus shared the kingship with Titus Tatius, King of the Sapines. These people, descended from Tubal-Cain, and the Sapine-Kittim children, were the ancestors and progenitors of a great empire.

There are several other potential hybrid creatures in the Cain Tradition, as seen in the Bible; one can consider the written description of those called the wild and hairy ones, such as Elijah, Ishmael, Esau—and then, there's the long-haired Samson.

The Saga of Samson

In the character of Samson, depicted as being in the 'Wildman Tradition' by scholar Herman Gunkel, we have a strong display of a Neon-Sapiens hybrid indication.

Author Gregory Mobley wrote an interesting article entitled, 'The Wild Man in the Bible and the Ancient Near East,' published in the Journal of Biblical Literature(Vol. 116, No. 2; 1997);

"There are many similarities between the biblical Samson and the medieval wild man. Though the Bible does not say a word about body hair, Samson's hair, uncut since birth, is his signal trait. Samson establishes his credentials as master of beasts in his inaugural feat of wrestling a lion (Judges 14:5-6). Samson display the perpetual aggressiveness of the wild man in his episodes of frenzied violence. His relationships with culture are of the wild man type; he is irresistibly drawn to culture by women and, once in culture, he is pressured to divulge secrets (Judges 14:15-17;16:5-17). Like so many wild men of myth and fairy tale, the Danite beast is humanized by a woman, Delilah."

There is a similar hint or clue given, of a captured satyr, who spills secrets when finally caught, according to Greek legend, and when a wild Samson comes into civilization, he too 'is pressured to divulge secrets.' When the cunning Delilah cuts the Wildman's hair, it is because the Wildman will *become like one of the human beings*(Judges 16:7, 11, 17).' During his psychological 'captivity,' Samson kills many of his enemies; several thousand Philistines die by his hand, as reported by the Bible.

In Richard Bernheimer's *Wild Men in the Middle Ages* (1952), Samson, and other wild men, are nicknamed 'Homo Ferus,' to indicate their not-quite-human status. We can consider Homo Ferus is really an indication of hybrid-hominid humanity, as the DNA admixtures swirled over eons of time. Samson was not a wolf, but a Neanderthal-Sapiens hybrid.

In the beginning, in a story plot somewhat similar to Enkidu and the Temple Seductress, before Samson is lured into civilization by Delilah's charms, he sleeps in a rock crevice, eats wild honey and lives off of the land, meaning, he doesn't eat civilized, human food. When he fights, he doesn't use human weapons, such as sword or spear; instead, the unstoppable Wildman slaughtered many of his foes with the jawbone of an ass. Similarly, Cain had killed his half-brother Abel, with the same type of weapon. If Samson was as strong as stated in the Bible, then he would have been a hairy, Neon-hybrid warrior, strong, extremely fast, and very deadly. In a way, while living in rocky crevasse, Samson reminds us of the cave-dwelling drakons in The Beowulf Saga. When Samson approached the ancient city of Gaza, he ripped up its gates with his bare hands; no tools or weapons were necessary. He is an outsider, who comes in from the wild. Samson's humanization, or civilized conversion, does not take, and in the end, he reverts to wildness in the wilderness again. His inner God did not speak to him while he was in the throes of Delilah, and captured by civilization—hence his return to wild nature, and his own God, before his eventual death. Samson the Wildman may have been 14–20% Neanderthal.

King David, Goliath, and the Gog-Magog

Amidst the many swirls and myths of the Christian Bible, and the early Jewish stories found in the Talmud, and elsewhere, we can still locate tantalizing hints and clues of a hidden, hybrid humanity, which are seemingly cloaked from plain sight by the various, often farcical, developments in in the Abrahamic literature. We must, at first, discard the many convoluted, nationalistic, and religious descriptions of King David as they are inaccurate, as was the traditional depiction of Jesus as a handsome, European white guy. King David, according to our best knowledge, lived in Israel around 1,000 BCE; however, that is nearly all that is known in the historical record. The degenerated, exacerbated legends of his existence now have the importance of children's tales. Several of these legends consider King David as a key ancestor of Yeshua, who became Jesus in Christianity—their unknown, humpbacked Savior.

Most of the biblical information we have concerning King David comes to us from the books of the prophet Samuel the Seer, who, we indicated earlier, may have had a hybrid-hominid father, along with his Sapiens mother St. Anna. This mating is disguised in the Bible as a 'divine birth from the Lord,' cover-up story. Interestingly, there are several scholars today, such as Stephen M. Miller, who consider that the myth of King Arthur, is akin to the myth of King David.

David's father was Jesse, in both the Jewish and Christian observances, yet his mother is infamously omitted in the curious Bible, while the Talmud readily states that she was an ancestor of the Kings of Judah—her name was Nitzevet.

There is no physical description of her; Nitzevet is simply referred to as an 'Israelite,' who bore nine children to Jesse, one of whom grew up to be King David. This particular son frequently visited the town of Ein-Gedi (Get, Geat, Getae?) near the Qumran caves of Israel, where, it was said, rather quaintly, *'to attend to his needs.'* Whether these 'needs' were for a safe haven, a meditative retreat, or a reference to sex in the caves, we'll never likely know. King David was known, as in his singing of the Psalms, to have a lovely melodious voice, which was capable of capturing both human and animal attention. We might imagine the wonderful echo of reverberating cave walls while an ancient man sang to his God. Perhaps King David's most famous legend, after considering his lustful exploits with Agrat bat Mahlat, the succubus, Queen Bathsheba, and his harrowing escapes to the caves from his enemy, King Saul, was that of his battle with Goliath.

Goliath, the Hybrid Giant

The early Christian authors depicted Goliath as a giant man, over nine feet tall, but this description must be seen as a morphing of the facts, as yet another fanciful biblical exaggeration, which modern Christians must still swallow, along with the Bible's many other, rather crazy stories. A better option, for the consideration of giants, is to employ paleo-psychologist Stan Gooch's idea that relict, or remnant hybrid human-Neanderthals, with their superior strength and stouter bodies, were secretly associated with the myth of a young King David, as he fought and killed Goliath, with several, well-aimed stones to the giant's face and forehead. There is no reason to doubt the truthfulness of this encounter; a fight between two hominid creatures, different in their admixture of DNA, may well have ensued in 1,000 BCE, in a similar fashion to that of King Beowulf and the huge Grendel, in the northern caves. The name of King David, who may also have had an unusual DNA admixture, stems from the root words of 'dev, deva, or div,' which can mean either angel or 'dev-il' in the ancient languages of the Levant, Greece, Arabia, and India. As both the extremely strong King Beowulf and the monstrous Grendel likely had different amounts of mixed hybrid DNA, we may also suspect the same of King Dav-id, and Goliath. IRRELEVANT TO HUMANS

In the Bible legend, Goliath was from nearby Canaan, or Lebanon, yet the Bible calls he and his tribe Philistines, perhaps simply to mark them as enemies. The descendants of Cain, the Cainites, were the early inhabitants of Canaan. The name of Goliath is also translated as 'Gath,' a name that may have considerable importance in the legend of King David and several others, including Alexander the Great, in the 3rd century BCE. Two of the five Philistine cities were called Gath and Gaza. The guttural sound of 'Gath' is also heard in the Hebrew legend of Gog and Magog. Indeed, Goliath may once have been pronounced 'Gog-liath.'

The sound of Gog, or of 'Gath' is similar to the aforementioned 'Get,' which is a primary translation of the name 'Cain.' Long-vowel chants display the close relations:

218

Goooooo-gh	(with 'gah' sound)
Gaaaaaaa-th	(with 'gah' sound)
Geeeeee-t	(with 'geh' sound)
Caaaaaaa-in	(with 'ca' sound)

These phonically related names may have resulted in Cain's alternative name of 'Get' moving into the northern tribes of the Getae and the Geats, where legend states, the monster Grendel, and his mother, are descended from Cain himself. The suggested cultural and DNA diffusion from the Levant to southern and northern Europe, is remindful, once again, of how journalist James Fallows' geneticist described his ancestry, and his high Neanderthal DNA count, as stemming from the migratory flow between Scotland and the humans and hybrid Neanderthal creatures, in the Levant, on the eastern Mediterranean shore, thousands of years ago.

In following the Jewish tradition, we suggest that an ancient Cain, born of a Sapiens named Eve and 'Satan,' (also known as Samael, whom we depict as a hybrid-hominid), may indeed have wandered, as an outcast from humanity, after he killed a human—his brother Abel, who was born of two human parents; Adam and Eve

GOG

REALLY YOU THINK ITS HISTORY. LIKE THE CRUCIFICATION IS HISTORY NOT METAPHOR

History doesn't record Gog as the name of any particular person; however, the names of Gog and Magog do indeed refer to a single unknown individual, and also his clan, or tribal lands. In the Abrahamic lore, Gog is frequently referred to as a monster, further suggesting his hybrid DNA makeup.

In the Bible, Gog and the Magog are referred to as 'unclean nations,' which we can also take as a prejudice against peoples who are hybrid-hominids, perhaps having 10–15% Neanderthal DNA.

Josephus the historian writes that Joel, or Japhetite, was the father of Gog and that the Gath represented one of the 'three races of man' mentioned in the Bible. Is it possible that the race of Japhetite (gath-etite?), the Gog-Magog, was a hybrid-hominid clan, not unlike the Shennong or Yandi clan, in ancient China? Both groups had their tribal leader's name, and the name of the clan, as one and the same.

In the hands of the early Christian writers, the Magog became the 'apocalyptic hordes,' and throughout the Medieval European period were variously identified as the Huns, Khazars, Mongols, Turanians or other nomads, or even the Lost Tribes of Israel. These authors were strangely correct.

As unusual as it seems, many of the peoples living today in the far eastern country of Mongolia—the Mongols, actually consider themselves as descendants of the Levant's Gog and Magog. This is rather astounding, plus, the names are phonetically similar. Magog became Mongol.

The biblical references to Gog and Magog are relatively few, but the Christian Apocrypha literature is well sprinkled with references to them. In the Qur'ān, Gog and Magog are seen as Yājūj and Mājūj, which are also phonically related.(yaj-maj). The earliest Christians, such as Ezekiel, tended to view these 'unclean tribes' as abhorrent—they were considered of 'Satan' and against the 'Lord.' Ezekiel may have been correct, if we take the Jewish interpretation here, which says that Eve mated with Samael, also called Satan.

Perhaps the Gog-Magog were actually one and the same as the Jewish legends of incubus and succubus, the wild creatures living in or near the caves of the Levant, where regular matings between Neanderthal hybrids and Sapiens seems to have occurred. At one point ancient tempers must have flared, for the biblical God said:

"Son of man, direct your face against Gog, of the land of Magog, the

prince, leader of Meshech and Tubal, and prophesy concerning him. Say:

Thus, said the Lord: Behold, I am against you, Gog, the prince, leader of

Meshech and Tubal."

The reference to Tubal is likely a reference to Tubal-Cain, further relating the name of the Cainites to the Gog-Magog. Ezekiel's God strongly suggests that Ezekiel and his hordes drive out the Gog-Magog by the sword, and so they, the 'clean' or more Sapiens-Israeli tribes, mass in large numbers and attack the nearby 'unwalled villages' of the Magog, the unclean Neanderthal-Sapiens tribe. Ezekiel's people relentlessly kill and plunder the unclean tribes, which is not unlike what the Gog-Magog most likely did themselves. Most of the Gog-Magog are driven off into the distant wilderness, never to return, to begin their wandering in the Land of Nod, as did the hybrid Cain (Get).

This Old Testament idea of 'Ezekiel's God' of course, is literally off the rails, having little connection to deep spirituality. Having a 'wrathful God,' the Old Testament prophets, such as Ezekiel and Elijah, murdered quite regularly. Elijah also wiped out the 'evil' priests at the Phoenician (Canaan) Temple of Baal, again, because 'God' told Elijah to do so. Basically, in this light, Ezekiel and Elijah can be seen as deluded murderers, killing others who were not of their faith, which is not uncommon in the history of Christianity. Not agreeing with them and their tribe would get you killed, and your temple robbed of its valuables; these were the early religious tribal conflicts. Yet the ancient folk of Canaan—the early Phoenicians—strongly influenced the early Jewish folk, providing them with language scripts, which eventually became the Habiri (Hebrew) language. The earliest Bible was actually written using the Phoenician alphabet. The Phoenicians even transferred their sacred religious symbols, which became the Tetragrammaton of YHVH (Yahweh) in today's Jewish faith. Although biblical scholars may disagree, it appears that the ancient Judaic attitude and vicious attacks against the 'unclean tribes' of Gog and Magog, eventually resulted in a northeastern exodus, or migration towards Lydia, or modern-day Turkey and then a subsequent migration towards China and Mongolia. While in Lydia, the Magog, or their descendants, may have become known as the Gok-Turks (gog-turk) where the term 'Turk' means 'extremely strong person.' While evolutionary scholars ponder over the ancient migrations of humans, they never consider that hybrid-hominids, such as the Gog and

221

Magog of the Levant, were also migrating, and changing their DNA admixture with the humans they encountered, while also experiencing severe xenophobia at every stage of their journey, until finally, they settled into Mongolia. East Asians today still have 20% more Neanderthal DNA than their European counterparts. Flash forward a few thousand years, and we find, later, in the 12th century AD, a powerful Magog (Mongolian) warlord named Genghis Khan, with his great strength, long flowing red hair and large brilliant green emeralds for eyes, would later unite many tribes of the East and launch vicious attacks against the West. This ferocious Magog, descended from hybrid ancestors in the Middle East, went on to become the second most famous person in history, ranking only behind Yeshua, the hybrid humpback, who went on to morph into the Jesus that is the caricature of the rapidly fading Western church. Truth is stranger than fiction, once again. The vicious and cunning Genghis Khan and his successors, the likely descendants of the wild Gog-Magog clans, eventually created the largest empire ever seen on Earth, stretching continuously from east Asia to medieval Europe. Perhaps the Khan would have tested for 8–10% Neanderthal DNA, which would have been normal for Mongols, the descendants of the Levant's Gog-Magog.

The Wandering Romani; Descended from Cain

After the unusual legacy of Cain, several millennia passed, and many wandering bands of Cain's descendants, known generally as the loosely assembled Romani tribespeople, traveled throughout India and Europe. These Romani 'roamers' were also known as the Kale tribes; notice the phonetic resemblance to 'Cai-l.' These people were considered unclean outcasts, who wandered from place to place. They were often driven off, murdered, or enslaved as they migrated.
Is it possible these wandering 'Roman-i' peoples were descended from the Sapine-Romano merger, where the influence of Tubal-Cain's descendants has been seen?
In 1323, Simon Simeonis, a traveling Irish Franciscan friar, described these social outcasts, while they were sojourning in Candia (cain-dia), on the island of Crete: "

"We also saw outside this city of Candia, a tribe of people who worship according to the Greek rite and **assert themselves to be of the race of Cain**. *These people rarely or never stop in one place for more than thirty days, but always, as if cursed by God, are nomad and outcast. After the thirtieth day they wander from field to field with small, oblong, black, and low tents, like those of the Arabs, and from cave to cave, because the place inhabited by them becomes after the term of thirty days so full of vermin and other filth that it is impossible to live in their neighborhood."*

The Iron Gates of Alexander

By the time of the Romans, a very telling story had sprung up about a certain exploit of Alexander the Great(356–323 BCE). According to this legend, the Greek King, during his campaigns near the Caspian Sea, had once constructed a mountain barricade called 'The Iron Gates of Alexander.' The barricade was built out of necessity, it was said, to prevent the wild Gog-Magog from attacking the Greek encampment in the dead of the night. The wild Magog tribe were considered cannibals, and so the Greek army, much stronger in total numbers, drove them out into a deep valley mountain pass, and then constructed the tall gates to keep them from their raids upon 'civilized' peoples.

Similar to the Jewish stories of the Levant's incubus and succubus, as potential hybrid creatures, we might imagine, that in a remote mountain area near the Caspian Sea, a single individual, or a small group of silent Magogs moving under the cover of night, might have broken into a Greek's hut or tent, and killed the men immediately. They would later eat the men, after stealing, raping, and enslaving the women, as was sometimes done in ancient warfare, regardless of hominid species.

The Giants of London

No, there were no werewolves in London, but there really were giants!

Ancient references to hybrid-hominids as giants are at least 4,000 years old, as witnessed by King Gilgamesh's repeated references to his friend Enkidu, as a giant, even the 'greatest' of giants.

As we saw with Jeremiah, also called 'Cai-l,' some of the Gog-Magog, or Cain clans, may also have traveled north from the Levant, and eventually settled in Great Britain, where there are numerous legends of giants, who are depicted as either monsters or heroes.

Geoffrey of Monmouth, in his Historia Regum Britanniae (1136), writes of a giant literally named Gogmagog ("Goemagot" or "Goemagog"), in the legend of the founding of Britain. The Historia reported that Gog-Magog and twenty of his fellow giants attacked a human settlement and caused great slaughter; Gog-Magog is observed as being so strong that he rips trees out by their roots and swings them as weapons, which certainly reminds of how Beowulf was felled by a dragon's (drakon's) tail, which we suspected may be a weapon, or an uprooted tree.

Another legend is more kind. In the saga of 'The Champions of London,' Gog and the Magog heroically rescue Princess Londona from the cave of the evil giant Humbug. There are also Gog-Magog reports in France and Ireland:

Works of Irish mythology, including the Lebor Gabála Érenn (the Book of Invasions), expand on the Genesis account of Magog as the son of Japheth and make him the ancestor to the Irish through Partholón, leader of the first group to colonize Ireland after the Deluge, and a descendant of Magog, as also were the Milesians, the people of the 5th invasion of Ireland. Magog was also the progenitor of the Scythians, as well as of numerous other races across Europe and Central Asia.

Gogmagog, **Wikipedia**

Basically, the *Lebor Gabala* states that the Irish are descended from the Gaels, who are partially descended from the Gog-Magog.

The name Gael (gae-l) seems to be a close approximation of the tribal words Geat, (gae-t), and Getae. Even the ancient tribe names of 'Gaul,' as well as the 'Goths' are likely derivatives of these older names. Most scholars will likely not agree, having their own dramatically different, yet outdated view of history, which doesn't even consider, yet, as of this writing, our hidden hybrid-hominids. They only write of history as the works of Sapiens—'human' people and characters.

The clarity of these British legends is lacking, but, even so, it's likely that the Gog-Magog, and the reports of Grendel in the Saga of Beowulf, a monster who is distantly related to Cain himself, are all somehow connected in the dim, distant past of hybrid humanity, as it constantly *migrated into new cave dwellings*, due to the constant pressure of dangerous contacts with human civilization.

The legends of the wandering Cai-n, perhaps sometimes heard as 'ka-i, or cog' and Gog, are names which are also phonically similar, makes great sense if the wandering through the 'Land of Nod' was simply a series of long hybrid-hominid migrations towards the east, west, and north, away from the motherland of the Levant.

As they migrated, ongoing, systemic violence of the humans against the 'unclean tribes,' the hybrid-hominids, likely contributed to their extinction. There really were drakon-slayers, or dragon slayers in the world, as they hunted down and killed their vicious hybrid-hominid wild brothers. Today, in small amounts, we still possess the ancestral DNA of Giants, Drakons, and the Gog-Magog, as our partial, Neanderthal heritage.

Giants, and Ogres, and Trogers; Oh My!

New language considerations

In today's urban English slang, a new, insulting word 'Troger' has sprung up, which is a combination of the words 'Trog' and 'Ogre.' This is quite a natural development. Something similar has been going on in many migrating cultures, for several millennia, yet unobserved by linguistic scholars.

~!~

A new suggestion stated here, is that the core, phonically similar, sound-words of **Drok, Trog, Gog, Og, Cai, and Get,** may all have been shifting monosyllabic descriptions of the ancient European, Middle-Eastern and Chinese peoples to describe our more monstrous, ancient hybrid ancestors. The premise presented here is that these similar, nearly identical sound-words later morphed and became imbedded into our modern English words of Drag-on, Trog-lodyte, Tro-ll, Gog-MaGog, Og-re, and also the European tribes such as the Geats, Getae and Gauls and Goths. There are additional 'morphed' words further below, some quite shocking. By not using the usual, weak etymologies for these words, we can avoid simply referring to pure, parroted myths which lead nowhere. The eons of migrating cultures swirled both their DNA and languages in ancient and medieval times, much of which has escaped notice.

~!~

As science ponders upon why the Neanderthals went extinct, perhaps we may consider a hybrid-genocide as a factor, as a large part of the reason was certainly due to a massive Sapiens response to rape, murder and plunder. For many of the hybrid folk were monsters, at one time, and killing them or driving them off was the only recourse. This response of Sapiens to monster-Neanderthals eventually morphed into the European medieval dragon (drok, drakon) slayers, where supposed, dramatic and

227

colorful myths are actually, faintly rooted in experience. Perhaps there really were, 'damsels in distress,' who had been attacked by a monstrous hybrid, optionally called a dragon, ogre, or giant.

"There were giants in the earth in those days."

Genesis 6:4

Although paleo-psychologist Stan Gooch often referred to hybrid-hominids as giants, trolls and ogres, he didn't realize there was a likely, yet hidden linguistic relation, as we consider the following explanations for giants, ogres and trolls.

The Giants

The English word of 'giant' stems from the middle-English and French word of 'gaent.' Note that this spelling, as gae-nt, is closely related to Cain's other primary name of 'Get.' The European tribal names of Getae, Geat, are also related to this original name of 'Get.' While modern usage of the word 'giant' tends to produce fanciful images of 60-foot-tall creatures in the cinema media circus, the 'real' giants were actually overwhelmingly strong and fast, and often deadly hybrid creatures. In Bristol, England, there is a rocky complex called The Giants Caves, yet the long entrance is only 4–5 feet high. Modern humans, as tourist visitors, have to bend over to enter; these cave homes were obviously *not* for tall giants! The Merriam-Webster, and other dictionaries, simply refer to giants as fabulous creatures, unusually large and powerful; these would be our hybrid-hominids, who were often monsters. In Greek and Roman Mythology, the Giants, also called Gigantes, were pronounced as 'Jye-GAHN-tees or gee-GAHN-tees.'
We can note that GAHN, GET and CAI, with ancient accents, are extremely similar phonetically, suggesting an extremely early, possibly prehistoric origin. These creatures were considered a terrifying race, having great strength and aggression, though not of tall stature.
Further, the mystery of the mythical *Centaur*, which in its original, non-embellished form, simply meant 'bull-killer' and not a half-man, half-horse myth, can be more properly seen as 'Cain-taur,' meaning, more

properly, a strong hybrid creature; a true 'giant' described as being capable of killing a bull.

The mysterious Arabian *Jinn*, known in Turkish as 'Cin,' were creatures of the night who attacked, raped and often killed humans, not unlike the exploits of the Jewish Incubus/Succubus. Is this name of 'Cin' or Jinn, a distant, now-forgotten reference to wild 'Cain' descendants?

Alternately, we can continue to believe the unfounded, parroted myths of a man-horse-centaur, and of a smoky desert Jinn, which have never been explained.

The Ogres

This word, ogre, meaning a man-eating, half-human creature, may be distantly related to the name of the vicious half-human Gog-Magog, whom we have mentioned. There is also Jewish literature referring to Og, the last of the giants, who were called the Rephaim; these were considered the ancestors of the early Hebrew folk. In the Bible, after their exodus from Egypt, the early Israelites were terribly afraid, for their new land was full of 'giants.' Thus, we can note the interchangeable reference to giants as ogres.

In addition to the Jewish lore, there is also the biblical saga of King Og, of the Amorite clan, who fought the 'chosen people' or the Tribes of Israel. Again, King Og, the extremely strong warrior, was the last survivor of the giant Rephaim. In the story, the more numerous Israeli tribes are divinely instructed to wipe out the entire Amorite clan—each man, woman and child was killed. Is it possible this was one of many species-related wars, where differing neighboring tribes, with different hybrid-hominid DNA admixtures, actually sought to exterminate, not just defeat, the other tribe, as a type of hybrid racial cleansing, or genocide? Scholars have strongly considered that prehistoric tribes, such as the 6,000-year-old Yamna culture, were also genocidal in the treatment of their neighbors.

The name of ogre, pronounced as 'Og-er' in today's English, may have been pronounced as Og-guh' in earlier times, which is nearly identical with the ancient sound of 'Gog,' suggesting a slang usage which developed to refer to a creature that was extremely dangerous to more Sapiens (human) tribes. Scholars also infer that a Greek word for demon, 'h-orkos,' contributed to the English Ogre. We should consider that Cain and his descendants could have been *related to, or even early founders* of the Gog-Magog. The names Cai'n and Get are also close approximations to Gog, in both sound and meaning. Thus, it is possible to consider that man-eating Og-res, or Gogs, were early hybrid cannibals. We might well deduce an origin of 'cain-ables,' which became 'cannibals,' as we describe our man-eating ancestors, the Monster-Hybrids, and disregard the standard etymologies. Is it possible that hybrid Cain, after murdering Abel with a jawbone of an ass, actually ate part of the corpse?

It's interesting to note that the first child of Cain was a boy named Enoch (En-och), which one may easily take as 'En-gog,' in our meaning, referring to a hybrid child. Further, in the Book of Enoch, it is clearly stated that ancient giants mated with the beautiful women of ancient Israel, which we may accept as Neanderthal-Sapiens intercourse.
In the Turkish lore, and even today, a creature known as a 'dev' is said to describe an ogre, giant, or the dev-il. In other cultures, such as the Hindi, the word 'dev' or 'deva' generally describes an angelic or godlike being, something totally different. We recall that, in the Levant, King David (deva'd) himself mated with Aghat bat Mahlat, a cave-dwelling animal-like succubus. Together, they produced a demon-child, called Prince Asmodeus. As we refer back to the Jewish/Levant cultures, where Mary and Hanna (Anna) are 'impregnated' by God, instead of a mortal man (sapiens), we begin to see the repeated notion of claiming that 'God has given me a child,' as a cloaking device, for the more likely ancient hip-bumping of a Sapiens-Neanderthal hybrid pairing, producing either Monsters, Philosophers, Saviors, or even Gods.

The Greek river **God** Oiagros, or Oregrus (Ogre-us), as the important father of Orpheus, and perhaps even Orphism, is yet another example of how ancient peoples thought; meaning, a **God can be indicated as an ogre** and vice versa, in the ancient lore and lingo. Perhaps Orpheus himself too, was a partial hybrid ogre, as another DNA anomaly.

Is it possible that Gog and God had several ancient meanings and sounds, which were poorly understood by scholars, and that, in certain references, Gog became confused as God?

A monument image of Orcus, in the Italian Gardens of Bomarzo, also known as 'The Park of Monsters' Credit: Alessio Damato, CC by SA 3.0

In the Italian legend of Orcus, an Etruscan God-Wildman, also represented the Ogre; indeed, our very word for ogre is indebted to him. Orcus was considered a red-haired giant who ate human flesh in his underground cave. The legend carries on where J.R.R Tolkien, author of The Lord of the Rings series, derived his terrible, man-eating Orc armies from Orcus, the ancient Ogre and in the Saga of Beowulf there are 'orcreus' creatures.

In the 2nd century BCE apocryphal book, "Ogias the Giant" or "The Book of Giants" the adventures of a giant named Ogias who fought a great dragon are depicted. Ogias is considered either identical with the Biblical Og or was Og's father. The core words of OG or DROG explain the confusion; when an ogre fought a dragon (drakon) it was really a battle

231

between two different hybrid creatures, with perhaps 15–20% Neanderthal DNA. Thus, we can note the interchangeable reference to ogres as either being giants or dragons—hybrid-hominids had many names.

Troll

Our childlike, fairytale depictions of half-human monsters, hiding under bridges, waiting to devour children, has a wisp of trueness hidden in the word 'Tro-ll.' The first syllable 'Tro-g' in the Greek Troglodatae, is similar in sound and meaning to Troll. Also, the key sound of Gog appears slightly garbled as 'Trog'; we may suspect the fleeing, migrating 'unclean tribes' of Israel, the Gog-Magog, at one time settled near the Red Sea, where the Grecian name of Troglodatae first developed. Later, the slang of Trog, as 'Troll,' developed in the myths of Europe, and thus, the threat of the monstrous creature hiding under the bridge was very real and most likely people were really killed and eaten by such wild monsters.

Let us do a brief, albeit gory, thought experiment, set in the ancient Levant. In 3,000 BCE, you and I are walking along near the caves, and suddenly spot a hairy hybrid creature, whose facial hair is covered in blood—it's sitting outside and actually feeding upon a human corpse, as they are believed to have routinely done. Observing this cannibalism (cain-ibilism) horrifies us—perhaps we knew the deceased. We quickly leave the scene and return to our Sapiens tribe to report the killing. A large group of armed men then departs to the horrid death scene. We are enraged, and trap, kill and mutilate the hated hybrid creature, which we possibly called a drok (dragon), Gog (ogre), Trog, or Get, or Cai, thousands of years ago.

Taming the Cyclops

It is difficult to dislodge mythical stereotypes once they become nearly permanently fixed in our brains. The wild Greek story of the Cyclops is one such example; it is not unlike the various dragon (drakon) myths that have gone wild around the globe.

When I was young, perhaps six years old, I had intensely vivid recurring nightmare dreams of being chased house-to-house by a 60-ft tall, one-eyed Cyclops, after I had watched an especially engrossing movie on the television, concerning the Greek legend of Odysseus, as he and his men encountered them while voyaging homeward. The legend of Odysseus, like my vivid dream, is a creative, wildly developed story, that likely bears little relation to the possible origin of ancient Cyclops.

Let us reconstruct an alternative view of the Cyclops, given what we know about the evolving hybrid-hominid presence in the Mediterranean Sea.

Homer the Poet and Hesiod the Philosopher, writing separately around 700 BCE, were the earliest Greeks to mention the Cyclops. Hesiod is kinder, portraying them as toolmakers for the Gods, while being strong, powerful creatures, with 'very violent hearts.' We may recall the Jewish legend of Tubal-Cain, the hybrid-hominid father of blacksmithing and tool-making. Homer, however, simply depicts Cyclops as powerful cannibals.

Our own first Euromerican translations of the Greek myths, stemming from the 18th century, favored the notion of 'one eye,' thus, the giant creature with one eye was born in the mind of many scholars. More recently, scholars are now considering that the Greek word 'Kýklōpes,' meaning *"Circle-eyes"* or *"Round-eyes"* is a more likely interpretation, rather than ol' one eye, and this linguistic development happens to be a perfect match for our hybrid-hominid theory. Let us recall that the Greek 'drakon,' which later became dragon, originally meant 'sharp-sighted one'—someone with extremely keen vision, and who had larger eyes than Sapiens.

The powerful Cyclops, or round-eyed ones, were said to live on 'The Island of the Kyklops,' which is believed to be the modern Italian island of Sicily.

These creatures were not 60-foot-tall giants, but were rather, as Stan Gooch had suggested concerning giants, extremely strong, overwhelming hybrid creatures, who had extremely keen, large, round eyes.

In Homer's clever myth, the Kyklops are portrayed as cannibals. One strong, sharped-eyed Kyklops easily captures, kills and eats several of Odysseus' men. The others watch helplessly, knowing they could be next, yet in the old Grecian story tale, they manage to escape.

The round-eyed Kyklops are a near-perfect match for our hybrid-hominid hypothesis, in that they are extremely strong 'giants' with powerful vision, who live in caves, and easily kill and eat humans. Cannibalism was certainly one of the many traits and behaviors of our own ancient past.

Considering a Cyclops as a creature with *large round, circled eyes* would be a good match for the huge stone statues found on the nearby island of Sardinia. These statues, called 'The Giants of Monte Prama' were sculpted in the 11th century BCE. On the western coast of the island, over forty stone carvings have been restored and assembled by archeologists. Could these statues have been monuments to ancient, large, circle-eyed creatures, that have historically been called Cyclops?

Homer also introduces us to another tribe of man-eating giants from ancient Greek mythology called the Laestrygones. According to the historians Thucydides and Polybius, these Laestrygones inhabited southeastern Sicily. In Homer's tales of Odysseus, the Greek wanderer also visited them during his long, wearied journey back home to Ithaca.

"There were giants in the earth in those days."

Genesis 6:4

Note the wordplay here: we may consider that the Laes*tryg*ones (Laes-Trog-ones) are actually the Kyclops, (cai-clops?) in a different guise of languages; both terms define a monstrously strong, man-eating giant. As Odysseus lands and investigates the island, they encounter many hundreds of Laes-trog-ones, who kill and eat a large number of his men, on the spot. As the humans try to escape Sicily, the giants ascend tall cliffs and hurl great stones upon the Greek ships, smashing eleven of the twelve sailing vessels, and then spear the men like fish, as they catch and eat them; Odysseus alone escapes.

Could these Greek myths of man-eating giants truly be the distant memory of an ancient hybrid encounter, well embellished by bards or scribes, who according to many scholars, were collectively known as . . . Homer?

The Dragon in The Land of Ogres

The Saga of King Arthur PenDragon

In a more recent etymology, just few centuries old, the word 'ogre' is considered of French origin, originally derived from the Etruscan God Orcus, who fed on human flesh. Its first use is seen in Chrétien de Troyes' late 12th-century verses of " Perceval, li contes del grail" (Perceval, the Story of the Grail), which contains the lines:

> Et s'est escrit que il ert ancore
> que toz li reaumes de Logres,
> qui jadis fu la terre as ogres,
> ert destruite par cele lance.

> *"And it is written that he will come again,*
> *to all the realms of Logres,*
> *known as the land of ogres."*

Many readers will be shocked, as was this author, to learn that British history is woefully incomplete, especially concerning the nature of its ancient hybrid-hominid communities, now imbedded in legend. Many British and Irish ancestral legends may actually have a hybrid-hominid glimmer of truth. We can recall the story of James Fallows, the Scottish journalist who was writing about the DNA of Neanderthals. He was shocked when informed by a genetic scientist that he, James, had a whopping 5% of Neanderthal DNA, a rather large anomaly.

The scientist went on to note the journalist's ancestry, with its particular DNA admixture, was the result of ancient Neanderthal-Sapiens mating and breeding that occurred on the shores of the Red Sea, thousands of years ago. James Fallows' mother's ancestry had then traveled north, finally arriving in Scotland, a long time ago, perhaps even during prehistoric times.

The premise of such ancient migrations, from the Levant, Red Sea area, and elsewhere, to China, Europe and the faraway isles of Great Britain and Ireland is also the basis for our truly provocative, hard-to-accept notion of King Arthur. In his many sanitized legends, we can still find several noteworthy clues that indicate we can treat the stories as part-fiction, and partly true, with hints and clues for our hybrid-hominid hypothesis.

Whatever his early origins, the fabled King Arthur and his fabulous entourage of knights and ladies at the Court of Camelot, and other mythical aspects of the legend, such as the Quest for the Holy Grail and the heroic exploits of the Knights of the Round Table, come to us from medieval literature rather than from pre or post-Roman British history. Thus, the popular Arthurian Legend is considered folklore, not historical fact, but we can peel the Legend back, to reveal further clues concerning the origins of ogres, giants, and dragons.

Ogres were the inhabitants of Britain prior to human settlement.

In the Historia Regum Britanniae, or the History of the Kings of Britain (1136 AD), by Geoffrey of Monmouth, it is stated that *ogres* were the early inhabitants of Britain prior to human (Sapiens) settlements. This simple statement has far-reaching implications. Given the focus of this book upon humanity's hidden, evolving nature, with its many DNA admixtures, there is no reason to doubt Geoffrey, in this particular case. Also, the many legends of the Gog-Magog, described previously as giants living in the British Isles, can be interchanged with the many legends of prehistoric ogres, and dragons, on the same islands. Disregarding the usual understanding of scholars, we can consider here that ogres, dragons and/or giants, are really descriptions of hybrid creatures with potentially 10–20% Neanderthal DNA, or more.

Today, the original legend, and life, of King Arthur is completely covered in mythical accoutrements, disguising, and obscuring his few historical records.

The shrewd Geoffrey, according to many British scholars, is thought to have created an amalgamated Merlin, and based his writing upon previous historical and legendary figures, such as Myrddin Wyllt, and a 5th century Romano-British war leader with a curious name: Ambrosius Aurelianus. Thus, it is said that Geoffrey's pen created the character known as Merlin Ambrosius, or Merlin Ambrose. But, is there a hidden pattern here, concealed in the naming conventions? Both Merlin and Ambrosius Aurelianus were considered prophets—enchanting soothsayers. And what of Merlin's relationship with King Arthur, who was mentioned as leading the fighting against the Germanic Saxon invaders, also during the 5th century AD period?

The Dragon in The Land of 'L'Ogreia

King Arthur's full name was Arthur PenDragon—we note the 'drok' or 'drakon' in his last name, identifying him as a likely hybrid-hominid. The name Pendragon referred to the 'chief dragon.'
It's rather amazing that this Dragon-King ruled in the curious Land of the Ogres (L'Ogreia). During his life, this hybrid King would have been fighting an enemy with a more Sapiens-like DNA admixture, in the more numerous, invading Saxons.

The 'Adventus Saxonum' literature, referring to the adventures of the invading Saxons, repeatedly refers to fights between the Red and White Dragons, subtly referring to King Arthur's Brits, and the German Saxon army. If we think about it, it's literally impossible for two hostile armies to have equivalent DNA admixtures. Perhaps both armies contained men of a hybrid nature, with varying amounts of Neanderthal or Sapiens. We are reminded of the legends about the old Kings of India, who had satyrs in their armies. In some cases, it appears that hybrid-hominid warriors may have fought alongside Sapiens fighting men. In this example, the ruler of the land of L'Ogreia, and his band of ogre-men, likely had more Neon DNA than their Saxon counterparts.

Knowing not much more about Merlin's birth, other than it having been born 'rough and grisly' is also of interest to us here and segues into the strange names. We recall that in the legend of King Arthur Pendragon, his father was named Uther Pendragon, whose brother was named Ambrosius Asmodeus.

Merlin's traditional biography casts him as a half-human, half-animal cambion, which, as we recall, was the exact same description used by the Kabbalists to describe Asmodeus, the so-called Prince of Demons. One of Merlin's many titles was 'Son of the Devil.' Notice the phonetic similarities between Asmodeus and Ambrosius. Both the sound and meaning of these two words are nearly identical, which is usually sufficient to indicate an ancient link. As noted earlier, the phonetic rendering of caam-bion is similar to draa-gon, and these two sound-names definitely have meanings akin to each other.

Although mainstream etymologists may faint here, it appears that the King's first name, Arthur, may be distantly derived from ogre, which would make sense. Over the millennia, we can consider that 'ogre' could have been repeatedly mispronounced and anglicized, perhaps morphing from 'Og-r' to 'au-tur', to finally arrive at the modern sound and name of 'Art-thur,' a more proper rendering for the son of Uther Pen-dragon. Thus, the key, ancient core sounds of Drok and/or Gog are at play here, both likely referring to a hybrid creature—an ogre, who was living and ruling in a land of ogres, as strange as it seems. Perhaps, in a morphed twisting of words, our kingly hero, was really an Ogre (Gog) and the son of a Dragon (Drok), with perhaps 10–15% Neanderthal DNA, running through his veins.

~!~

According to many British scholars, there is only one person who could have been the historical source of our legendary Arthur. This is a man named Riothamus, or Rigotamos, also called Arturius by some sources. He is mentioned in *The Gothic History* written by a 6th century historian named Jordanes, who lists him as a 'High King in Briton,' who lived in the 5th century AD. Eventually, Riothamus fights against the Visigoths, but his army loses and he gets lost in history. This story, however, can tell us about a few similarities between Arthur and Riothamus:

240

Riothamus led an army of Britons into Gaul and was the only British King who did (just like Arthur, according to the legend).

Riothamus was betrayed by a deputy ruler who cooperated with barbarian enemies, just like King Arthur was betrayed by Mordred. Later, variants of the legend characterized Mordred as being Arthur's villainous bastard son, born of an *incestuous relationship with his half-sister, Orcades*, the Queen of Orkney, in the Scottish northern isles. These two names, Orcades and Orkney, are also highly suggestive of a hybrid-hominid root, which we are calling Ogre, or Orc, at the moment.

Riothamus disappears after a final battle, without any recorded death. His legend states that he is going to a town called Avallon—King Arthur also left for Avalon after his final battle.

British academic Léon Fleuriot has argued that the name of Riothamus is nearly identical to Ambrosius Aurelianus, whom we have mentioned before. He suggests that "Riothamus" was an Aurelianus title, as overlord of all early Briton territories. We saw earlier that 'Myrddin the Wylt' was also referred to as Merlin Ambrosius, in the Arthurian Legend. Hopefully, the reader can persevere, and even appreciate, the severe morphing of misspoken, misunderstood words that developed over the past several thousand years.

We return to the curious name of Ambrosius Aurelianus, who was reported historically as a war hero of the Romano-British tribes, yet, eventually, given the misty myths of time, transformed into the uncle of King Arthur, the brother of Arthur's father Uther Pendragon.

Thus, we have clues of both 'half-man, half-animal' cambions and drakons being seen in these legends, as well as many other cloaked names.

Because of the deep respect and mythical leaning of many people who love the hoary legends of King Art-thur and the Round Table, it may be extremely difficult to accept that King Og'r, King Arthur, or King Riothamus, if we prefer, was really a hybrid fellow, with perhaps 10–15%

or more of Neanderthal DNA, in his blood and bones.

Who else could rule the people of L'Ogreia, but the Kingly Dragon?

The Truth of the Troglodytes

I magine you and a few friends were casually walking along the coastal shoreline and plains of the ancient Red Sea, perhaps 4,000 years ago. Suddenly, your group spies a humanlike creature, near a small cave or hole, perhaps 1,000 meters away. The unusual figure, nearly covered in long red hair, also perceives your group approaching, and darts away quickly, making a hasty retreat back to its cave, quite literally diving back into the safety of its darkness. Such sightings were not uncommon in those days—hence the legends grew. These cave creatures were called the 'Troglodytae' by the early Greeks—the name means 'hole diver' or cave-goer'—and they are good candidates, given their unusual traits, for our hybrid-hominid list of Monsters, Philosophers & Saviors. There are, however, scant historical references to these remote-living people.

Herodotus referred to the Troglodytae in Libya and the Red Sea area in his Histories, as being a primitive people who were mercilessly hunted by the Garamantes tribe, who attacked the cave-dwellers with four-horsed chariots. The well-traveled Herodotus curiously stated that the Troglodytae were a physical anomaly. As he recorded, they were:

"The swiftest runners of all humans known in

the entire world, as fast as horses."

This is a high compliment, if we consider that the Greeks themselves highly valued the art of professional running in both their warfare and their sacred Olympic games.

One can only imagine a few scattered Troglodyte hominid creatures out hunting or fishing near the ancient coast of Libya, and then suddenly encountering a more human tribal group, perhaps hunting them as a lesser species, with their huge four-horse chariots, as described by Herodotus. Could this extreme foot speed of the Troglodytes, reached during full throttle while running in desperate fear, be related to an admixture of DNA slightly favoring the nearly extinct Neanderthal species? There is

243

also the possibility that the more numerous Garamantes tribespeople were hunting the few members of the cave-dwelling Trog tribes because they may have been seen as vicious criminals, and something to be loathed. As murderers, rapists, plunderers, and cannibals, still living outside of the walls and fences of civilization, they yet required a certain proximity to it. Science now considers that Neanderthals possessed much greater leg strength, and greater heart and lung capacity, than their more Sapiens counterparts, nearly doubling their abilities. We can assign these greater physical traits, to a lesser degree, to their hybrid descendants as well. Herodotus also wrote that the Troglodytae appeared 'different' and separate from other tribal folk; they spoke with a strange 'screeching' language, and mainly consumed lizards, snakes, and other reptiles.

Another historian, Flavius Josephus, refers to a large location surrounding the Red Sea called Troglodytis while discussing Genesis, and states that the descendants of Abraham conquered the land and formed colonies in that area, by killing or forcing the Trogs out of their cave dwellings. These migrating Troglodytae 'tribes' later spread westward to Libya and also northward, to the Black Sea area.

The historian Strabo, in his work Geographica, wrote that a wild, northern group of Troglodytae lived alongside the Crobyzi, a Getae tribe in Scythia Minor or the modern Romania-Bulgaria area. Perhaps these tribes were related, in their DNA. As we saw earlier in the sagas of Spartacus, Beowulf, and Cain, these curious Getae/Geate tribes play an interesting, continuing role in our hybrid hypothesis.

As we discuss the evolving nature of the ancient sound-names of Og, Gog, Drog & Trog, eventually becoming Troglodyte or dragon (**drak**on) to the earliest Greeks, we find, repeatedly, that several different cultures, with distinctly different DNA admixtures, were involved in warlike exchanges.

As a genetic-cultural observation, we can note that many of the wars normally attributed to differing 'Sapiens' or human tribespeople in the past, were really conflicts between disparate genetic pools, of both Neanderthal and Sapiens. The ancient Libyan conflict between the Garamantes and Troglodytae tribes, and Abraham's descendants conquering the Trogs surrounding the Red Sea, perhaps 5,000 years ago, is a good example of earlier conflicts between incongruous DNA groups.

Paleo-psychologist Stan Gooch describes the nature of prehistoric migrations of Eurasia after the last glacial age, over 10,000 years ago:

"There are no roads and no maps in this vast area, just tens upon tens of thousands of square miles of territory, mostly virgin forest. It is not difficult, for the time being, for tribe to remain separate from tribe.

The main point here is this: The mixture of Cro-Magnon and Neanderthal genes is appreciably different in various modern peoples (both in and outside Europe). The mingling of cultures is similarly uneven. Some pursue, very much, the path of earth magic and moon worship, others that of hunting magic and sun worship.

*Nowhere, in any case, is there any longer either moon worship or sun worship, as they once separately existed, before the **great mingling**."*

The Sons of Japheth

The ancient Hebrews considered that there were three races of humans living in their part of the world. These were known as the Sons of Japheth, the Sons of Ham, and the Sons of Shem. The Bible (Genesis) relates a tale of how these three groups were said to be created by the three Sons of Noah, after the Great Flood, and provides a long list of descendants.

The Sons of Japheth can be considered as a hybrid-hominid race, as the Gog-Magog tribes are of that group. The wandering Tubal-Cain was a son of Japheth who later migrated from the Levant to Spain.

In the map below, the other tribes of the Sons of Japhet include the tribes of Gomer (Gog-mer), Thubal (Tubal), and Thogarma (th-og-arma). These are also likely hybrid-hominid tribes. The inhabitants of Thrace, which we have previously discussed, are also listed as descendants of the Sons of Japheth race. The map below shows the likely hybrid-hominid migrations and dispersion, after God ordered Ezekiel to drive the Gog-Magog out of the Levant, thousands of years ago.

THE WORLD AS KNOWN TO THE HEBREWS
ACCORDING TO THE MOSAIC ACCOUNT.

Riphath

Rosch

S C Y T H

Gomer

Magog

CASPIAN SEA

J

Dodanim

Thiras
Thracia

BLACK SEA

Caucasus Mts.

Elisha

P

Riphath

Mesch Gog Magog

Cyrus

Ararat

Oxus R.

Ludit (Lydians)

Javan

Ashkenaz (Phrygians)

Sardis

Gomer

Thogarma
(Armenians)

Chaldeans

Mt. Ararat

Araxes R.

Taurus

Tarsus

H

Arphaxad

T

Madai
(Medians)

Rages

Rhodus

Ur

Mash

Assyrians

MEDITERRANEAN SEA

Kittim
(Cyprus)

Helbon

Carchemish

Hena

Calneh

Arad

Kutha

Susa

Arpad

Hamath

Damascus

Babel

R. Euphrates

Tigris

Zidon
Zoar

Canaan

Amorites

Amalek

Edom

Ishmaels

Dumah

Hagarites

Paras
(Persia)

Lehabim
(Lydians)

Phut

Memphis
(Mophi)

Lud

Naphtuhim

Midian

Kedar

A r a b i a n s

Havilah

Persian Gulf

Mizraim
Egyptians

H

Pathrusim

No Ammon
(Thebians)

Syene

Dedan

Abimael

Sheleph

Havilah

Almodad

Jobab

Nubia

A

Meroe

Havilah

Uzal

Hazarmaveth

Sephar

Seba

M

Ophir

Jarah

Seba

Haldoram

GULF OF ADEN

C U S H

AETHIOPIANS

Str. of Babel Mandeb

Sabthecha

SONS OF

JAPHET
SONS OF

HAM
SONS OF

SHEM

and EBER

with his descendants the
Hebrews. Ishmaelites.
and Edomites.

Extent of the ancient
Assyrian Empire.

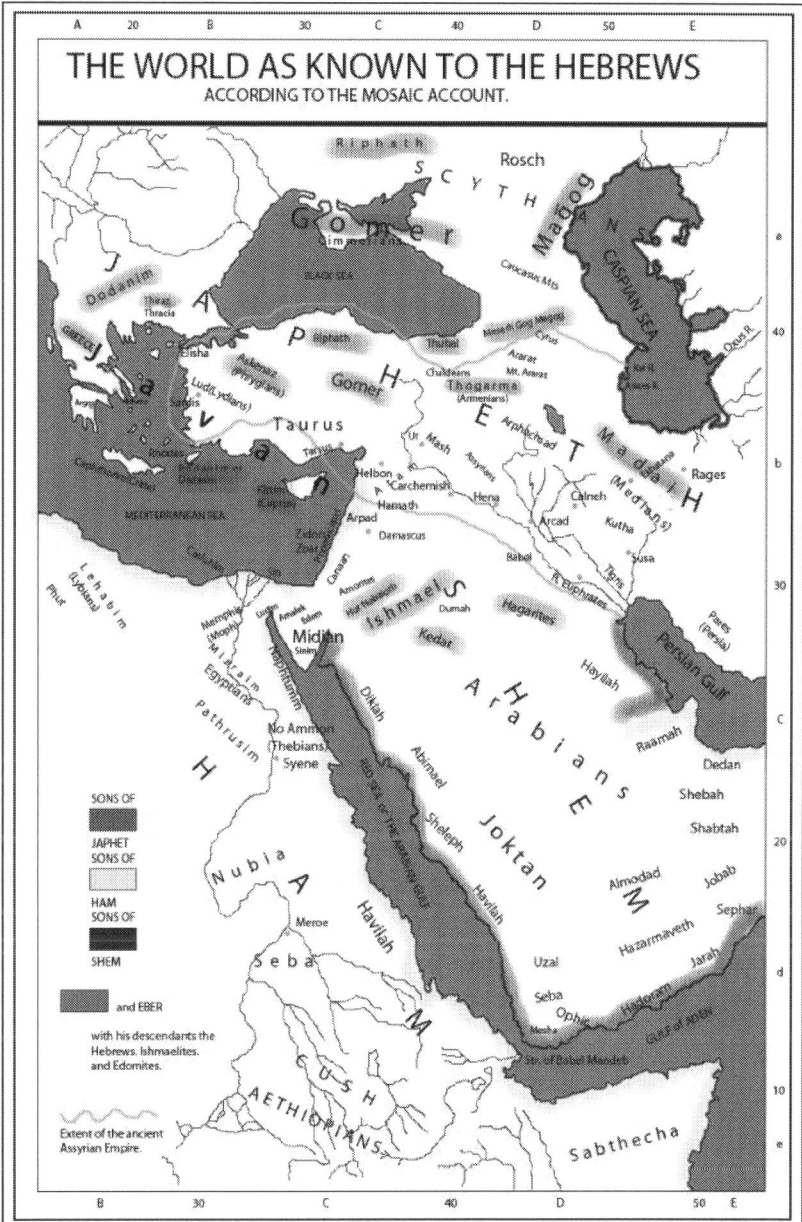

*Map from "Historical Textbook and Atlas of Biblical Geography (1854)"
by Lyman Coleman. Public Domain
Tribes: Red: Son of Japhet, Yellow: Son of Ham, Blue: Son of Shem*

247

Another key hybrid-hominid figure is Togarmah, the son of Gomer and grandson of Japheth, as listed in Genesis. Togarmah is an ally of Tubal-Cain. The Book of Ezekiel relates how Tubal and Togarmah worked together to supply the armies of Gog, so a tribal alliance is indicated. Togarmah is also important because he is considered to be a mythical ancestor to the tribes that migrated northward, which were later known as the Turks, Phrygians, Kharzas and many others between the Black and Caspian Seas.

The Great Mingling of Troy

The Gog ~ Trog ~ Trojan ~ Migration
~!~
A New Look at The Trojan War

W e discussed earlier how some Neon-Sapiens tribes called Gog-Magog left the Levant and wandered to the far east and became the ancestors of the Mongols. We know there were Troglodyte Neon-Sapiens cultures on both coasts of the Red Sea before they were driven off by ancient Jewish people (Abraham's descendants). We have seen how Tubal-Cain traveled west to Spain and Italy. Togarmah, the ally of Tubal, left the Levant with his tribes of hybrids, the Gog-Magog, traveled north, and were responsible for populating great swaths of land, between the Black and Caspian Seas. Now we will focus on one particular tribe in particular, living in the famous, ancient city of Troy.

We are interested in both the Trojan War, and also the Exodus of Troy. Once upon an ancient time, a great war occurred in what is now western Turkey, the remnant tales of which smack of many suspicious inklings of a hybrid-hominid past. Scholars today are split upon the meagre historical evidence concerning the famous historical event known as the Trojan War. It is generally accepted that Homer, the historical poet, and/or a Homeric scribal group, penned the Iliad, which describes the 10-year war, composing it around 800 BCE. The conflict itself is dated several hundred years earlier, around 1,200 BCE.

The validity of Homer's depictions in his tome, is subject to interpretation. Since today's scholars are largely in disagreement about the many details found in the Iliad, we will focus mainly on the noteworthy Neanderthal-Sapiens observations that can be shown. Specifically, we will show how Gog-Magog tribes migrated eastward and then northward. We saw earlier how the Gog hybrid peoples became known as Troglodyte by the early Greeks and were living around the Red Sea, before they were conquered or driven off, according to the story of Abraham in the Bible. The premise here is that several groups of hybrid-

249

hominid tribes, the Trogs, migrated northward to Turkey and the areas of the Black and Caspian Seas. In his work *Geographica*, Strabo the historian, mentions a tribe of Troglodytae living along with the Crobyzi in Scythia Minor, near the Danube river, fairly close to Troy. The Crobyzi are a strong, red-haired Thracian-Getae tribe, whom we have previously indicated as having hybrid-hominid blood. In the Trojan War lore, the Thracian tribes are listed as allies of the Trojans, suggesting a DNA kinship. Several historians mention that these Troglodytae invented, and played, musical instruments, which smacks of their humanness, as a Neanderthal-Sapiens admixture. Did the Troglodytae mate with local sapiens in the Black Sea area and slowly intermix into human society over several thousand years, eventually forming hybrid-hominid tribes?

Archaeological evidence points to 3,500 BCE as the date for the first building of Troy. The ancient site contains nearly a dozen levels dating back over 6,000 years. Our interest here is in level 7a, which was destroyed in 1190 BCE, most likely by the invading Greeks, as they finally conquered Troy, after years of trying.

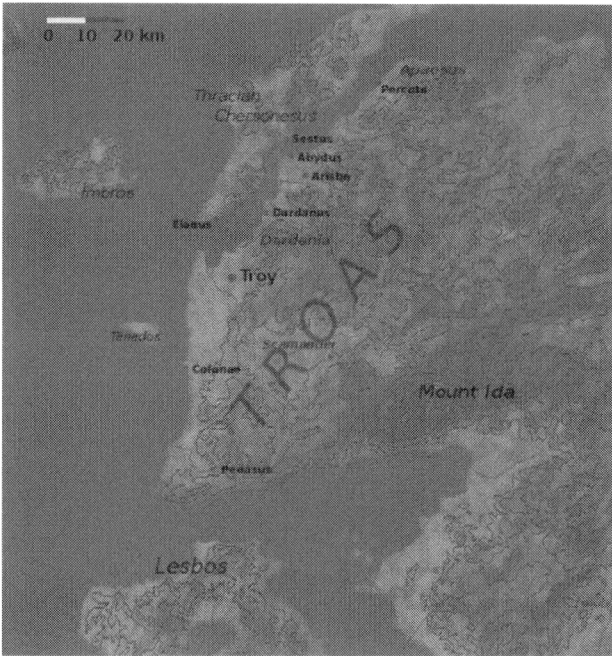

*Map of the Troad (Tros) and surrounding areas, in the times of Troy.
Credit: Wikipedia, CC: SA 3.0*

While we are suggesting the Trojan War had warriors that were Neon-Sapiens hybrids, as usual, there is no DNA analysis available for these ancient combatants. However, our evaluation for Troy as a possible hybrid city is assisted by observing a few special characters seen in Homer's Iliad: King Tros, Hector, Achilles, Aeneas, Brutus, and Helen, the most beautiful woman in the world, in olden times.

King Tros

The Greek historians wrote that the prolific Zeus was said to be the father of King Dardanus, who later sired Erichthonius, and the entire tribe of the Dardanoi, in ancient Anatolia, or modern-day western Turkey. King Erichthonius mated with a river nymph, Astoche, who begat Tros, who became the King of Troy and the Troad, or Troas kingdom. Thus, at the

251

time of the Trojan War, there were two royal houses in the city: The House of Troy and the House of the Dardanoi. Some ancient writers thought that Dardanus had migrated from the west, and, as the earlier map of the tribes of the Sons of Japheth revealed, one of the hybrid tribes in prehistoric northern Greece was called the Dodanim, which is phonically akin to Dardanus, and the Dardanoi people.

The sound of 'tros' is phonically similar to our discussion of Og, Trog, etc. We should consider that tribes of Troglodatae were reported nearby and may have intermixed for centuries with Sapiens folk in the area. As a speculation, to pronounce Astoche as 'ast-oche' might suggest she was a female Orc or ogre, hybrid creature, who lived in a cave by the river, not unlike Agrat (ogre?) Bat Mahlat (Magog?), the cave-dwelling Succubus in the Levant, who mated with King David? Perhaps we could call them Ogres of the Magog.

It's noteworthy that both King Dardanus and King Tros had issues with their parents, the former having a divine father and a human mother, and the latter having a human father but a so-called river nymph for a momma. We once again declare all divine or semi-divine myths and claims to be elaborate religious cover-ups and try to determine if a Neon-Sapiens hip-bumping was involved in the birth. There were numerous mixed-breed tribes in this area for thousands of years, many having originally migrated from the Levant, long ago, as the 3rd race of humans—the Sons of Japheth.

Strong Hector

How does one become the greatest fighter in Troy? Odysseus said that Hector fought like a raging, crazed maniac. Let us suggest greater strength, speed, agility, and Neanderthal genetics.
King Priam was the King of Troy during the long war, and ruled along with Queen Hecuba, with whom he sired seventeen sons. This promiscuous Queen, however, is said to have also 'bumped hips' with Apollo and had two sons in this fashion: Hector and Troilus. Once again, we must ignore the mention of divine births and focus upon the possibility

252

of a hidden hybrid-hominid mating. The unspeakable, mixed-breed mating, quite oddly, become acts of God, gods, or goddesses. A teenage Troilus is ambushed and murdered by Achilles early in the war, at a watering hole outside the city gates.

The earliest known depiction of Hector, upon a bronze coin, 300 BCE
Credit Wikipedia ~ Public domain

In Hector's image, we note the excessive thickness of face and body, resembling that of a Neanderthal-Sapiens hybrid. Scholars speculate that Hector is wearing a helmet in the left-image, but we may disagree. As we mentioned earlier, hybrid-hominids in the Black Sea area have been reported to have had pointed ears on several occasions, according to Stan Gooch, and pointed ears are routinely depicted in ancient images of giants, ogres, trolls, etc. Occasionally, even today, humans are born with pointed ears, possibly because they have a higher amount of Neanderthal DNA.

Hector is mentioned several times in the Iliad as having great strength, which is indicated by his lifting and hurling massive rocks to break down the Greek gates; he then kills them with large stones. We are reminded of the mighty, powerful Samson, when he broke down the city gates of Gaza in the Levant.

On the Greek side, Ajax the Greater, a man said to be of great frame and strength, also hurls large stones as weapons, even while swords and spears are also available. In some respects, these feats of great strength remind us of a hybrid-hominid Stone Age battle, but the many embellishments of the ensuing millennia have greatly polished this ancient war into a 'classic,' classy Greek motif. The public now looks back and sees the Trojan War through the classic lens of academia, with its cast of handsome white, Caucasian heroes; it's a scene not unlike the European whitening of Jesus, the small Jewish humpback teacher.

Achilles; Born in a Cave by the Sea

When I was younger, I was entranced by reading about the powerful fights between the Greeks and the Trojans, especially the heroes, Hector and Achilles. I didn't realize, that although I enjoyed academia's interpretations and portrayals of these ancient cultures, just how much I was missing. Achilles, the great Greek warrior, is the most famous of all Trojan War characters, but history has spun several ruses concerning him. The famous story of his Achilles Heel is well known, yet this tale was an add-on, created more than a thousand years after the ancient battle.

"Although the death of Achilles is not presented in the Iliad, other sources concur that he was killed near the end of the Trojan War by Paris, who shot him in the heel with an arrow.
Later legends (beginning with Statius' unfinished epic Achilleid, written in the 1st century AD) state that Achilles was invulnerable in all of his body except for his heel because, when his mother Thetis dipped him in the river Styx as an infant, she held him by one of his heels."

Achilles; **Wikipedia**

In the earliest Greek lore, there is no trace of any reference to Achilles' general invulnerability or his famous weakness at the heel. On the Greek vase paintings presenting the death of Achilles, the arrows of Trojan Prince Paris are shown striking Achilles in the chest and torso.

Another remarkable thing about ancient Achilles is that there are no facial images or depictions in existence that clearly show his countenance. With Homer, there is only the single coin from 300 BCE so we really can't study their facial features and must focus upon their great foot speed and powerful strength, as we look for hybrid-hominid clues.

In a turning point in the war, Hector kills Patroclus, Achilles best friend. Achilles, enraged, then re-engages with the Greek forces and runs amok, slaughtering them in his fury, with his much greater strength, speed and agility. No one can stand before him. The Trojan river gods, Scamander and Simoeis, cry out for help in the fight against Achilles:

> *"Come to our aid with all speed and*
> *rouse a mighty roar of timbers and rocks,*
> *so we can stop this **savage man who***
> ***in his strength is raging** like the gods."*

The enraged, better-armed Achilles finally encounters Hector. Having only a short sword for a weapon against Achilles' many spears, Hector is outmatched in weapons, and decides to flee. Achilles, known as the 'swift-footed,' for his great superior speed, could not outrun the equally fast Hector, but the Trojan finally stopped to face his Greek foe, after running three times around the city walls. Wanting to go down fighting, he bravely charges at Achilles with his sword, but is speared several times by Achilles, and goes down. Accepting his fate, Hector begs Achilles, not to spare his life, but to treat his body with respect after killing him. Achilles tells Hector it is hopeless to expect that of him, declaring that:

> *"My rage, my fury would drive me now*
> *to hack your flesh away and **eat you raw***
> *– such agonies you have caused me."*

Achilles then kills Hector and drags his corpse by its heels behind his chariot before the walls of Troy. In this author's view, these two combatants were equally matched in strength and speed, but Hector had the misfortune of fewer weapons; these two never fought a long, standing combat, with equal weapons and armory. A sword against thrown spears is a mismatch, and Homer makes it seem so in his writing of the Trojan War.

Because Achilles has a divine parent, was born in a sea-cave, and has greater strength and speed than his Greek associates, he qualifies as a likely hybrid-hominid, Neon-Sapiens candidate.
Ancient historians offer several different opinions on the birthplace and residence of Achilles, ranging from the southern Greek land of Achaea, located in the Peloponnese islands, to the land of the Scythians, further north, towards the Black Sea.

If **Ach**illes was Scythian, then his place of birth, around 1200 BCE, would be surrounded by several hybrid tribes we have mentioned, such as the scattered Gog-Magog, the Troglodytae and the early Getae tribes. Pliny the historian refers to a mysterious 'Island of Achilles' and its 'port of **Ach**aei'; these are general references to the land of **Ach**aea on the northern portion of the Peloponnese islands, which houses similarly named regions **Arc**adia and **Arg**olis. Neanderthal and Sapiens fossils have been found in sea-caves in the Peloponnese region, dating back over 100,000 years. Is it possible that these older cave peoples mixed with the numerous migratory waves of Sapiens and Gog-Magog hybrids, in ancient prehistoric Greece? These Achaeans are said to have been founded by King **Ach**aeus.

Although Greek academics and historians will be loath to admit this, having their own locked-in etymologies for these similar-sounding names, let us consider an older, yet unknown meaning. Many boldfaced names in the paragraph above have a particular sound-similarity, a sound extremely close, or identical to one of the important name-sounds we have been following, that of Og, Gog, and Ogre. Scholars consider that 'ogre' may have come from 'Gog' in olden times, but haven't made the same connection for the ancient 'ogres' living in the Peloponnese area of southern Greece. This appears to be an oversight. Modern scholars, interpreting the Achilleid, written in the first century AD, consider that Achilles name was pronounced as 'A- Ki-Re-U', a very distant sound from the modern English. They consider that this name translates as *'his people have distress,'* or something similar. A pattern is seen in the translation of King Achaeus. His name also means grief, pain, & woe.

As the ancient Jewish folk had written that there were three 'races' of humans into which the tribes of the Levant were divided, the ancient Greeks also may have ethnically divided their own peoples into four major tribal groups: the Achaeans, Aeolians, Ionians, and Dorians. The Achaeans may have been the 'distressed' tribes. They may have been descended from the migrating Og tribes, also known as the Gog-Magog clans, which were certainly distressed themselves, being called 'unclean' tribes by the ancient Jewish people. Is there a strange DNA connection here, resulting in distressed, unclean peoples? Can we compare these descriptions to the name of Mar(y) the Bitter One, a thousand years later, whose son was also slightly deformed?

Och-illes

A better fit for the name of Achilles, in this author's opinion, would be to recognize that the ancient sound of OG is being heard incorrectly by modern linguistics, as 'ACH' or 'ARC' or ARG', which is a sound heard in so many Peloponnese names.

This old sound of OG was already heard in nearby Tuscany (Italy) in the name of the Ogre-God, Orcus, whom we previously discussed as another hybrid-hominid 'monster' candidate. As difficult as it is for classical Greek scholars to admit, our Greek warrior's name was really closer to Och-hilles, Orc-hilles, or something similar. As a speculation, ancient Achilles may have had 10–15% Neanderthal blood, a bit more than Socrates, a thousand years later. This Neanderthal blood is what made Achilles (Och-illes) so unstoppable—he was faster, stronger, and more lethal than other Sapiens warriors.

The only way to kill him was with arrows, which is how he died.

I was somewhat shocked when I realized this, and instantly thought of the relationship to King Arthur (art-r, Og'r) Pendragon, who ruled the land of Ogres.

There are two wildly differing tales concerning Och-illes' birth and the nature of his parents, his human father Peleus, and his sea-nymph mother Thetis.

We mentioned the famous, charming story earlier, of how sweet Thetis lovingly dipped her son, Achilles, the spawn of Peleus, into Styx, the Greek river of death, to help him gain invulnerability, but, alas, missed the heel.

The other, lesser-known and older tale describes her more like a monstrous creature. In this myth, Thetis, as a sea-nymph, whom we will consider as a hybrid-hominid living near the sea, gave birth to Och-illes in a damp Peloponnese sea-cave, in the dim, misty past. Thetis was promiscuous and had twenty children by various suitors and gods. The first six children that she had with human Peleus, it was said by several historians, were actually murdered by their mother, by burning them alive on a cavern funeral pyre, and possibly eating them, as we should realize that ogres are often cannibals, and to those, meat is meat.

These Neanderthal-Sapiens children must have been undesirable, and possibly deformed after a human male mated with a hybrid-hominid female. After Och-illes was born, he was placed on the pyre to burn, but his father finally intervened and snatched the hybrid child from the fire. Thus, Achilles was said to have six dead brothers in this telling. The ancient Greek tribes were well known to have practiced infanticide, and crossbreed mating may not have produced the goodly desired results. After nearly losing his child, Peleus then gave the distressed child to Chiron, the great and wise centaur, to raise. Later, Achilles became known as a most beautiful child, as he grew, perhaps . . . but, in whose opinion?

Chiron

As we noted in an earlier chapter, the mysterious, mythical centaur, in its original, non-embellished form, simply meant 'bull-killer'; the half-man, half-horse embellishment came much later. Thus, Chiron was not a half-man, half-horse creature, but a powerful, fast-running, hybrid-hominid creature who was friendly with certain Greek tribes—especially the Achaeans. His well-known images of having the lower body of a horse may have been Grecian artistic symbolism of both his great speed and his great lust, which is a trait of both centaurs and satyrs. The romantic term 'centaur' can be more properly seen as having morphed from 'Cain-taur,' meaning, more correctly, a strong hybrid creature; a true 'giant' described as being capable of killing a bull. One can speculate that, as Herodotus observed that the Troglodytae hybrid people were as fast as horses . . . in his words, that this statement became popular amongst the Greek people and later morphed into legends, where these hybrids were artistically portrayed as having horse bodies, on their lower torso, while still being called 'cain-taurs' or creatures strong enough to kill bulls.

Chiron's father was Apollo, so another divine birthing is being claimed, while a hybrid mating is being hidden, in the Greek lore. Stan Gooch had mentioned how Nean-Sapiens hybrid humanity was responsible for 'gifting' many attributes to Sapiens, thus, Chiron the 'caintaur' is a good example of Gooch's notion, as he was known for his knowledge and skill with medicine, and thus was credited with the discovery of botany and pharmacy, the science of herbs and medicine, as was King Shennong further east.

After Achilles, the swift-footed, extremely strong warrior was trained by Chiron, he was unstoppable at Troy in hand-to-hand combat. The only way to kill the overpowering fellow was by shooting him with arrows, which is how he died.

AJAX

Both Och-illes and Ajax, the great, powerful brute, were said to have been trained by Chiron, so the suggestion here is that hybrid-hominid creatures, Nean-Sapiens, were regularly mixing with their more human counterparts, and that the unusually strong, rock-throwing Ajax, is also implicated as a powerful hybrid. Ajax was also an Achaean, who, like Achilles, had divinity in his parentage; his mother was a nymph. He was possibly the child of a hybrid mating in ancient Greece and thus was overwhelming powerful on the battlefield, as compared to a Sapiens warrior. Ajax nearly defeated Hector in battle by hurling and injuring him with huge stones, but nightfall ended the Stone Age fray, and Hector survived for another day.

Like Achilles and King Achaeus, Ajax's name has a negative connotation, meaning 'one who laments and mourns.' Finally, we should not omit the 'AJ' prefix in his name. In what surely can't be a mere coincidence, with a different pronunciation, we can see the AJ-prefix can really represent the ancient sound of OG, once again. Thus, Og-x, might be a truer representative sound, than that of the modern, anglicized Ajax.

The Abduction of Helen

In looking through our Neon glass lens for hybrid DNA clues, we can now move back to the actual cause of the great war, where the Iliad states that Prince Paris of Troy abducted Helen of Greece, said to be the most beautiful woman in the world. The Greeks wrote that many Gods were instrumental in causing the Trojan War, taking positions on both sides. However, could this well-embellished tale be seen differently, if Paris, a lustful 'Trog-an' Prince, was actually a slightly hybrid creature, who were well known to the ancients to regularly abduct human females from their dwellings, as the Jewish Incubus and Gog-Magog were also said to do? Abduction and rape are both Neanderthal and Sapiens' negative tendencies, so a hybrid-hominid type of violent abduction remains a possibility. We must disregard the many medieval, European paintings of all-white Greek and Trojan cultures, as they are but an incorrect distraction and an unconscious portrayal of Caucasian-Sapiens mentality. The entire assemblage of hundreds of Greek and Trojan tribes in 1,200 BCE, along with their many allies, likely had an anomalous mix of Neanderthal and Sapiens bloodlines, with characters like Hector, Achilles, and Ajax standing out, because of their superior speed and strength, as compared to the battlefield warriors with less Neanderthal, and more Sapiens DNA. In addition to the reported abduction, history also records that Troy may have engaged in piracy in the seafaring lanes which they controlled, and that a low-scale feuding between the Greek and Trojan coalitions had been simmering during most of the 10-year conflict, as Homer's Iliad only focuses upon the last days and ending of the great war.

The Exodus of Troy to the New Lands

Aeneas & Brutus

~!~

I've got three ships and sixty men, a course for ports unread

Land Ho! ~ **The Doors**

The famous Trojan Horse, which contained hidden Greek soldiers who opened the gates of Troy, is another of history's great embellishments, and like the spurious ruse of Achille's heel, is greatly exaggerated, and now merely fodder for young children. Besides the concept of a huge, hollow wood horse, we must accept another tale: when the Trojan chief priest thought the huge horse was a trick, two huge serpents suddenly emerged from the sea, sent by the gods, and devoured him. *Ahem*.
So, after such a divine sign, the Trojans decided to open their gates, after looking around to make sure the Greek armies weren't nearby. Yawn. Alternatively, historian Michael Wood has proposed that the 'Horse' was actually a huge, wooden battering ram, with a raised, painted horse's head ramming against the gates of Troy. The battering ram was long and wide enough to cover, or hide, the 20–30 Greek warriors underneath. It might be possible for portions of the Greek fleet of 1,200 ships to be used in the artful construction of such a large, wooden weapon. Respecting the horse for its speed, the Levant's Phoenicians, perhaps the best sailors in the ancient world, were known for using wooden horse-image figureheads on their boats, which could be used as battering rams against unfriendly ships. Using our alternative plot, one can see how the scene unfolds, in a more natural way:

Attacking quietly, in the dead of the night with no moon or starlight to reveal them, a small, stealthy band of men approached Troy unseen, carrying a heavy 25-foot, wooden battering ram, colorfully painted. Lifting the battering ram over their heads for protection, basically, 'hiding inside' from Trojan arrows, spears and rocks, the strong Greek men heave

262

the battering ram's horse-shaped head into the strong gate, again, and again. The gate weakens and splinters under the repeated blows and begins to break. Trojan voices sound the alarm and guards rush to the attack, but they are a step too late. The Greeks breach the gates and the hordes of Greek warriors and their allies, carrying thousands of torches, sweep into the doomed city. Inside the walls of Troy, a horrible, loud din of warriors roaring, and women and children screaming and wailing begins, and doesn't stop for many long hours, into the daylight hours, as the crazed warriors rampage through the city, killing and burning as they go. Dismembered bodies line the once-glorious, now bloody streets. Somehow, as the great slaughter of the outnumbered Trojans is going on, a few key characters manage to escape the deadly carnage.

Aeneas

Our main focus here will be upon the ensuing adventures of Aeneas and Brutus, two more hybrid-hominid candidates. Below is the standard myth of Aeneas:

"Aeneas was a Trojan hero in Greek mythology, son of the prince Anchises and the goddess Aphrodite. He is more extensively mentioned in Roman mythology and is seen as an ancestor of Remus and Romulus, founders of Rome.
*Aphrodite made all Greek gods fall in love with mortal women, and Zeus, to punish her, made her fall in love with Anchises, who was a herdsman near Mount Ida. Aphrodite appeared in front of him, and the herdsman was smitten by her beauty. After sleeping together, Aphrodite revealed her true identity to him, who feared for any consequences that might afflict him. Aphrodite reassured him that there would be no problem as long as he **kept it a secret.** She also told him that she would give birth to Aeneas. In the Iliad, Aeneas was the leader of the Trojan Dardanians, and the main lieutenant of Hector. Aphrodite protected him throughout the war, and was also helped by Apollo, and even Poseidon who normally favored the Greeks. In Roman literature, mainly the Aeneid written by Virgil, he was one of the few Trojans not killed during the Trojan War. He travelled to Italy, where he settled in the region where Rome would later*

263

be built by his descendants, Remus and Romulus."

www.Greekmythology.com

As we are trying to avoid myth-making with Aeneas, it's important to note that while he has Anchises for a human father, he has no human mother and Aphrodite won't do, thus, another religious cover-up is suggested, to hide a wild hybrid mating, which likely occurred on that ancient green hilltop, surrounded by unconcerned flocks of sheep. In Virgil's *Aeneid*, penned in 25 BCE, twelve hundred years after the great war, a greater light is thrown upon Aeneas, than is in the Iliad. Virgil has great respect for Aeneas and his migratory band, as he considers them early ancestors of Rome. Like Achilles, Ajax and Hector, Aeneas is also exceptionally strong and a fierce warrior; he is reported to have killed nearly thirty Greeks in battle. If this were true, he would be truly dominating and overwhelming to the average Sapiens fighter. For Aeneas, we have no facial depictions to evaluate, only the single 300 BCE bronze coin of Hector, Aeneas's good friend and captain, where Hector appears to have Neanderthal-Sapiens facial traits.

His wife is killed during the Sack of Troy, but Aeneas, his father, son, and some of the few remaining Trojan warriors manage to escape Troy. They depart for the nearby land of Thrace, who were their allies during the war, and whose tribes also indicate signs of Neanderthal-Sapiens crossbreeding, several thousand years ago.

Aeneas's name usually translates as *'terrible grief,'* another dismal name in the same vein as Achilles and Ajax; however, a second, prominent translation, developed later, renders *'dweller in the body,'* which is seen by several scholars as referring to the ancient concept of a God descending into the body. The Story of King Gilgamesh, written nearly a thousand years before the Trojan War, also depicts this concept, as King Gilgamesh is repeatedly referred to as 'one-third man, two-thirds God; *'Lo, the flesh of the gods in in his body.'* Thus, we might join the two disparate meanings and say, as spiritual folk often do, that we are spiritual creatures having a human experience, and yes, there is grief and distress in life's journey. Apollodorus the historian wrote that;

"...the Greeks let him alone on account of his piety."

In Virgil's Aeneid, Aeneas and his father Anchises are shown to have considerable psychic and spiritual capacities; they both have remarkable prophetic dreams and visions, telling them to go to distant Hesperia (Italy). After Anchises dies during the long journey, Aeneas later meets him in the Underworld of Hades, which we might consider as an ancient description of what is called today an 'After-Death-Communication' (ADC). Socrates the satyr was also both a great warrior and a spiritual man. Gooch was right when he said the Neanderthals and their descendants transmitted their spiritual gifts to humanity, along with a bevy of lesser things. When the Trojans and Aeneas arrived in Italy and defeated the indigenous Latin tribes, the powerful Aeneas easily overwhelmed King Turnus, in another show of mismatched strengths. Being both strong and spiritual, Aeneas became the much-loved ancestor of mighty Rome.

Brutus and Britain

Brutus, or Brute of Troy, the great grandson of mighty Aeneas, has a noteworthy story, related to our theme following Neanderthal-Sapiens admixtures. His legend relates that he had a human father, Silvius, the son of Aeneas, but his mother is unknown, and died in childbirth.

An interesting chapter in the 9th century (AD) Historia Brittonum traces Brutus's genealogy back to the biblical Sons of Japheth, the Jewish 'third race' who were comprised of 'unclean tribes' such as the Gog-Magog and other similarly named hybrid tribes. This chapter, concerning the older history of Britannia, supports our general thesis that the sound of Og and Gog eventually morphed into Trog. The fast-as-horses Troglodytae were spread between Libya and the Red Sea. These wild, strong hybrid tribespeople of the Levant continued to migrate and mixed with Sapiens clans living in the Turkish area, eventually populating the land of Troad and the city of Troy thousands of years ago. These Neandertal-Sapiens migrants eventually became known as the strong tribes called Trojans (trog-ans), and it's remarkable that the Historia Brittonum successfully recorded such a long, remarkable, ancient journey of hybrid tribes, which spanned several thousand years.

The Historia Brittonum also recorded that Brutus arrived in the area, and renamed the land Britain, after himself, as conquerors often do.

Geoffrey of Monmouth's 12th century account, in his Historia Regum Britanniae, tells much the same story, but in greater detail. According to Geoffrey, a magician predicts great things for the unborn Brutus but also foretells he will kill both his parents. A strong brute grows up, and does so, perhaps by accident, in some reports, nonetheless he is banished. Traveling to Greece with a small band of loyal men, he discovers a group of Trojans enslaved there. Brutus frees them and becomes their leader. Together, they travel on, and the exiled Trojans land on a deserted island and discover an abandoned temple dedicated to Diana. After performing the appropriate ritual of respect and devotion, Brutus lies down and dozes in front of the goddess' statue. During his sleep, he is given a vision of the land where he is destined to settle, an island in the western ocean, which is inhabited . . . but only by a few *giants*.

Sailing on, the seafaring Trojans come upon a second band of Trojans, who had escaped and survived by moving to the west coast of Italy. Brutus joins forces with Corineus, their leader, who is also a prodigious warrior. They press on and eventually land on the south coast of England, then called Albion. The Historia Regum Britanniae recorded that Brutus and Corineus encounter vicious giants (Neanderthal-Sapiens admixtures) living in the area and defeat them. Brutus renames the island after himself and becomes its first King, while Corineus rules in Cornwall, which is named after him. While there, at a festival, they are again attacked again by giants (hybrid-hominids) and kill all of them but hold the largest giant, whose name happens to be Goemagot (Gog-Magog), for a wrestling match with Corineus, who must also be a strong hybrid warrior, for he throws Goemagot over a cliff to his death. Brutus then builds a city on the river Thames, which he calls Troia Nova, or New Troy. As we noted earlier, years later, New Troy is renamed London, in honor of Princess Londona, who was rescued by kinder, friendlier Gog-Magog giants than those encountered by Brutus and Corineus.

The most remarkable point in this saga of Brutus, is that the long cycle of migrating giants, called Gae-en-tes in those days, and who were also known as Og-res, is finally complete. The Gog-Magog tribes left the Levant, being driven off by the early Jewish folk, and migrated north, west and east. The northern migration of the Gogs landed them in Albion, or prehistoric Britain, where legends grew of giants and ogres, basically the same hybrid creatures. The western migration of some Gog-Magog people was led by Tubal-Cain, an ancestor of Cain himself, where Spain and Italy were populated by his hybrid people.

The longer, eastern migrations of Gog-Magog landed them in Arabia, by the Black, Caspian and Red Sea areas, and also in far Mongolia. As the Gogs became the Trogs, which later populated the Troad over several thousand years, Brutus of Troy, with his royal lineage, and being a distant descendant of the Gog-Magog, the third race of the Hebrews, the Sons of Japheth, completed the extraordinary 'circuit of hybrid movement,' by arriving back in Britain, as its first King, according to Geoffrey.

Et Tu, Siddhartha?

Siddhartha Gotama; The Buddha; The Son of a White Elephant?

Dark Night, Wind is still

I, Flying to yon Door

You'll know my Love

O NCE Upon a Time . . .
as we recall from the Introduction, is not just a playful reference
to a fairy tale, but rather, in its first use, the phrase has its roots
in the earliest Pali language; the ancient language spoken by Siddhartha
Gotama, the Buddha of India. Thus, his sole biography, in Pali, begins
with those very words: *Once upon a Time*. Perhaps the charged words
referred to the mating of the true parents of the Buddha. Truth is, well . . .
you know.

~!~

As we have seen with the Trojan War myth, the various Bible stories and
the Jewish Cain Tradition, there is a strange penchant for Western
religious 'divine birth' myths, to not be as they seem, and are likely an
ancient cover-up of sorts, for the Neanderthal and human interbreeding
that must necessarily have happened in the dim past, in order for the
reader and the author to possess 2–4% Neon DNA or more, today. These
religious stories are really the stories of hybrid humanity hiding in dark
caves in the Levant, and occasionally mixing with other nearby
indigenous or migratory peoples.
In the East, we have already seen hybrid-hominid clues in the Sherpas, the
Tibetan-Chinese Clan of Shennong, as well as the Mongols, who declare
that they came from the wild Gog-Magog tribes of the Levant.

And now, we must turn our attention once more to the East, where the story of Siddhartha Gotama, the Buddha, looms large with hints of a hybrid-hominid past, if we can successfully link several old, relatively unknown clues together.

Siddhartha, born in the 5th century BCE, was the founder of the early Hinayana (Little Raft) style of Buddhism, with his intense experience and subsequent teaching of Nirvana (Nibbana, in Pali). Today's Buddhist sect Mahayana (Big Raft) is more socialized, and its members do not experience Nirvana, if we are to believe the Dalai Lama himself, who states in his books, that he does not know what it is, or if it exists. So, things have changed in Buddhism over the millennia.

Gotama was said to be a Prince, or knight, in a small township in the mountainous northern India-Nepal area. As his spiritual fame grew, it was forbidden for over 300 years after his death to have any iconic image portray him, as the true Buddha is considered transcendent, and not a mortal. But we can ask, is this the *real* reason for the non-disclosure, or mention, of what he looked like? Thus, his physical appearance is totally unknown, regardless of the many iconic, serious, sad, and even humorous Buddhist statues created over the centuries since his death. Our focus here will be upon Siddhartha's own clan, the Shakyas, and also upon the importance of his mother, known as MayaDevi, and also Queen Maya. Maya of course, is a key word in India and Tibet, and having Maya for a mother, is obviously referring, as a huge clue, to the great illusion of life. Queen Maya, in the early Buddhist legends, dies seven days after the mysterious birth of her son, and then communicates with him from heaven as he grows into adulthood. Much of his biography is actually a developed legend, and not truly believable, and like their Christian counterparts, today's many Buddhists have to look the other way or face a rather farcical myth of their founder's strange and unusual beginning. Below is the 21st century view of the now-accepted 'biographical form' concerning the birth of Siddhartha. Note the similarity to the Jewish legends, where sterile women did not conceive and then, years later were 'visited' by God.

269

"Māyā and King Suddhodhana did not have children for twenty years into their marriage. According to legend, one full moon night, sleeping in the palace, the queen had a vivid dream. She felt herself being carried away by four devas (spirits) to Lake Anotatta in the Himalayas. After bathing her in the lake, the devas clothed her in heavenly cloths, anointed her with perfumes, and bedecked her with divine flowers. Soon after a white elephant, holding a white lotus flower in its trunk, appeared and went round her three times, entering her womb through her right side. Finally, the elephant disappeared, and the queen awoke, knowing she had been delivered an important message, as the elephant is a symbol of greatness. Referring to the prophetic dream Queen Maya had prior to conception, the life story of the Buddha according to the Pali Canon say that his mother did not engage in sexual activity or entertain any thoughts of other men during her pregnancy. It does not say that Siddhartha was conceived without sexual activity between his parents. However, some parallels have been drawn with the birth story of Jesus."

Queen Maya (Mother of Buddha), **Wikipedia**

Who's Yo' Daddy?

Indeed, the potentially related names of Maya and Mary (the Bitter One) may contain many secrets from the past, as yet unknown to academia. So, in a great, surreal thrust of biographical poetic imagery, we find Queen Maya swept away, presumably in a lucid dream, where she becomes naked, and is washed in a mountain lake, then then adorned with special clothing. Somehow a White Elephant made its way over to her, to father and later manifest the child Siddhartha Gotama . . . and Voila! A Savior is born, for the world to misunderstand yet again. It's strange to consider Buddhism as a truly atheistic religion, as they claim to be today, while the unusual claim of the founder's divine birth is simply ignored. As in the Cain Tradition of Jewish history, we once again have the questionable divine birth, appearing as a cover-up story, possibly due to the embarrassing implication of the hybrid-hominid implications, which would cause great oriental loss of face, as they say. Taken literally, the ludicrousness of the White-Elephant myth is only matched by those seen in the previously concocted Biblical and Jewish myths and stories of the Cain, Hannah, Mary, and Jesus early traditions. There, the truth is more involved with the caverns of the Levant, which contained hybrid creatures, known as the incubus and succubus, the 'unclean' ones, or the Gog-Magog in ancient Jewish history.

The various cover-up myths often seem to take the texture and direction of a common, modern, soap opera, with all of their romantic intrigue. We can take note that the word 'devas' in Queen Maya's dream, has a root base of 'dev,' which, in another culture, may be expressed negatively as 'dev-il,' or devil, or even a King, as in King David (deva'd). We recall that King David is reported to have mated with a succubus, Agrat Bat Mahlat, who was likely a Gog-Magog; which produced Asmodeus; Prince of Demons. As we shall see, Siddhartha's wife is accused of adultery . . . with a Moon Demon!

The Pali Canon states that MayaDevi was 'not with any man' but this might be a deceptive ruse, like Christianity's Mother Mary. For hybrid-hominids were not considered men, but rather devas and/or dev-ils were very often not angels, but rather, lustful, cunning devils.

In our alternative hybrid-hominid hypothesis, a scene akin to those in the Levant is developing. Sneaking under the veil of the myth of Buddha's mom for a moment, might we suggest that she, under the lustful full moon, may have run off, or have been carried off, for a wild tryst with a hybrid fellow, or perhaps a few of them? Stranger things have happened, and yes, the taboo subjects of strange births *must* be covered up, to save the 'oriental face,' as it seems. In the sagas of Siddhartha's own Shakya clan, there are, as in the Shennong Clan, reports of ancient Shakya kings mating with 'dragon princesses,' but the details are few, yet suspicious, for these other 'divine births.'

~!~

Perhaps we should challenge each and every ancient story involving divine birth, given what we have seen, but space is limited.

These ancient fabrications are simply unnecessary and may be purposeful fomentations of a deluded left brain. This does not mean that we throw the spiritual baby out with the dirty religious bathwater; no, indeed, it's important to stay focused on the ancient universal message: We can consider that All Births are Divine, including, obviously, those of the reader and the author. This is not an opportunity for the Ego to gloriously thrash about inside itself again, but rather represents a spiritual doorway to the deep Wisdom Body of the human nature, wherein, if you are a Yogini, you will find God or Goddess in the left ventricle of your heart. Go there if you can, because in the labyrinth of the mind, only glimpses will be given to you, and possibly not even those, while you live in the deep, hypnotic Maya of your mind. Ananda K. Coomaraswamy, the Hindu sage who informed both orientalist Heinrich Zimmer and a young Joseph Campbell, wrote *The Living Thoughts of Gotama*, a small book wherein a great deal of spiritual wisdom is distilled, which has been lost to today's Mahayana Buddhists. It's noteworthy that today's leading Buddhists, such as the Dalai Lama, no longer experience, nor understand, the true nature of Nirvana, according to the Lama's own printed word, in his own books. Thus, young aspirants should not enter into Buddhism, thinking to experience the illusive Nirvana, or Nibbana, as it is known in the old Pali language, for no one ever does, according to the Buddhist report.

I can't see the end of me

My whole expanse I cannot see

Oh Me! **Kurt Cobain; Nirvana**

Yet, the pain and enlightenment of Nirvana is still experienced by a few.

The Sweetened Life (lie) of the Buddha

In returning to the life of Siddhartha Gotama, after his very unusual birth (no matter which incredible story you believe), we find another clever obfuscating ruse has been well established concerning his upbringing and his entry into adulthood. A type of cleansing and sanctification has occurred in Buddhism, not unlike the morphing of a dwarfish, humpbacked Jesus into his sweetened, nearly angelic Euro-American form, complete with halo. Below is the 'standardized and approved' version of Siddhartha's life:

"Siddhartha was brought up by his mother's younger sister, Maha Pajapati. His father is said to have shielded him from knowledge of human suffering. When he reached the age of 16, his father arranged his marriage to a cousin of the same age named Yaśodharā. According to the early Buddhist Texts of several schools, and numerous post-canonical accounts, she gave birth to a son, named Rāhula. Siddhartha is said to have spent 29 years as a prince under his father's rule. Although his father ensured that Siddhartha was provided with everything he could want or need, Buddhist scriptures say that the future Buddha felt that material wealth was not life's ultimate goal. At the age of 29, Siddhartha left his palace, and despite his 'human' father's efforts to hide from him the sick, aged and suffering, Siddhartha was said to have seen an old man. When his charioteer Channa explained to him that all people grew old, the prince went on further trips beyond the palace. On these he encountered a diseased man, a decaying corpse, and an ascetic. These depressed him, and he initially strove to overcome ageing, sickness, and death by living the life of an ascetic. Accompanied by Channa and riding his horse Kanthaka, Gautama quit his palace for the life of a mendicant. It's said that "the horse's hooves were muffled by the gods" to prevent guards from knowing of his departure."

Siddhartha Gautama; **Wikipedia**

~!~

Author's note: In this sanitized version, Siddhartha's assumed human father (a step-in stepdad?) was named King Śuddhodana, while the white-elephant-daddy story remains in the background. It's rather incredible to read that a man could get married at age sixteen to his cousin, and then have to have life and death concepts 'explained' to him at age twenty-nine. In each human culture on earth, children observe and learn that aging and death occur at a much earlier age than twenty-nine, say perhaps 10–12 years of age.

At age twenty-nine, Prince Siddhartha has been married for thirteen years, yet must be expected to be a blithering idiot, concerning life, disease, and death. Are not royal persons supposed to be well trained in the important philosophies and conditions of life? Yes, of course. Thus, the entire scene is a contrived religious smokescreen, which apparently is either bought (hook, line and sinker) or totally ignored by today's Buddhists, since Siddhartha is said to be their sacred founder. Apparently, the young Prince had to sneak out of the palace, and so the legend of 'horse hooves being muffled by the Gods' was added as icing, to the luscious, thick cake of Buddhist legend.

Buddha's Son Rāhula: A Child of the Moon Demon?

There are several conflicting legends (as always) involving the Buddhist stories of Siddhartha, his assigned wife and cousin, Yaśodharā, and their supposed son, the unusual boy known as Rāhula. The well-scrubbed version, available for the general public consumption, states that Rāhula is Siddhartha's son, and that he grows up and becomes a Buddhist under his father's tutelage. Thus *All's Well That Ends Well*. This myth of Rāhula, however, is also ripe for exposure, under the scrutiny of our hybrid-hominid hypothesis. As in the pattern seen of Buddha's mum, Queen Maya, Rāhula's mother Yaśodharā also has a background that requires investigation. Scholars generally accept the name 'Rāhula' as meaning '**hindrance**,' a strange name indeed, for a baby boy. The common storyline depicts Siddhartha leaving his home and palace, just as Rāhula has been born to Yaśodharā, earlier that day. The spiritually romantic (altered) plot states that Siddhartha is so intent upon beginning his quest towards Nirvana, that, (tears and sobbing here), he even foregoes touching his wife and child as he is leaving; he doesn't say goodbye, but rather, with his charioteer, the princely knight departs into the deep woods, beyond the protective walls of the kingship. Briefly, Gotama starts his spiritual journey, meets several monks in the forest and later sits under the Bo tree, where he achieves enlightenment, which the public thinks, or is informed that, is Nirvana. Again, we have a wonderful *All's Well That Ends Well* Buddhist concoction. After yawning, we still must ask: but what really happened? If we examine alternative texts, usually ignored by academics, we get our necessary clues.

So Rāhula, the supposed son of Siddhartha, is born on the very same day that the Prince decides to renounce the throne and begin his quest. That's rather curious, isn't it? The Pali language account states that when Siddhartha receives news of his son's birth, he replies, *'A Rahu is born; a Fetter has arisen.'* These are strange words, but scholars consider that Rahu, meaning hindrance or a fencing (fetter) simply refers to the notion that Siddhartha would rather get on with his spiritual quest, rather than to stay and be a father. According to the romantic storyline, the Prince takes one look at the baby and his wife, and doesn't touch or speak to them (sob), fearing he may lose his spiritual resolve; he bravely leaves for the forest, leaving his precious family behind, to become a spiritual hero (Yawn). Sometimes, cover-up myths become nauseating.

Other texts derive Rahu much differently. The Apadana, and other accounts in Buddhist monastic traditions, consider that the name Rahu is derived from the:

'Eclipse of the moon, which is caused by a demon, named Rahu.'

And so, we have our first clue, or suspicion, that a hybrid-hominid presence may be seen in this strange story of the Buddha's son.

The Difficult Birth

Alternatively, the Mūlasarvāstivāda tradition relates, that Rāhula is *conceived* on the very evening of the renunciation of Prince Siddhartha, and was born *six years later*, on the very day that his father achieves enlightenment, which was during a lunar eclipse. What a coincidence! And, being born a full six years after the last parental tryst is quite a mental distraction to absorb. Its nearly as hard to explain six years of Yaśodharā's pregnancy, as it is divine birth; to continue further into the many Buddhist myths and legends is simply to invite endless paradoxical chaos. The history of Siddhartha, Yaśodharā and Rāhula is entirely shrouded by huge amounts of embellishments.

An alternative view of Rāhula can be attained. It is reported that, as an adult he had an unusual, large 'umbrella'-shaped head, coupled with a face that had a large nose and bulging eyes. The unusualness of the head may suggest Denisovan or Neanderthal physical characteristics; Rāhula didn't look like other human folks. As in Queen Maya's story, where she didn't have children with her husband the King, but rather got divinely 'carried away' and had an *ahem*, 'divine birth,' by a white-elephant-deva, Yaśodharā's bed may have been shared by the moon-eclipsing demon, Rahu. If so, Rāhula is the child of the Moon Demon, which we may view as 'de-mon' or de-vil, once again. In other words, Rāhula is *not* Siddhartha's son. This certainly explains, psychologically, why a young Prince would depart in great haste on the day of the birth of his own ill-begotten son. Siddhartha was under great psychological duress. Could Rāhula really be the misshapen hybrid son of a hybrid creature, lurking nearby, who had sex with Siddhartha's royally assigned wife Yaśodharā? When Siddhartha first saw the newborn, he would know at once it was not his, with its unusual skull and face. And so, broken-hearted, but at last free of suspicions of his wife, he then departed, leaving a broken family behind. Siddhartha's mind would be on fire with the birth of a crossbreed creature, and all that it implied, with his wife's somewhat-bestial adultery. The resultant shame was so great upon Siddhartha, as his wife had, like many women today, consistently lied during her pregnancy. A severe social taboo of a mixed race, or worse, a mixed species, is often found in ancient and modern peoples. The young Prince, whose own mother may have had sex with a 'white-elephant-deva,' was shocked and overwhelmed by Rāhula's ugly birth, and this is the better reason for his departure into the deep woods. His questionable romance with his wife was forever broken, due to her lies concerning conception, and the deformed child she gave birth to.

Some try to tell me, thoughts they cannot defend.
The Moody Blues

The notion that Siddhartha became 'enlightened' on the very same day of his son's birth, is also macabre; perhaps the romantic light bulb finally came on, when he realized Rāhula was not his, and that his wife had lied to conceal her illegitimate relationship with a near-human creature, who passed along his unusual skull and facial traits to his son, Rāhula.

If you think about it, our hybrid-hominid hypothesis is much more believable than the stories of divine births, moon-demons, and white, horny elephants. Truth is stranger than fiction.

~

Let us put ourselves in the position of young Siddhartha for a moment and ignore the 'sanctified' biographical version of his life.

At age twenty-nine, your life has been entirely upended by the appearance of a strange baby. Your wife has not been faithful; perhaps you suspected this for a long time. Worse, the entire kingdom will soon know.
Now totally broken-hearted, Siddhartha departs and lives the life of a mountain forest ascetic, barely subsisting, perhaps at times starving. His mind is seething with emotional pain. He slowly wanders, or trudges, mindlessly and aimlessly. The woods are full of wild animals—some are large predators, such as tigers, who prowl at night. Safety is a major issue for Siddhartha and the monks he tries to befriend; they don't have the protection of the tall walls of the township. Fear of predators should not be underestimated; it is reported that over one million people have been eaten by tigers in the last five centuries, in this very area of India, Nepal, and South Asia.
Having come from being a well-respected, wealthy, provided-for royal member, Siddhartha is now dirty, poor, destitute, and is often terrified during his nights in the wild woods. The non-stop pain of thinking of Yaśodharā, Rāhula and the great embarrassment that resulted from knowing that 'everyone knew' of his wife's strange affair, even his father the King, wore heavily upon him. Under the pressure, the young knight's mind began to bend.
Later, as Yaśodharā was accused of a secret adultery by the village townsfolk (we can only imagine with whom?) she undertakes several 'Acts of Truth,' or supernatural accomplishments, such as floating stones on water, etc. to show everyone the boy is truly Siddhartha's, and that she is truly a Princess. This last 'miracle' is one of the worst Buddhist concoctions; quite often the left brain will stop at nothing to produce lies and confabulations to avoid the psychological, painful truth.

After he left his small kingdom, Siddhartha's mind was not fit for meditation—far from it. He was intense, and psychologically desperate, and perhaps seriously frail in health, as he quickly deteriorated from the trials of his life. Flat broke, and not being able to return to the place of his birth, Siddhartha finally sat down beneath a large tree and completely broke down. The pain was so great he couldn't even cry out; his mind was going numb at the thought of ongoing existence, and the suffering he had seen and now experienced. He may have wanted to die, to escape the pain of life. But he didn't die; instead, something of a spiritual, neuropsychological miracle occurred.

Break on Through (to the Other Side)

The Doors

"When One Perishes, but the Body does not Die;

That One Knows Eternal Presence.'

The Tao Te Ching; **Lao Tzu**

What is Nirvana?

Form is Illuminated by Light?

Thomas Edison's first light bulb. Wikipedia: SA: CC 2.0

The Greater Self

As a hybrid Socrates once stated to 'Know Thyself,' while also stating that he conversed often with his 'Daimon' or the spiritual entity inside himself, Siddhartha also advised his monks to connect with the Inner Self, which he referred to quite often, as 'The Lovely' or 'The Lamp.' This was Siddhartha's own spiritual connection, which occurred after his own crushing, devastating Nirvana, which is a form of psychological death!

After this great adjustment, a powerful enlightenment occurs, which is always expressed differently by those having the conscious experience. Neuropsychologically, with Siddhartha, we may consider that the left-brained Ego, the constructed 'Self Module,' as it's known to neuroscience, finally collapsed, suffering in the greatest of pain, and that a great torrent of enlightenment took over, no longer occluded, as the Wisdom Body (right, rear & heart brains) gushed forth, in an unbelievable river of conscious awareness. So, indeed, the young knight did become a Buddha, and reached the 'other shore,' which is said to be the mysterious goal of ancient Buddhists. Siddhartha began to teach the forest monks of his extremely convincing, poignant experience, where he became 'intimate with the Lovely'—his own Lamp.

"Literature is the faint remembrance of Experience."

Steven A Key

Today's schools of Buddhism cannot 'teach' this naturally occurring experience, with its resultant yogic method of acknowledgement, knowledge, and connection. Thus, their meditations are often vague, and unguided; aspirants quickly fade from their chosen paths. No one seems to experience Nirvana in the many Buddhist schools.
Yet, the Buddha, as he taught his monks, went so far as to say that, *'unless one is intimate with the Lovely,'* they should **not** attempt the vaunted Eight-fold Path which he had laid out for his followers. Today, this is forgotten Buddhism.
Buddhist Scholar I.B. Horner and Ananda K. Coomaraswamy, both early translators of the Pali Canon, wrote this now-forgotten translation of Siddhartha's earliest words, in a section entitled the 'Great Self,' where the Buddha is speaking:

"Does the Order of Monks expect that I should not attain utter Nirvana until I have left some instructions concerning it?

*I do not see any other single condition by means of which the Ariyan eightfold Way, if not arisen, can arise, or, if it has arisen can be brought to perfection of culture, except by this **friendship with the Lovely**.*

Just as the dawn monks, is the forerunner, the harbinger of the sun's arising, even so is Friendship with the Lovely the forerunner, the harbinger of the arising of the seven limbs of wisdom in a monk.
Do you make of the Self a Lamp?

The Living Thoughts of Gotama

It's important to note that the little-known Coomaraswamy was a primary mentor to a young Joseph Campbell, and Heinrich Zimmer, the German Orientalist.

Aside from this beautiful, spiritual reading, we find that Siddhartha was actually psychologically damaged in his relations with women. Ananda, his chief monk, had been trying to persuade Siddhartha to allow women into the newly formed spiritual order, which Siddhartha resisted, and then finally allowed.

The young knight was so bothered by his prior relation with his wife and son, that he once informed Ananda, according to Coomaraswamy, in his book, *The Living Thoughts of Gotama* that;

All women are stupid.

The shocked reader, if female, need not take offense at this deranged comment. The key is to see beyond the outer, social arrangement, and to realize that a terrible tragedy has occurred, which has a misogynistic side effect. If the tragedy happened to a spurned woman, she may likely develop into man-hater as well, while also walking a spiritual path.

In this sense, Nirvana is similar to a psychological, spiritual Phoenix, rising from the fire-burned Ashes of Life, regardless of gender.

Achieving an intimate connection with 'The Lamp' is the equivalent of the ancient Yogini reducing her obstructing Ego, and connecting neurally with the greatness of the God-provided Wisdom Body. In today's lingo, we may say that these words of Buddha are referring to an 'inner light.' In

Jungian psychology, we might say that we connect with our inner archetypes when the right hemisphere of the Wisdom Body is finally free to express itself, and when the obstruction of a reluctant Ego is removed. This is how The Father and Son become One—to use the phrase of Jesus. Jesus, Siddhartha, Lao Tzu, and many other spiritual savants of the past were actually poor, homeless wanderers, even hybrid-hominids, slightly different from humans, with perhaps 8–15% Neanderthal DNA. We should recall paleo-psychologist Stan Gooch's view that the Neanderthals and their hybrid descendants were the ones who gave religion to a Sapiens culture, long ago. We have seen many varieties of Monsters, Philosophers & Saviors, to be sure.

One is reminded of the poor, homeless folk today, who wander and beg, moving from town to town, as they too exist, on the outskirts of supposed 'civilization,' perhaps with their own quiet saints.

As he passed from this life, an aged, eighty-year old Siddhartha, the likely son of a hybrid-hominid himself (or a White Elephant), spoke his final words to his monks, upon his deathbed.

'Be Your Own Light.'

And thus, ends the truly remarkable story of his little-known life.

Once Upon a Time.

~!~

Be Your Own Light.

Conclusions

The author wishes to thank the persevering reader for having the resilient ability to absorb the many pieces of shocking, new information about Sapiens, Neanderthals, Denisovans, and our hybrid-hominid past.

As I was researching and writing, I was always fascinated by the questions of:

Who gave us Neanderthal DNA?

Who were the famous hybrid Neanderthal-Sapiens creatures in the long road of history?

Several times, I was shocked, and perhaps you were too, at the famous, familiar names that were involved, and now must be looked at in an entirely new way. Our conclusion here, of course, is both one of speculation and one of fact. The summary of names given below, of the various hybrid candidates, are not a perfect nor comprehensive list of the unknown creatures in our past, yet it remains that our own hybrid DNA must be explained, as stated from the very beginning.

Enkidu, Huwawa, Zana, Spartacus and the Getae, Socrates, Silenus & Satyrs, Bes, the Sherpa clans, Asmodeus, Quasimodo, Merlin, Beowulf/Grendel, Jesus, Mary, Cain, Goliath, Gog-Magog (Mongols), King Arthur, King David & Agrat bat Mahlat, Achilles, Ajax, Hector, Chiron, and Brutus, King Shennong, Siddhartha and their eastern clans, which were also founded by Dragons.

Ogs Trogs & Drogs:

Dragons, Ogres and Trolls really did exist; and were often really strong, deadly killers, as they were really Neon-Sapiens admixtures, like Grendel of Beowulf. Sapiens-Ogres children were a historical reality, usually via Neanderthal rape.

Today, only fables and myths dimly remind us of a very stark previous reality, of an unknown hybrid-hominid history.

Elizabeth Kubler-Ross, the precocious German woman who became the world's first death psychologist, once commented, to my surprise, that she considered the human race to date back over forty million years! This was long before the more recent advancements in DNA analysis and the newer views presented here by anthropologists, some of whom are now considering Neons as humans, or humanlike. Joseph Campbell, the author of the popular *Hero of a Thousand Faces*, once summarized the theme of his book:

"A hero ventures forth from the world of common day into a region of supernatural wonder: fabulous forces are there encountered, and a decisive victory is won: the hero comes back from this mysterious adventure with the power to bestow boons on his fellow man."

Hairy Heroes

We can expand Campbell's view, by joining it with Stan Gooch's contemplations on Neons, Denisovans, and their hybrid descendants, and thus include perhaps 50,000 years of prehistoric hybrid-hominid existence into the dim past. We should forever forget the naïve notions that heroes, in general, are really just Western white men. Rather, we should consider that a darker, hairy hero's face was large, with a larger skull than Sapiens; these would be our prehistoric heroes, as Philosophers and Saviors, who existed alongside the many unfortunate Monsters of the past.

Neanderthal with face paint glitter.
Credit: Viktor Deak – Scientific American, June 2010

After considering the above list, its rather startling to consider that genetic scientists now consider it feasible to be able to recreate a Neanderthal-Sapiens hybrid using a few bits of DNA from the skull fossils.

Genetic science is moving fast. The Neanderthal genome was first sequenced in 2010. Meanwhile, new gene-editing tools have been developed and technical barriers to 'de-extinction' are being overcome. Technically, science could attempt the cloning of a Neanderthal. It would involve introducing Neanderthal DNA into a human stem cell, before finding a human surrogate mother to carry the Neanderthal-esque embryo. However, there'd likely be mismatches between mother and the hybrid embryo that might make the endeavor unfeasible. As in the past, many deformed and stillborn children will likely result from the cloning attempts. And, given that the Neanderthal is our closest relative, its cloning would likely be regulated as whole human or reproductive cloning, which in most countries is still illegal.

Only time will tell of their eventual success or failures to restore a Neanderthal-like creature. As in the cases of the naturally occurring Cain, Mary, and Jesus, many scientific crossbreed clonings would likely produce a strange set of new and unusual creatures, some deformed, perhaps some with humpbacks. If it were possible, recreating a pure Neon

285

creature with a brain case that has a 400% larger vision center than Sapiens, would certainly be a psychological challenge for analytical scientists to ponder, but Stan Gooch intuited, and understood their deeper, visual nature, being a paleo-psychologist.

There are still a certain few conservative anthropologists who debate amongst the more liberal-minded members of their kind, that the ancient, dull Neon couldn't appreciate and/or use flowers, let alone decorate burial sites with them. Whenever Neon dig sites indicate burials with flowers, the conservative scholar's response is that they were haphazardly brought in by burrowing rodents. Fragile flowers don't last, and so perhaps we'll never know, if we rely solely upon the archeological spade. Concerning the Neons and their potential prodigies, the knowledge supplied by paleo-psychologist Stan Gooch, author/researcher Colin Wilson, and others, lies in stark contrast to the limited theories outlined by mainstream academia.

Summary of gifts or contributions

With an open mind, let's consider that, according to Gooch, and more recent science developments concerning Neanderthal, considerable social and spiritual gifts were passed along during the Neon-Sapiens hybrid-hominid exchanges in the distant past. We can also consider the newer, comprehensive archeological theories of their development. Below is a possible list of such 'gifts,' formulated by the author:

Children's toys,
Pets, animal training, horseback riding,
Sports and athleticism, sprints, fighting contests,
Mountain climbing,
Religion-shamanism and psychological health,
Chanting (Gooch suggested HMMM)
Deep knowledge of dreams and inner worlds.
Talismans and jewelry,
Speech, writing,
Fire-making, hot water,
Sexual practices & knowledge,
Knowledge of herbs, (and flowers),

The use of paints for body and domicile,
Canoeing, boating, swimming,
Hunting and trapping animals, animal husbandry,
Cavern house-making, bedroom, bathroom living room,
Vegetarianism, cannibalism,
Knowledge of weapons and war, including spears, stone clubs, archery,
Fire-breathing, fire-defenses and fire-dancing,
Singing, music, flutes, drums,
Strong, sentient interaction with nature. (the Universe was alive).

Many anthropologists consider that horse domestication is only 5,000 years old, and first developed with the creation of ancient chariots. They don't consider that Neons or their descendants rode horses, however, this view may be premature. It has been shown that Neanderthal fossils showed a frequency of such injuries comparable to that of modern rodeo professionals, showing frequent contact with large, combative mammals. There is no reason not to include hunting and even riding horses. Further, the remarkable Bhimbetka grottos and caves in central India are liberally sprinkled with ancient artwork concerning horses. These caves were inhabited from 100,000 to 10,000 years ago and the artwork clearly shows seven figures riding on horseback. Other images show figures riding upon elephants, and warriors wielding bows and arrows.

Shamanism is considered by academics to be only 10,000–20,000 years old and this conservative estimate certainly doesn't include the notion of Neons being early shamans. While Gooch's idea of Neanderthal gifting of shamanism to humans may seem unusual, new findings and reports are claiming that shamanism is actually nearly a half-million years or more, based upon evidence of an ancient cult of Bird-Shamanism, which was located in Israel and the Levant; the very areas we have been targeting as ancient Neanderthal hotspots. Even in our modern times, Bird-Shamanism is still practiced in many cultures, such as the American Indians, those folks with a higher Neon DNA count than most other humans.
One thing the conservative scholars may not have realized, as did Gooch, was that, perhaps the development of human culture was the other way

around and that Sapiens learned from the bright Neons, with whom they had sex, children, and a hybrid lifestyle we can hardly recognize.

"We passed on all we know. Ten thousand generations live in you now."

Neon

'Tis The End

~!~ Peace, Love, Lessons, Wisdom, Flight ~!~

Author's Appreciation Page

~!~

If you enjoyed reading this book,
please consider posting a favorable review
for the author and book on Amazon.com.
All help is greatly appreciated. Thank You.

~!~

Appendix A ~ Sacred Locations

Many thanks to Sacred-Texts.com for the use of their excellent website.

The entire 1927 translation of The Story of King Gilgamesh can be found here:

https://www.sacred-texts.com/ane/eog/index.htm

The Saga of Beowulf can be found here:

https://www.sacred-texts.com/neu/eng/tsb/index.htm

The Story of the Trojan War can be found here:

https://www.sacred-texts.com/cla/bulf/bulf26.htm

Appendix B ~ Ancient Festivals

Although many of the Neons and hybrids were surely monsters and violent cannibals, it remains that a more harmonious relation also existed between Neons and Sapiens, where love, lust, youthful romance, and peaceful co-existence prevailed. The simple acts of sharing may be seen as a natural Neon-Sapiens experience:

Sharing things that I know and love, with those of my kind

Deacon Blues, **Steely Dan**

We must certainly acknowledge, of course, that much of our hybrid humanity, both in history and the vast prehistoric past, has had a strong penchant for war, violence, theft, rape, and slavery, all of which are monstrous behaviors. However, let us conclude on a good note, even if romantic, and perform a brief thought experiment, where ancient humans, either Neons, Sapiens or their hybrid offspring, also experienced a few good times in life, away from the terrors of large animals and the general pain and drudgery of daily living. Our species seems to require a periodic break from the stresses of living; this is most likely true in both ancient prehistoric and modern times.

Early humanity, including Denisovans, Sapiens and Neons, may have had a somewhat playful and childlike side to themselves, for nearly everyone died at an early age; getting past forty was rare. The overall population would be smaller and more youthful than in modern times, where large, aging populations are seen. Somehow, in the ancient past, the simple act of relaxing and playing with others of your own kind eventually spawned the concept of planned festivals, where people could gather to meet, talk, eat, drink, play, engage in sports and music, and maybe even a little hanky-panky.

We can imagine how ancient hybrid-hominid tribes may have gathered, in a large field, or perhaps a forest, for the purposes of holding a peaceful festival. Let us consider the Neon DNA ranges from 3–8%, in the attending tribal groups, however, no violent ogres are allowed. This is a time of peace. Several hundred people were in attendance at this festival, which was just getting underway; it was the very first day of a weeklong celebration, within a few hundred yards of the Black Sea.

A stout, dark, and hairy young man, of unknown hybrid-hominid heritage, spies a beautiful girl, with delicate skin, and begins to desire her. As the gala, where brightly colored festival activities begins, we hear shouting, music, and a small hum of mixed voices. Many tables are abundantly stocked with many different foods, producing an exotic smell. The young man pours a fermented beverage into two cups, and slowly walks over to the girl he has been admiring. Offering a small, hesitant smile, he hands the cup to the girl, who accepts his gift, and looks him directly in the eye. Their gaze interlocks.

Smile at me, I will understand,

even if we are not of the

same language.

The young man and woman are from two distinctly different tribes, one perhaps more hybrid-hominid than the other, yet a peaceful friendship has grown up between the local tribal groups. They don't yet know each other's language, yet the young man attempts a soulful exchange and slowly articulates key words of his tribal religion, to show he is a decent fellow:

Manspeak: HA AB KA BA MA TA RA

(My body, heart, mind,& soul are of justice; and from the Earth and Sun)

(note: these monosyllabic words are actually prehistoric Egyptian)

The young woman remains silent, and slowly sips her beverage while she ponders what the rough-looking young fellow could be saying. She is now staring deeply into his remarkable, large green eyes, which are very sincere. The beverage is strong, she's beginning to feel exceptionally good; she likes the friendly, powerful stranger, even his musty smell. Her father and family are nearby, and nervously watching her every move with the dark, red-haired fellow. The young girl smiles back at her new companion, and finally opens up and begins talking, in her own strange language, which is unknown to him:

Womanspeak: *The sunsets go, the clouds roll by, the earth turns old.*

The young man doesn't understand a word, but is mesmerized by the graceful, melodious sound of her voice; her eyes are also sincere, and a bit wild. One good beverage deserves another, and several rounds are downed.

Come on out, dance, make romance.

The wild night is calling.

Domino; **Van Morrison**

The full yellow moon is announcing the dusky evening. The festive crowd is becoming more and more raucous; now many folks, of both tribes, are dancing wildly around a roaring bonfire, in the middle of the festival grounds. A constant drumming is heard in the background.
And then an ancient choreographed scene develops; several of the fire-dancers take a white liquid made from plant resins into their mouths; they light their fire brand sticks and begin twirling circles of fire in unison. Then, at the right moment, they blast forth huge 20-foot-long torrents of flames from their mouths, wildly exciting the half-drunken crowd, which roars with approval. The young children watch in raptured amazement.

With just a little imagination, one can see how both fire-breathing and fire-dancing could easily have been weaponized in the distant past, but that is not the case today, at the festival celebration of the full moon.

Over the years, the festival grows and grows; a thousand people from several slightly different tribes, in peace together, further develop festival products; various crafts and exotic foodstuff are sold at the market of the festival. Firepits are roasting wild boars and rabbits.

The music dance and sing.

They make the children really ring

Roundabout; **Yes**

New competitive events are scheduled to include feats of prowess. There are stone-throwing contests, along spear chucking, the forerunner of the modern javelin. Even prehistoric archery contests can be considered, given that Neon-hybrids were using sophisticated glues, made of ocher, beeswax, and plant gum, with their knowledge of fire, to produce a strong glue to secure the sharp arrowheads. The Neons and their descendants, having greater lung capacity and stronger legs, would likely engage in sprint contests. Fighting contests to prove strength were another likelihood, although perhaps not to the death, since they were at a festival.

Ancient tribes morphed their DNA as they developed, however, they also came into existence and later died out, for various reasons. The famous movie, *The Last of the Mohicans*, centered around this notion, of a disappearing American Indian culture. Another popular film, *Dances with Wolves* illustrates the point of slightly disparate DNA admixtures co-existing in tribal cultures. In this story, two white folks merge with a Western Indian tribe, whose Neon-Sapiens DNA were slightly different from their own. Our depiction of an ancient Black Sea forest festival is similar, as we suggest tribal, DNA admixtures for eons, into the past.

~

At our festival, the young, odd couple are still together; they seem like an ancient Romeo and Juliet, from different clans, slightly different in DNA. They began to drift away from the many campfires and from the noise of the raucous festive crowd. They begin walking down to the river with its best view of the moon, lighting its soft-flowing waters. No further speech is attempted, but a warm feeling is now mutual: they are attracted to each other. The young girl begins to hum a melodious tune; her man is once again mesmerized, as they walk along the river. He pulls a simple flute from his pocket . . . and amazingly, matches the musical tune of her voice quite easily, as if by magic.

Be on my side, I'll be on your side.

Come a little bit closer

Harvest Moon, **Neil Young**

They stop for a moment. The young man points to his chest and softly says his name: 'Ruk.' The beauty points to her chest and responds, 'Lana.' The dark, hairy fellow reaches over to touch her by the arm; he feels the soft skin of his beautiful companion and marvels. Feeling her breath suddenly taken away by his touch, Lana responds, by taking Ruk's strong hand. Under the moon, by the river, they embrace for the first time . . . and the rest is a hidden history.

Girl, you gotta love your man

Take him by the hand

Riders on the Storm, **The Doors**

And perhaps, such crossbreeding of slightly different tribes containing various admixtures of Neon-Sapiens continued for eons. Long ago the pure Neons had since died out, perhaps because of powerful Neon males mating with beautiful Sapiens females.

Appendix C: The Human Dragons

What is about to be explained requires an extremely open mind. The mythical dragons that we see depicted in the world today, are 100% artistic portrayals, which have little connection with the real origins of dragons.

Dragons were a form of Neanderthal-Sapiens human monster.

The public's myth-making capabilities, and Hollywood, did the rest in forming the concept in the public mind. This subject is so crazy, yet luscious and true, that I decided to provide more information about how dragons were really humans, as we discussed in an earlier chapter on Beowulf, Grendel & the Dragons. The subject may overwhelm the reader and cause rejection. We are escaping from the myths of dragons and say that they were more than a legend; Beowulf really did fight them in caves. He won some, lost one, and died. As crazy as it seems, his myth is rooted in forgotten truth.

I SEE YOU

Like King Arthur, Buddha's clan was also started by a 'dragon,' or more properly 'drakon,' one who has extremely sharp, keen eyes. Neanderthal eyes were one-third larger than Sapiens, and the rear vision braincase was 400% larger; their hybrid descendants would have retained some of their superior visual capabilities. Buddha had dragon blood in him too, as did his son, Hindrance (Rāhula). King Shennong, the founder of China, had a drakon (dragon) daddy. His early images portray him as a benevolent humanlike monster, not a dragon.

King Shennong: God of the Wind of Fire

We saw earlier in the picture of the human blowing his 'dragon's breath', that it's fairly easy to conceive that prehistoric humans breathed fire, in some cases using their fire-breathing as a terrible weapon. In returning to King Shennong and his birthplace of Shennong's Cave, as it is now called, we find a very curious legend manifested, of how the good King

Shennong was said to have been born to a human princess and a divine dragon. Dragons are, of course, a primary Chinese mythological symbol and ostensibly not hominids, but rather winged, fire-breathing beasts, right? Today, in modern psychological terms, dragons are considered mythical fixations of the human mind, which is creating and playing along with fanciful notions, while also knowing they are not real. Dragons are often depicted in Western media culture as being as large as those huge flying, flame-throwing beasts in the television portrayal of the hugely popular Game of Thrones. This portrayal, however, is entirely mythical. The stereotypical, public view of what makes a dragon must be totally dismantled, as it is an obstacle of itself, in seeing a potentially deeper truth.

We should strongly consider that the longer history of human fire-breathing may have been 'gifted' to Sapiens by Neanderthals long ago. Thus, King Shennong was called 'God of the Wind of Fire,' and this is also why Huwawa, in The Story of King Gilgamesh, was said to have 'flame in his jaws.' At some point in pre-history, hominids found that a white, possibly edible substance, was highly flammable, and many eons ago, simple fire-breathing began, as a trial and error process, and was eventually weaponized. A 20-foot blast of flame will terrorize and kill, and such things actually happened, but have been rendered to myth.

While this marvelous prehistoric Chinese story of Shennong having a dragon for a father initially smacks of being totally myth, it turns out that there may be a way to understand how one's parents could be both human and dragon, if we consider, as an example, a somewhat distant, faraway archeological solution found in an ancient cave in Austria. In Europe, the image of flame-breathing, flying dragons are nearly as ubiquitous in folklore as they are in China. Dragons now can be seen as a worldwide, mythical, cultural phenomenon. The public's view of dragons, both ancient and modern, is steeped in mental confusion and fear, yet the public expression is what actually propels the mistaken notion of the myths of flying, fire-breathing dragons. In his book, *An Instinct for Dragons*, anthropologist David E. Jones reveals that belief in dragons was extremely widespread among ancient cultures because evolution slowly created an innate fear of predators in the human mind. Just as monkeys have been shown to exhibit a fear of snakes and large cats, Jones considers that the trait of fearing large predators such as pythons, large birds of prey, elephants, lions, bears, and other fearful animals, has been permanently imbedded in the subconscious mind of all Sapiens. We can easily compare Jones' statements to those of Stan Gooch, who considered that humans were often terrified of hybrid-hominid creatures they called ogres, giants, trolls, etc. In more recent times, Jones argues these 'universal fears' have been frequently combined in folklore and created the myth of the dragon. Might we include our huge-faced, large-eyed Neons and their hybrid offspring in the list of terrifying creatures? It turns out to be a good idea. Though usually depicted as a winged creature, the dragon is generally to be found in its underground lair, in a cave, which identifies it as an ancient creature of the earth. The typical portrayal of dragons (drakons) in Europe's medieval Christian is usually seen as protecting a dark cavern; the dragon is then slain by a religious hero. But let's iconoclastically break this mistaken portrayal.

The most recent etymology for the word '**dragon**' does indeed basically translate as '**winged serpent**,' however, in earlier origins of the word, the meaning is entirely different and doesn't relate to a winged, flame-breathing beast at all. The modern English word of 'dragon' derives from Old English and Old French, which stems from the earlier Greek 'drakon,' usually translated as 'dragon.' However, the word '**drakon**' more properly, originally meant, '**I see**,' or perhaps '**sharp-sighted one**,' which dramatically alters the portrayal of a mythical dragon. Our keen-eyed hybrid-hominid, living in its cave, would be an exceptionally good match, for a drakon/dragon, before the myths morphed into legend. And there is more.

The Greek translation is thought to stem from eastern languages, such as Sanskrit, Aryan and possible older proto-Indo-European sources. The Greek word 'drakon' probably derives from an Aryan root of derk- meaning "to see" and the Sanskrit dṛç- also signifying "to see." So, the reader can see that over the eons a word meaning 'to see' or to be 'sharp-sighted' fantastically morphed into a whimsical notion of a flying, fire-breathing creature, not particularly known for its eyesight. The worldwide folkloric portrayal of dragons is totally incorrect. There is no etymological connection between far-seeing 'drakons' and the flying monsters of modern myth. There is, however, a lesser myth in Germanic folklore, which author Rudolph Koch symbolically calls, 'The Dragon's Eye,' which disregards the flying, flaming type of creature and focuses entirely upon the Eye of the Drakon. Now, which of the creatures that we have discussed would be known for their superior eyesight? The answer would be the Neons, with their large rear-brained visual cortexes four times larger than modern humans, and also their long line of hybrid descendants. Socrates, the short, stout Greek hybrid with large bulging eyes, was said to have a peripheral vision noticeably advanced over the common Greek man, according to Plato.

So, now, we may interpret a dragon more properly, as an ancient creature, without mythical wings, and who is far-seeing, with terribly intimidating eyes. This creature, who lives in a cave, has a deadly glance and is extremely formidable. Not called an ogre or giant in this case, but rather a 'drakon,' this type of creature sounds like a powerful Neon-Sapiens hybrid, not unlike Huwawa, the hybrid forest monster in The Story of King Gilgamesh, who is slain by the King.

The great tendency of humans to mythologically assign dragon attributes to simple hominid features cannot be underestimated. An example follows of how a hybrid fossil became known as a dragon's tooth. In 1935, anthropologist Gustav von Koenigswald came across several strange teeth in drug stores in Hong Kong and southern China. The specimens, sold as 'dragon teeth,' to be ground up for use in Chinese medicine, were special. They were apelike, but huge—much bigger than the molars of any other fossil or living primates. Their size (and that of four fossilized jaw bones) suggested that Gigantopithecus blacki was the largest primate ever discovered, towering nearly three meters in height. But without any skulls or skeletons, researchers didn't know whether the animal, which lived from roughly 2 million to 200,000 years ago, was a relative of today's orangutans, today's African apes, or something else entirely.

Many worldwide cultural myths, including those of the Chinese, also state that dragons could shape-shift into human form, and vice versa. Generally, this was done for a lustful purpose, of raping or having sex with mortal women and men. Hybrid-hominid homosexuality or bi-sexuality in those ancient days, may have been more prevalent than today's modern society. As we shall see, there may be a subtle history hiding behind these myths, now morphed into extreme forms. King Shennong and his curious clan are prime examples of this myth, likely having a Neon-Sapiens root basis. Let's remember, *Shennong was said to be born of a dragon father*;

Who's Yo Daddy?

The extreme sex drives of the Neons and their hybrid offspring, as described by Gooch, would be another good match here, to describe our Neon as a sharp-eyed, lust-driven drakon, who lives deep in his cave-lair.

How Dragons Fly

There are no wings involved. Those were peasant misunderstandings eons ago. If a Neanderthal, or a hybrid human creature flies at all, it is with his dream-imagination, and his psychic flying, or remote viewing capabilities, which may have been four times more powerful than our own, given the larger rear-brain vision cortex. Humans were also reported flying in ancient times, not just dragons. The ancient 'public mentality' simply didn't understand the real, much deeper nature of flying, and so incorrect myths sprang up.

To get behind the crazy legend, we should not take the subject of dragon flying too lightly but must convert it to a psychological, psychic sense. Modern governments and institutions, such as the United States Military, and the University of Princeton, are quietly known to have run decade-long psychic experiments, where a remote-viewing process, as it is commonly called, basically constitutes the ability of a Sapiens hominid, to project its mind beyond its body, basically *flying in a psychic fashion*. Ongoing, relentless testing of these experiments in numerous international institutions, including Russia and China, confirms a human's psychic abilities, except to the most hardened left-brain-dominant skeptic. This ability was not unknown to ancient shamans around the world, who used special herbal concoctions to dramatically alter their state of consciousness, and still do, to this very day. Milarepa, the famous legendary Tibetan Yogi of past centuries, was popularly considered to have the ability to fly in the air at will, not unlike our fire-breathing dragons, launching upwards from their dank, dark caves. We may consider both myths to likely be more representative of psychic flying, such as related below.

There's a place down in Mexico

where a man can fly over mountains and hills.

Hypnotized, **Fleetwood Mac**

Underneath the ordinary public mentality, many modern people, such as artists and creative folk, often discuss their psychic capabilities, such as clairvoyance, which is similar to remote viewing. Is it possible that Neon-hybrids actually had similar, if not more powerfully developed capabilities? This was Stan Gooch's position; these hybrid ancestors were unusually psychic. Their greater visionary braincase may suggest a powerful greater potential for psychic phenomenon, such as remote viewing, and if so, most primitive Sapiens, with their dominant left brain all a-chatter, mistook this psychic 'flying' capability, or out-of-body experience, to be something entirely different, and over thousands of years a greatly mistaken, fabricated notion took root in the legends of dragons. This reminds us of the old kindergarten exercise, where a large ring of children hears 'white horse' whispered in one child's ear, by the teacher, the first child whispers into the next child's ear, and so on around the ring of twenty-five children. The last child to hear the whispered words would hear something like 'purple, polka-dotted zebra.' This children's play exercise illustrates how primitive myths may have spread around ancient migratory campfires, with many dull, and dim-witted minds telling their laughable tales about fire-breathing, flying dragons. And yet, there is much more to tell about the earliest, original drakons (dragons), in the hoary legend of Beowulf, which will be revealed in his upcoming chapter.

The Dragon-Hole

The archeological dig that we mentioned earlier, in Austria, is called 'Drachenhohle' or, in English, it renders as the 'Dragon's Cave' of Mixnitz, a nearby township. Archeologists have speculated that European peoples of the Middle Ages, in the 5th to 15th centuries AD, named this cave 'dragon-hole' because of the larger-than-human bones found there. These fossils were mainly from cave bears, lions and some wolves, but a later dig found Neanderthal fossils at a deeper layer. There were of course, no 'dragon' bones ever found.

The story of the Dragon-Hole later culminated in the saga of the 'Dragon Slayer of Mixnitx,' where a human entered a cave and managed to slay a drakon hybrid-hominid. This plot is the same as in a subsequent chapter concerning Beowulf the Hero, who also fights a cave dragon (drakon) and loses his life. But we must know by now, that we are dealing with an ancient concept far different than understood today. Perhaps the Dragon-Hole is really named from a far-off, ancient memory, where humans and Neon encountered each other, and possibly mixed together. The Dragon-Hole represents the old traces of Neon and Sapiens presence in Austria, dated between 65,000 and 31,000 BCE, yet might there be a hidden, more recent hybrid-hominid presence? If we refer to Dragon-Hole, as housing a fearsome 'sharp-sighted creature who lives in a cave,' the meaning is entirely different, and suggestive of a Neon-hybrid presence. With his superior nocturnal eyesight, if you entered his dark cave, Neon could easily see you, but you likely could never see him, in the near pitch-black recesses. In returning to King Shennong's ancient cave in China, one can build a far better case for his father being a 'dragon' if we substitute 'drakon,' as the far-seeing Neon, who mated with a prehistoric Chinese princess, and the rest is truly a forgotten Sino history, or simply a mythical folklore, depending upon your preference of interpretation. Once again, we have a potential mating between crossbreed species, resulting in offspring that should have a greater Neanderthal DNA percentage than modern humans. This would be King Shennong, the son of a princess and a sharp-sighted drakon (dragon). As in the other hybrid offspring examples, the early Shennong Clan, possibly composed of Neanderthal, Denisovan and Sapiens DNA, would slowly diminish over the eons since the early first matings, devolving into lesser amounts of hybrid DNA, until the current levels of 4+% are seen in the modern Chinese, which are some of highest Neon percentages in the world. The Shennong Clan, with its nickname of Yandi, may have been red-haired also, as depicted in a few of the artist portrayals. Yan means flame or red-colored, thus Yandi translates traditionally as the 'Red Emperor.' Scholars have taken Yan to mean simply the color red itself, but this may be simply an assumption. The Red Shennong Clan is said to have interbred with humans and produced the clan of the Yellow Emperor, which should also have been a hybrid-crossbreed mix, with a slightly lower Neon DNA percentage. King Shennong is sometimes said to have fathered the Yellow Emperor, who was the next ruler of prehistoric China. Perhaps like his drakon grandfather, The Yellow Emperor, was said to have turned into the form of the Yellow Dragon at the end of his life, to ascend to Heaven. Since the Chinese consider him to be their first human ancestor, they sometimes refer to themselves as "children of the dragon." A truer, less mythical statement would be 'children of the sharp-eyed drakon.'

"Truth is stranger than fiction.

Literature is a faint remembrance of Experience."

The New Muse Suggested Reading List

For those who would know yet more.

Like many others, this author, a former technocrat, researches via the internet for both well-known and esoteric information. If interested, the diligent reader-researcher can find much of the material contained in the *New Muse Book Series* via a series of well-planned, heuristic internet searches. During the creation of the *New Muse Book Series*, the following books were researched or referenced by the author.

A History of Psychiatry, Ed Shorter

A History of Western Philosophy, Bertrand Russell

A New Earth: Awakening to Your Life's Purpose, Eckhart Tolle

A Simple Path, The Dalai Lama

A Stroke of Insight, Jill Bolte Taylor

A Theory of Everything, Ken Wilbur

A Traveler's Guide for the Afterlife, Mark Mirabello

Ageless Mind, Ageless Body, Deepak Chopra

All you Need Is Love, Jewelle St. James

Alphabet and the Goddess, Leonard Shlain

Ancient Egypt: The Light of the World, Gerald Massey

Ancient Egyptian Symbols: 50 New Discoveries, Meader & Demeter

Ancient History, Israel Smith Clare

As a Man Thinketh, James Allen

Aspects of Christian Mysticism, William Major Scott

Atlantis and the Kingdom of the Neanderthals; 100,000 Years of lost History, Colin Wilson

Autobiography of a Yogi, Paramhansa Yogananda

Autobiography of Wolfgang von Goethe

Barbelo: The Story of Jesus Christ

Beelzebub's Tales to His Grandson, George Gurdjieff

Beyond Belief: The Gospel of Thomas, Elaine Pagels

Beyond the Robot, Gary Lachman

Beyond Theology, Alan Watts

Bhagavad Gita-As It Is, A. C. Bhakti Vedanta Swami Prabhuppada

BioCentrism, Robert Lanza

Biotechnology Unzipped: Promises and Reality, Eric S. Grace

Black Elk Speaks, John Neirhardt

Brave New World, Aldous Huxley

Broca's Brain, Carl Sagan

Buddha and the Gospel of Buddhism, Ananda Kentish Coomaraswamy

Captain of my Ship: Master of my Soul, P. H. Atwater

Care of the Soul, Thomas Moore

Carl Sagan, William Poundstone

Chaos, Gaia, Eros, Ralph Abraham

Chaos, James Gleick

Christian Monasticism, David Knowles

Christian Mysticism, William Ralph Inge

Chuang Tzu: Basic Writings, Burton Watson

Cognizant Mind, Arnold Trehub

Conscious Acts of Creation; The Emergence of a New Physics, Tiller, Dibble, Kohana

Consilience: The Unity of Knowledge, Edward O. Wilson

Contact, Carl Sagan

Cosmos, Carl Sagan

Creative Evolution, Henri Bergson

Croiset: The Clairvoyant, Jack Harrison Pollack

Dancing Wu Li Masters: Seat of Soul, Gary Zarkoff

Dying to Wake Up, Rajiv Parti

Easy Journey to Other Planets, A.C. Bhaktivedanta Swami Prabhupada

Ecstasy: A Study of Secular and Religious Experiences, Marghanita Laski

Embryos, Galaxies, and Sentient Beings: How the Universe Makes Life, Richard Grossinger.

Entangled Minds, Dean Radin

Essential Philosophy, James Mannion

Evolution Isn't What It Used to Be, Walter Truett Anderson.

Extrasensory Perception: Support, Skepticism, and Science, Vol I, II, Edwin May, Sonali Bhatt Marwaha

Filters and Reflections, Jones, Dunne, Jahn

Fire in the Mind: A Biography of Joseph Campbell, Stephan and Robin Larsen

First Steps in Egyptian, Sir Wallis Budge

Freudian Psychology, Calvin S. Hall

Future Shock, Alvin Toffler

Gandhi: An Autobiography

Ghost in the Machine, Arthur Koestler

Guns, Germs, Steel, Jared Diamond

Healing Ancestral Karma, Steven Farmer

Hello from Heaven, Bill and Judy Guggenheim

How Can One Sell the Air? Chief Seattle

Iamblichus' Life of Pythagoras, Thomas Taylor

In Search of the Miraculous, P. D. Ouspensky

Induced After-Death Communication: A Miraculous Therapy for Grief and Loss, Alan L. Botkin, Craig Hogan

Journeys Out of the Body, Robert A. Monroe

Jung, Diedre Bair

Land of the Fallen Star Gods, J. S. Gordon

Leaves of Grass, Walt Whitman

Life after Life, Raymond A. Moody Jr., M.D.

Light on the Yoga Sutras of Patanjali, B. K. S. Iyengar

Living Buddha, Living Christ, Thich Nhat Hanh

Living Consciousness, Metaphysical Vision of Henri Bergson, Barnard

Loitering at the Gate to Eternity: Memoirs of a Psychic Bystander, Louisa Green

Man and His Symbols, Carl G. Jung

Margins of Reality, Robert Jahn, Brenda Dunne

Matter and Mermory, Henri Bergson

Meditations, Marcus Aurelius

Memories, Dreams, and Reflections, Carl G. Jung

Metaphysical Meditations, Paramhansa Yogananda

Milarepa: A Biography, edited by W. Y. Evans-Wentz

Mind to Mind, Rene Warcollier

Mirrors of the Soul, Kahlil Gibran

Modern Philosophy, Roger Scruton

My Religion, Helen Keller

Mysticism and the New Physics, Michael Talbot

Mysticism, Evelyn Underhill

Myths of the Hindus and Buddhists, Ananda Kentish Coomaraswamy, Sister Nivedita

Names of God, Nathan Stone

No One Here Gets Out Alive: a Biography of Jim Morrison, Jerry Hopkins and Danny Sugarman

On Death and Dying, Elizabeth Kubler-Ross

Our Roots in the Great Pyramid, Mostafa Elshamy

Peak Experiences, Abraham Maslow

Philosophical Writings, Rene Descartes

Popal Vuh, Dennis Tedlock

Powers of Mind, Adam Smith

Psychic Discoveries Behind the Iron Curtain, Ostrander and Schroeder

Psycho-Cybernetics, Maxwell Maltz

Quantum Healing, Deepak Chopra

Raising the Earth to the Next Vibration, Richard Grossinger

A Brief History of Time, Stephen Hawking

A History of God, Karen Armstrong

Reflections on Life after Life, Raymond A. Moody Jr., MD

Remote Viewers; The Secret History of America's Psychic Spies, Jim Schnabel

Remote Viewing Secrets, Joseph McMoneagle

Science and the Akashic Field, Ervin Laszlo

Science Set Free, Rupert Sheldrake

Selected Poems: Keats, Edited by George H. Ford

Serpent in the Sky: High Wisdom of Ancient Egypt, John Anthony West

Serpent in the Sky; The Ancient Wisdom of Ancient Egypt, Jonathan Anthony West

Seth Speaks, Jane Roberts

Stalking the Wild Pendulum: On the Mechanics of Consciousness, Itzhak Bentov

Still Here, Ram Dass

Surely, You're Joking, Mr. Feldman, Richard Feldman

Tales of Wonder, Huston Smith

Tao Te Ching, Lao-Tzu, Gia-Fu-Feng, Jane English

Teachings of Sufism, Carl W. Ernst

Tertium Organum, P. D. Ouspensky

The Afterlife of Billy Fingers, Annie Kagan

The Akashic Experience: Science and the Cosmic Memory Field, Ervin Lazslo

The Ancient History of Egyptians, Assyrians, Vol. 1 & 2, Charles Rollin

The Ancient Wisdom, Annie Besant

The Art of Thinking Clearly, Rolf Dobelli

The Autobiography of Mark Twain

The Autobiography of Rudolph Steiner

The Bicameral Critic, Colin Wilson

The Biology of Transcendence, Joseph Chilton Pearce

The Black Swan, Nissan Nicholas Taleb

The Body Electric, Bob Becker

The Body of Myth, J. Nigro Sansonese

The Book Your Church Doesn't Want You to Read, Tim Leedom

The Christian Conspiracy, Dr. David Moore

The Closing of the American Mind, Allen Bloom

The Collected Wisdom of Heraclitus, Brooks Haxton

The Coming Era in Science: New York Times, Edited by Holcomb B. Noble

The Complete Illuminated Books of William Blake

The Complete Works of Count Tolstoy: Walk in the Light While Ye Have Light

The Complete Works of Swami Vivekananda

The Conscious Universe, Dean Radin.

The Crack in the Cosmic Egg; Challenging Constructs of Mind and Reality, Joseph Chilton Pearce

The Crown of Life: A Study in Yoga, Kirpal Singh

The Dance of Siva, Ananda Kentish Coomaraswamy

The Dancing Wu Li Masters, Gary Zukav

The Dead Sea Scrolls Uncovered, R. Eisenmann, M. Wise

The Dialogues of Plato, Erich Segal

The Divided Brain and the Search for Meaning: Why Are We So Unhappy? Iain McGilChrist

The Doors of Perception, Aldous Huxley

The Dragons of Eden, Carl Sagan

The Dream Culture of the Neanderthals, Stan Gooch

The Egyptian Book of the Dead (and Great Awakening), Dr. Muata Ashby

The Egyptian Book of the Dead (and Great Awakening), Sir Wallis E. Budge

The Elegant Universe, Brian Greene

The End of Faith, Sam Harris

The End of Suffering and the Discovery of Happiness: The Path of Tibetan Buddhism, The Dalai Lama

The Essential Blake, Stanley Kunitz

The Essential Jesus, John Dominic Crossan

The Field, Lynn Taggart

The Flight of the Eagle, J. Krishnamurti

The Four Agreements Companion Book, Don Miguel Ruiz

The Future of the Mind, Michio Kaku

The Future, Al Gore

The God Delusion, Richard Dawkins

The Gospel According to Jesus, Stephen Mitchell

The Gospel According to Zen: Beyond the Death of God, Robert Sohl and Audrey Carr

The Gospel of Sri Rama Krishna, Vivekananda Center

The Great Chain of Being, Arthur Lovejoy

The Hand, Frank R. Wilson

The Heart's Code, Paul Pearsall

The HeartMath Solution, Childre & Martin

The Heart-Mind Matrix, Joseph Chilton Pierce

The Heaven at the End of Science, Philip Mereton

The Hero with a Thousand Faces, Joseph Campbell

The Hidden Jesus, Donald Spoto

The Holographic Universe, Michael Talbot

The Illuminated Rumi, Coleman Barks

The Inner Treasure: An Introduction to the World's Sacred and Mystical Writings, Jonathan Star

The Intention Experiment, Lynn Talbert.

The Invisible Gorilla, Cristopher Chabris, Daniel Simons.

The Joseph Campbell Phenomenon, Lawrence Madden

The Joyous Cosmology, Alan W. Watts

The King James Version of the Holy Bible

The Lady Tasting Tea: How Statistics Revolutionized Science in the 20th Century, David Salsburg

The Life of Sir Isaac Newton, Sir David Brewster

The Living Thoughts of Gotama, Ananda Kentish Coomaraswamy

The Lost Years of Jesus Revealed, Rev. Dr. Francis Potter

The Lost Years of Jesus, Elizabeth Clare Prophet

The Marriage of Heaven and Hell, Aldous Huxley

The Masks of God: Creative Mythology, Joseph Campbell

The Masks of God: Occidental Mythology, Joseph Campbell

The Masks of God: Oriental Mythology, Joseph Campbell

The Masks of God: Primitive Mythology, Joseph Campbell

The Master and His Emissary: The Divided Brain and the Making of the Western World, Iain McGilChrist

The Mind-Boggling Universe, James McAleer

The Mystical Mind: Probing the Biology of Religious Experience, D'Aquili, Newburg

The Myth of the Eternal Return, Mircea Eliade

The Myth of the Machine: The Pentagon of Power, Lewis Mumford

The Mythic Image, Joseph Campbell.

The Notebooks of Leonardo da Vinci, Edward MacKurdy

The Origin of Consciousness and the Breakdown of the Bi-Cameral Mind, Julian Jaynes

The Origin of Species, Charles Darwin

The Other Bible, editor William Barnstone

The Outline of History, H. G. Wells

The Pentagon of Power, Lewis Mumford

The Philosophies of India, Heinrich Zimmer

The Portable Jung, edited by Joseph Campbell

The Power of Now, Eckhart Tolle

The Prema-Sagara (Ocean of Love), Kavi Lal

The Presence of the Past: Morphic Resonance and the Habits of Nature, Rupert Sheldrake

The Psychology of Transcendence, Andrew Neher

The Quotable Einstein, Alice Calaprice

The Republic, Plato, translated by Benjamin Jowett

The Rosetta Stone, Sir Wallis Budge

The Scalpel and the Soul: Encounters with Surgery, Allan J. Hamilton

The Search for Bridey Murphy, Morey Bernstine

The Search for Omm Sety, Jonathan Cott

The Secret Path, Paul Brunton

The Secret Teachers of the Western World, Gary Lachman

The Selfish Gene, Richard Dawkins

The Singing Neanderthal, Steven Mithen

The Song of God: Bhagavad Gita, Christopher Isherwood, Swami Prabhavananda

The Supreme Adventure, Robert Crooke

The Tao of Physics, F. Capra

The Teachings of Don Juan: A Yaqui Way of Knowledge, Carlos Castaneda

The Teachings of Rumi, Andrew Harvey

The Tibetan Book of the Dead (Great Liberation), W. Y. Evans-Wentz

The Travelers Key to Ancient Egypt, John Anthony West

The Universe in a Single Atom: The Convergence of Science and Spirituality, The Dalai Lama

The Universe Within: The History of the Human Body, Neil Shubin

The Untethered Soul, Michael Singer

The Upanishads, Sri Aurobindo

The Vanishing Peoples of the Earth, National Geographic Society

The Varieties of Religious Experience, William James

The Wanderer, Kahlil Gibran

The World of the Druids, Miranda J. Green.

Think on These Things, J. Krishnamurti

Through My Eyes, Gordon Smith

Thus Spoke Zarathustra, Friedrich Nietzsche

Unconditional Life, Deepak Chopra

Varieties of Anomalous Experience, Cardena, Lynn, Krippener

Vistas of Infinity, Jurgen Ziewe

Waking Up in Time: Finding Inner Peace in Times of Accelerating Change, Peter Russell

Why God Won't Go Away: Brain Science and the Biology of Belief, Newberg; Andrew; D'Aquili; Eugene

Why Socrates Died, Robin WaterField

Your Eternal Self, Craig Hogan

Index

About the Author

A High-Low Bio

Steven A. Key, in a former technological life, had a career taming the largest computer systems in the world—those rascally mainframes folks often hear about. As a deep-researching computerist and technocrat, he was readily primed to combine his investigative skills with his deep personal interests in all things pertaining to Body, Mind & Spirit. Combining unique approaches to neuroscience, psychology, consciousness, and ancient history, Steven created the **New Muse Book Series**. His initial book, *The Vikings Secret Yoga – The Supreme Adventure,* is the first book of its kind in that it reveals the hidden Yoga of the tenth-century Norse poets. This secret has been extremely well kept and is now revealed anew for the first time in over a thousand years, via the skeleton key of Raja Yoga.

~!~

The above loosely assembled biographical information gives the public and the publisher sufficient insight to establish an author's persona but, on the other hand, defeats the entire purpose of the author's writings concerning consciousness and neuropsychology as Yoga.

The real biographical information of people should include a description of their deepest nature and selves. Socrates referred to his deeper nature as his spiritually guiding Daimon. Siddhartha mystically informed his disciples to be "intimate with the Lovely" as a guiding lamp. We are the House of the Holy. It's important to put that in the bio, otherwise, it's simply an egotistical expression of personality.

Another aspect of a high-low bio involves an appreciative association with one's parents, as the Upanishads state. Thus, in the light of Yoga, one's mother and father are seen as godlike beings—goddess and god—

for the fantastic provisions, whether good or bad, that they provide to the child, their living, breathing representative of themselves. It's good to be an apple from that tree. A high-low bio should include the entirety of humanity, as sisters and brothers, for we are all gifted in the same neurological fashion, in having a lower and a higher nature. We then extend, sentiently, into the universe for all creatures large or small. We are all of the same root. As for springing from my karma and its reincarnation via my parents, it's essential to point out that, generally, people have only a single-life view, that of their Ego. This is what the Greeks called anamnesis, the great forgetting. As one forgets at birth, the Ego grows and believes its life to be the sole reality. As one proceeds along the path of life that all humans must journey, additional glimpses and insightful experiences of past lives can result in one's accepting a multi-life view, which this author endorses as another deep, essential facet in this high-low bio.

You know how little while we have to stay.

The Way You go up is the Way You came Down.

The Labyrinth . . . is in You Now.

Steven A. Key

Manufactured by Amazon.ca
Bolton, ON